THE FOUNDATION
OF
MYSTICISM

SPIRITUAL HEALING PRINCIPLES
OF THE INFINITE WAY

Other Writings of JOEL S. GOLDSMITH

Living by the Word

Living the Illumined Life

Seek Ye First

Spiritual Discernment

A Message for the Ages

I Stand on Holy Ground

The Art of Spiritual Living

God Formed Us for His Glory

The Journey Back to His Father's House

Showing Forth the Presence of God

The Only Freedom

The Infinite Way

Practicing the Presence

The World Is New

Consciousness Transformed

God The Substance of All Form

Man Was Not Born to Cry

Living Now

Consciousness Is What I Am

Gift of Love

The Art of Meditation

The Altitude of Prayer

The Contemplative Life

Conscious Union with God

The Art of Spiritual Healing

The Spiritual Power of Truth

The Thunder of Silence

Awakening Mystical Consciousness

Realization of Oneness

A Parenthesis In Eternity

Living Between Two Worlds

Rising In Consciousness

Consciousness In Transition

Our Spiritual Resources

Living the Infinite Way

The Master Speaks

Beyond Words and Thoughts

Leave Your Nets

Consciousness Unfolding

Spiritual Interpretation of Scripture

The Foundation of Mysticism

The Early Years

1954 Infinite Way Letters

1955 Infinite Way Letters

1956 Infinite Way Letters

1957 Infinite Way Letters

1958 Infinite Way Letters

1959 Infinite Way Letters

The Heart of Mysticism:1955-1959

The Mystical I

THE FOUNDATION
OF
MYSTICISM

SPIRITUAL HEALING PRINCIPLES
OF THE INFINITE WAY

Joel S. Goldsmith

Acropolis Books, Publisher
Santa Barbara, California

THE FOUNDATION OF MYSTICISM
SPIRITUAL HEALING PRINCIPLES
OF THE INFINITE WAY
© 1998 by Acropolis Books, Inc.

Printed in the United States of America.
Third Printing, 2007

For information contact:

Acropolis Books, Inc.
Santa Barbara, CA

http://www.acropolisbooks.com

Library Of Congress Cataloging-in-Publication Data

Goldsmith, Joel S., 1892-1964.
    The foundation of mysticism: spiritual healing principles of the Infinite Way /
Joel S. Goldsmith.
    p. cm.
Class lectures delivered by the author Apr. July 1959 in Hawaii. Includes
bibliographical references.
ISBN 1-889051-22-5 ISBN13: 978-1-889051-22-2
1. Spiritual healing. 2. Spiritual life.   3. Mysticism.
I. Title
BP610.G6419 1998
                                                    98-45907
                                                    CIP

This book is printed on acid free paper that meets the American National
Standards Institute Z 39.48 Standard

Except the Lord build the house,
they labour in vain that build it. . . .

—Psalm 127

"Illumination dissolves all material ties and binds men together with the golden chains of spiritual understanding; it acknowledges only the leadership of the Christ; it has no ritual or rule but the divine, impersonal universal Love; no other worship than the inner Flame that is ever lit at the shrine of Spirit. This union is the free state of spiritual brotherhood. The only restraint is the discipline of Soul; therefore, we know liberty without license; we are a united universe without physical limits, a divine service to God without ceremony or creed. The illumined walk without fear—by Grace."

—*The Infinite Way* by Joel S. Goldsmith

TABLE OF CONTENTS

PART III
LIVING THE HEALING PRINCIPLES:
HAWAIIAN VILLAGE CLOSED CLASS

TABLE OF CONTENTS

The Foundation
of
Mysticism

*Spiritual Healing Principles
of the Infinite Way*

INTRODUCTION

In 1981, at a time in my life when I was bereft of
spiritual understanding and deeply in need of a foundation for spiritual living, friends introduced me to the
teachings of Joel Goldsmith. The previous year I had
walked out of a monastery, leaving behind twenty-three
years of prayer, meditation, and humanitarian service;
leaving behind a secluded life dedicated to seeking and
serving God. This was a giant leap into an unknown
world characterized, at least for me, by the struggle for
daily existence. And at that time it seemed I had forever
lost an extraordinary nurturing of inner fulfillment and
a beautiful, harmonious environment that provided the
outer necessities of human living, while sustaining an
inner contemplative life–communion with God.

My first experience with Joel's writings was not
uncommon. I was moved by the profound wisdom of
The Infinite Way, and then read *Realization of Oneness;* the
concept of this one title alone embraced the goal of my
life. I was filled with joy. I told many of my friends, "I
have found the answers to all my questions!" And,
literally, I had. I later discovered that Joel authored at
least thirty-two books; that there were in existence
approximately twelve hundred hours of his recorded
classes–something for everyone–especially the soul
hungering and thirsting after righteousness, the truth of
Spirit.

"And you shall be filled," promised the Christ. These
teachings became manna for my new existence, and to

this day, nearly seventeen years later, I feel I have hardly scratched their surface. Truly speaking, these teachings are an "infinite way." One never seems to plumb the depth, realize the allness, or exhaust the spiritual wisdom they contain. Joel has a marvelous way of reaching the hearts and minds of ordinary people, those looking beyond the mundane life for a vision, an understanding and realization, of the magnificent promises of spiritual unfoldment given by illumined sages in every century, men and women of all faiths who understood the darkness that blinds our human eyes to spiritual light.

If you are new to the message of the Infinite Way and this is the first book of Joel Goldsmith's or one of the first, you are reading, fasten your seat belt! You are about to take off into a revelation of timeless wisdom that, to the best of my knowledge, has never before been revealed in scriptural writings of the world. With irrefragable insight into the nature of God and the nature of error, developed through more than thirty years of an intense spiritual search that was inflamed by a remarkable healing gift, Joel presents in this book *principles* of living that unfold for mankind the mystical experience of communion–union, realization of oneness–with the infinite source of being.

If you have studied the Infinite Way teachings for many years, the lectures compiled in this book were given especially for you and me. We know that Joel Goldsmith was truly a world teacher, traveling ceaselessly for more than a decade-and-a-half to teach students of many nations, in cities scattered all over the globe. While in Amsterdam in late 1958, he was inwardly led to discontinue his tour and to return to his home in Honolulu, there to await further guidance from Spirit. At that time in his ministry, Joel had begun to teach the message of the Infinite Way from a higher state of illumined consciousness, the Christ consciousness,[1] and he did not realize he was talking "over the heads" of his students, teaching beyond their grasp–that they were not prepared to enter with him into the mystical union, realization of oneness: a state of self-realization in which an exact correspondence with truth, with Spirit, is experienced as one's own being.

In Honolulu, he remained in seclusion for several weeks. During this period he was instructed to re-teach the fundamental spiritual healing principles of the Infinite Way message. Students had failed to grasp them and put them into practice and, because of this, they had not laid the foundation for actual communion–union–with God.

I need to digress for a moment to explain why healing principles are a foundation for the mystical experience of God-realization. Because the ministry of Joel's life really began with the bestowal of a remarkable healing gift–which he did not at all understand–he turned to the Christian Science teachings to begin his spiritual search. As in my own experience, many Infinite Way students do not come to these teachings from a background of Christian Science healing, and it is a

---

[1]Realization of oneness with God expressed as individual being. Although Joel said many times that neither he nor any of us could expect to demonstrate the fullness of the Christ-consciousness revealed by Jesus, nevertheless the grace of God is not withheld from any individual. God's presence can be realized, experienced, and demonstrated through sincerity and dedication to spiritual living.

revelation to learn that spiritual healing as taught by Mrs. Eddy in the latter part of the nineteenth century opened a door to understanding and demonstrating an aspect of Jesus Christ's teachings almost unknown to Western civilization for more than seventeen hundred years Joel learned that healing itself was not the purpose of spiritual living but rather its natural outcome. Through thirty years of healing physical and mental diseases (including cases that to medical science were terminal), through an intense study of the world's religions and ancient scriptural texts that seldom left time for more than three hours' sleep at night, and through his own progressive inner revelation, Joel realized that living the spiritual life meant understanding the *nature of God:* God is, and God is individual being; the *nature of error:* that which forces humanity into an existence of ignorance; and the *nature of prayer*, rising above the error through communion with God. Spiritual healing results naturally from this knowledge.

As mentioned, Joel's quest originated with a healing gift, and his search for what it was and why it had been given to him led to the unfoldment of the Infinite Way message. Joel devoted his life to teaching this revelation. He concurrently demonstrated, not only the healing of diseases that commonly afflict our human bodies, but also the healing of situations in our every-day living that present to us failure in relationships, employment, financial stability–in other words, healing of the lack of harmony that naturally demonstrates fulfillment in our lives. Spiritual living, constant awareness of the presence of God, is the goal. Spiritual healing is its natural outcome–and also its measure. If one is living spiritually, harmony is demonstrated. There could not be a higher, more exact standard. And so, although the principles given in the Infinite Way teachings are actually principles of spiritual living, they are most referred to as spiritual healing principles. These are the basis of the higher revelation–mysticism.

The classes Joel was instructed to give in Hawaii in 1959 covered a period of three months, from April to July. In this one period he gave fifty-eight classes; and in the last class he identified twenty he felt best expressed his review of the healing principles. It is these twenty classes that comprise the material for this book.[2] By reiterating the principles again and again, each time in a different context, Joel enabled his students to understand and practice the spiritual healing principles of the Infinite Way.

Publishing this material in one volume gives to the reader the tremendous impact of Joel's teaching style, bringing with it the realization that his intention was to forever free human consciousness from the influence of error, to irrevocably establish human consciousness in Christ-consciousness. Profound truths occur right in the middle of a paragraph, truths that feed the soul. These truths are effortlessly spoken, uttered from lifetimes of spiritual growth and unfoldment. Joel always said the message was never his, but was revealed in and as his

---

[2]Ed. Note: Tape recordings of these classes are available from The Infinite Way, P.O. Box 2089, Peoria, AZ 85380-2089, 1-800-922-3195. Catalogue numbers are as follows: the ten tapes comprising the twenty classes to which Joel refers are: 1959 Maui Advanced Work, #247 (tape #5) & #248 (tape #6); 1959 Hawaiian Village Open Class, Catalog; #260 (tape #3) & #261 (tape #4) and the 1959 Hawaiian Village Closed Class, Catalog #262 (tape #1), #263 (tape #2), #264 (tape #3), #265 (tape #4), #266 (tape #5) & #267 (tape #6).

consciousness by the one universal truth that is forever freely given to all humanity. The student of the Infinite Way learns that God's light, God's grace, shines impartially upon a stumbling humanity, illuminating the consciousness, the awareness, of saint and sinner alike–that error was never established in creation but became an impartial imposition on the mind of man. Joel Goldsmith proved these through spiritual healing. The fulfillment of his ministry is a ceaseless giving of wisdom, an outpouring of truth that, like a waterfall, cascades into the endless river of human existence. Through the Infinite Way message, the grace that characterized Joel's life floods ours.

Allen Marsh
Bellevue, Washington
1998

PART I

PREPARATION

"So shall my word be that goeth forth from my mouth: it shall not return unto me void, but it shall accomplish that which I please, and it shall prosper in the thing whereto I sent it."

Isaiah 55:11

1959 Maui Advanced Work

~ 1 ~

LAYING THE FOUNDATION:
THE HEALING PRINCIPLES

Good evening.

For the balance of 1959 our work has taken a definite shape and now we know where we are going. We have reached that place in our unfoldment where we are going to assume full responsibility for the activity of the Infinite Way on this island and wherever else it may lead. You can no longer sit back as if you were beginners, sheep standing around who have shepherds protecting and prodding you. Now the time is here for you to be a light unto this community and show by the fruitage of your own lives what others who seek in this direction may look forward to. In every community there must be groups standing on their own feet spiritually, not only showing forth the Infinite Way activity in their community, but also contributing to its 'round-the-world prosperity (the least of which I'm talking about is money).

Now I'm going to illustrate this for you: We will begin by taking up the work necessary to establish the Infinite Way activity in this community. This work is not of a material nature; it does not call for the use of your bodies or your pocketbooks; it is purely a mental and spiritual activity. You can sit in the quietness of your own home, or anywhere else you please, and silently do the work within which will bear fruitage.

In preparation for the meeting to be held here tomorrow night, you will undertake the spiritual work for its fruitage, whether that fruitage is to appear in numbers of people or whether it is to appear in the form of healings for those who are here. As you know, we are not so concerned with numbers as we are for attracting those really and truly seeking this, and then giving them the fruitage after they come. You will not follow a formula. You will not have a set prayer for treatment. Your work must be inspirational, but it must cover and embrace the major principles which constitute the prayer and treatment work of the Infinite Way. Those who enter this meeting are not merely entering a room. They are entering the Infinite Way consciousness of truth. As they enter this room, they enter our conscious- ness, our spiritual household.

Everyone in this meeting is a guest of God. Everyone in this meeting enters the household of God as a brother, sister, son, or daughter. Divine consciousness, which is individual consciousness—your consciousness and mine— embraces and enfolds everyone who enters this meeting. Embraced in the consciousness of truth, God's grace permeates their being and touches their mind, their soul, their body. "Know ye not that ye are the temple of God?" Those who enter this temple which you are, are entering the temple of God, and God is there, blessing, redeeming, raising up, restoring.

When imbued with truth, your mind is a law of harmony, healing, health, happiness, peace, and pros- perity. That is why those who come into the presence of an individual who lives with the word of God—not only with it, but by it—enter a consciousness which is a benediction, and they feel that. Therefore, if you have permeated your mind with the word of God before you come here, then all who enter this meeting enter that word and receive light, blessing, benediction, courage, freedom, joy, and "the peace that passeth understanding."

Now I am speaking as if I were each one of you:

My mind is filled with the word of God because I keep my mind stayed on God, from rising in the morning to sleeping at night. Always there is some spiritual truth active in my consciousness, some scriptural passage kept alive within me. My mind is permeated with truth, it is constituted of truth, and all who enter the realm of my mind find truth, life, love, eternality, immortality, the grace of God, the benediction of God. My mind imbued with truth is a law of elimination to all discords, all inharmonies, all injustices, all sins, all diseases, all false appetites. I of my own self am nothing, but "I and my Father are one," and he that is within me is greater than any error that exists in the world. Therefore, when I fill my consciousness with truth, with love, with wisdom, I am a law of harmony, of healing, of peace unto all who enter my spiritual household, my consciousness, my mind. "I can of my own self do nothing," but since "I and the Father are one . . . and all that the Father hath is mine," through grace I am given all of the dominion, all of the healing influence, all of the forgiving influence. When my mind is filled with truth and love, "neither do I condemn thee."

All who enter this hall are forgiven their sins of omission or commission. They come into his grace because my mind is filled with his grace, with his word, with his truth, and all who enter here enter the divine presence and receive forgiveness and regeneration. They even find that the lost years of the locust are

red to them by the divine grace which God has given me as
th.

"Man shall not live by bread alone, but by every word of
God that proceedeth out of the mouth of God." Every word of
truth which constitutes my consciousness is bread and wine,
water, meat, life, and resurrection unto all who enter my
consciousness. Truth is the divine influence; love is the divine
influence. If my mind, my consciousness, my soul is filled with
truth, spiritual truth and love, all who enter my consciousness
partake of that divine bread, meat, wine, and water which is
life eternal. Through the truth embodied in my consciousness, I
am a law unto you: a law of healing, a law of forgiveness, a
law of grace and benediction, even a law of supply.[1]

Just think, this is you talking to yourself, thinking
within yourself. You are not an isolated person separate
and apart from every person in this room. I am in you,
you are in me, and we are in God. So the truth which
you embody in your consciousness embodies God in all
those who come into this room to be a part of your
consciousness, and we are one. We are not two, or three,
or four, or five, or six as we seem to be; we are one. I
am in your consciousness, you are in my consciousness,
and we are in God- consciousness. One. All partaking of
the divine name or nature.

Do you see why it is given to priests to forgive sin? It
is given by virtue of the authority of truth embodied in
consciousness, not by virtue of the authority vested by

---

[1]The italicized passages that appear throughout the book are
outpourings of inspiration that came to Joel spontaneously as he
was lecturing. A form of contemplative meditation, these passages
were not intended by the author to be used as affirmations, denials,
or formulas but are an example of the free flowing Spirit.

an organization–that is only an outer sign. That is the same as a physician who has a license to practice. His license doesn't give him the authority to heal anybody, it is his knowledge of medical science which he has embodied. The license is only a formality. It would do no one any good if there were not a developed consciousness of the healing arts behind the license.

So with this. Even if you were ordained by a church, you could not heal or bless anyone unless your developed consciousness was behind the authorization. The truth embodied in your consciousness is the healing art, the forgiving authority, the redeeming power. Without this truth in your consciousness, you are nothing: "If I speak of myself, I bear witness to a lie," but since "I and my Father are one," I am endowed with dominion from on high. "The spirit of the Lord God is upon me and I am ordained to heal the sick." Ordained? Yes, ordained by the grace of God by virtue of the word of God which is now embodied in my consciousness.

Each one of you who has been studying one, two, five or ten years must have a mind filled with truth. Even if you have not memorized statements of truth, you have the substance of truth, the knowledge of truth within your consciousness, and this authorizes you as a healer, forgiver, redeemer–one who sets free all who come within range of your consciousness.

So you will now begin to see yourself in a new light; you will now begin to realize you have spent these years filling your mind and soul with God's word. And now that word of God has come to fruition, and all who reach you and touch you are blessed. They receive benediction–darshan. Then realize that all who come to this meeting tomorrow night are coming, not into a room or to hear a man; they are entering the temple of God which is your consciousness. Your consciousness which is imbued with truth is the temple of God, and they enter here to receive healing, to receive freedom, joy, bliss, and harmony–the grace of God.

Now, at each meeting held here, whether I am in this chair or another–or when you have your own meetings–always remember that you must consciously prepare yourself for it during the day of that meeting by becoming quiet for some length of time. Realize that all who enter the room enter not a room, but enter your consciousness, and your consciousness is filled with truth and love. Your consciousness is constituted of the word of God. In fact, these years of your study have dissolved your old consciousness and built a new one for you, a new consciousness made up of truth and love, a new consciousness made up of the word of God which is "quick and sharp and powerful."

This word of God which constitutes your new-born consciousness is life and truth and love to all who enter. You don't have to direct your thoughts at them; they enter your consciousness and partake of its nature. If your mind or consciousness were full of sin, false appetites and false desires, they would enter there and feel it, be disturbed by it and become restless. But you have no such consciousness anymore and you know that whatever remains of human consciousness in you is not a power. Only the word of truth given to you by the grace of God is power. Therefore you will now begin to see yourselves as temples of the living God, filled with his word. And remember that all who enter that consciousness enter the spiritual realm of freedom and harmony.

Yes, but we go a step farther: You will now undertake a work before you leave your homes in the morning to go about your daily activities, whether they be shopping, taking care of your business, profession, or teaching. You will remind yourself of this truth: that you have died to your human sense, that you have been reborn through the word, and that your consciousness is constituted of the word of God. As you leave your home you carry God's grace everywhere you go, everywhere you walk, run, or ride. All who enter your consciousness during the day, whether they be storekeepers or customers, clients or patients, students or friends—and sometimes enemies—must feel the power of God which is stored up through your years of opening yourself to the word of God, truth, and now constitutes your very being. God, truth, is the fiber of your being, searching even to the bones, the marrow, the joints of your body. Every bit of you is filled with God, for even your body is the temple of God; your body is the storehouse of God's power and God's grace.

Now you will learn never to leave your home without giving yourself and your community this treatment. We call it treatment rather than prayer because we think of prayer as that part of our work performed after this treatment is given. In other words, first must come conscious realization and declaration of truth, the part of our work we call treatment. When we have completed this we will sit quietly—"Speak Lord thy servant heareth"—and then wait in that receptive atmosphere until we feel the seal of God upon us, the release, or click.

You must remember that two of the most neglected parts of the teachings of Jesus Christ are praying for your enemies and forgiving unto seventy times seven.

~7~

These are two of the important parts of our work. "Forgive us our debts as we forgive our debtors." Do you see what a responsibility that places on you? You are virtually saying, "Don't forgive me as I don't forgive." You are setting the price of your own freedom or bondage. Therefore, in your treatment work, you must provide a minute to consciously release all who have offended, whether it is an offense against you, against democracy, against justice, against nations, or against the word of God. Set them free. Release them. Ask God's forgiveness. Be willing that they be forgiven without penalty regardless of the nature of their offense, even as Jesus forgave the adulteress, even as he forgave the thief dying on the cross. Be sure you are praying that God opens the minds and souls and consciousness of those whom we call enemies, those of materialistic minds or of whatever name or nature we may believe their offense to be. All of this, you see, must be included in your treatment work and cannot be neglected, for only what you put into your treatment demonstrates as fruitage.

The fundamental principle of your treatment is, first of all, to know why you expect your treatment to be effective. It isn't because of you or me. It is because the word of God entertained in our consciousness is "quick and sharp and powerful." It is because you are knowing the truth that makes you free. But you must know the truth and you must know it fully and completely. You must be able to remember the principles which constitute this message and put them into active expression. They have no power up in the air; they have no power in a book; they have power only when they are taken into consciousness and expressed. Do you not see that is the reason so few prayers are answered? It is because truth remains in a book or is expressed as lip-service rather than taken actively into consciousness and realized.

The Master asks, "What did hinder you? Rise, take up your bed and walk." That's an astonishing statement. Here's a crippled man and he's asked, "What did hinder you?" Common sense would have said, "I'm crippled, that's what's hindering me." But the Master saw that and still he said, "What did hinder you? Rise, pick up your bed and walk." In other words, that which is binding you isn't power; you are bound by your acceptance of it as power. Every treatment you give must embody the specific truth that there are not two powers: a good power and an evil power. Every treatment must embody the truth that God is power and not this appearance, whatever name you give it—paralysis or Pilate. If it is a temporal power, it is not spiritual law; it is not power. Whether you are giving treatment to forms of sin, disease, lack, limitation, unemployment, or unhappiness, your treatment must include the statement that this you hold binding isn't a power. Every treatment must include the realization that we are not invoking a God-power to destroy a sin- or disease-power. The truth we are declaring is: "What did hinder you?" Nothing is power but God. You see, if your treatment contains any element of belief or hope that God's power is going to do something to some other power, you might as well go back to your old-fashioned prayers which have always proved so ineffectual.

Yes, the world is reaching out for a higher concept of God. In a statement by Dr. Alexis Carrel[2], he says:

---

[2]Alexis Carrel, 1873-1944. French Surgeon, sociologist, and biologist who received the 1912 Nobel Prize for Physiology.

"Generally, the patient who is cured is not praying for himself but for another." That's a tremendous observation. When you are doing this work for those who are to enter your consciousness, even if they are the enemy, the unenlightened, the truth that you are praying for them becomes effective. It demonstrates in your own experience. And I was very surprised and happy to read an article on Sanford Ballard Dole, the pineapple king here in Hawaii, who also had a religious side that very few people knew about. He says: "Prayer in its highest exercise is an opening of the gates of the soul to the divine influence. The mere asking of favors from God is tiresome and discouraging." That was written in the 1880's!

You see, there have always been men and women who rose above their surroundings. Mr. Dole made an observation to that effect too, in this same article: "Doubtless a great deal of doctrinal teaching of the time was a hindrance rather than a help to the spiritual life because it encouraged such things as asking God for something for me, or for mine, or for my nation." Now the world has come to a place where it is ready to outgrow all forms of prayer and religious belief that were formerly taught about God, especially those that have been so ineffective. That is reaching out for a concept of God that more nearly approaches truth and demonstrates God in our experience.

Whatever is entertained in your consciousness is also known to your neighbors. They are not mind readers anymore than I am, but they can intuitively feel whether your consciousness is a blessing or a curse, or whether it's just a vacuum doing nothing either of a constructive or a negative nature, just vegetating. You know when you're in the presence of a mentally strong person, whether they're mentally strong on the good side or mentally strong on the evil side, just as you know when you're in the presence of a wishy-washy person who is thinking neither good nor evil but just going along for the ride.

It is part of our responsibility to be a neighbor to our neighbors. We do not have to project ourselves into their human affairs; we do not have to be their advisors or proselytize and bring them into some teaching for which they have not been prepared. Our responsibility as a neighbor isn't in that direction. Our responsibility is to be a positive influence for good, and we are a positive influence for good only in proportion to the activity of truth in our consciousness, only in proportion to the truth that fills our consciousness and that we are consciously uttering silently, sacredly, secretly. All who engage in the study and practice of a metaphysical, spiritual, or mystical teaching are really responsible to be examples to this world for what truth entertained in consciousness can do. All the world is seeking that.

When you pray, enter into your sanctuary and pray in secret. You don't have to tell anyone that you are praying for them or that you hope to be a blessing to them. Be satisfied if God's grace touches them without your getting any personal credit for it. Let God have the glory. But be a good steward of the word of God, not one that just hoards it in the mind and lets it rest there. Put it to use.

So we now have a program in which we will not leave home in the morning without sending the word before us to make the crooked places straight, without realizing that wherever I am, the word of God is, for it constitutes my new-born consciousness. My consciousness is a benediction and a blessing. It is a healer. It is bread, wine, meat, water, and supply unto all who touch my consciousness, be they friend or foe. Then, whether you attend our meeting here or whether you are alone, you have specifically given these treatments. Always remember that you are inviting the guest of God into your spiritual household, those who are ready for entrance into the spiritual realm. When they come, don't let them find your house empty. Don't let them find your consciousness devoid of truth and love. Be sure it is filled. This will be the beginning because if you successfully show forth the fruitage of your morning work and this meeting work, you will then be prepared for the next step, which will be undertaking treatment work for specific healings of those among you who require it and all others who ask for it.

Now I am as convinced as I can be that when individuals ask me for help, whatever benefit they receive is due entirely to the measure of truth which constitutes my consciousness. I am equally certain that all who wish to devote their consciousness to truth, who wish to die daily to their idle human thinking, wishful thinking, time-wasting thinking, and fill their consciousness with truth can be healers. Always remember: *Now* truth constitutes my consciousness; *now* I am a law; *now* I am an authority; *now* I am ordained to heal the sick, forgive the sinner, raise the dead, and feed the hungry by virtue of truth entertained and expressed in my consciousness. Specific truth.

The specific truth is that there is only one power. The specific truth is that none of this that's hindering you has the power to hinder you. Why? The specific truth is that your consciousness is an annihilation to everything unlike good; your consciousness filled with truth is a law of benediction and grace unto everyone who enters your spiritual household, your consciousness. Do you see the need for specific truth, specific principles of truth, consciously expressed?

Then, when you have completed your statements of truth, your realizations of truth, your utterances of truth, you now enter the second phase: "'Speak, Lord, for thy servant heareth.' I am listening for thy voice. Put the seal on this treatment. Let me know that I have reached the throne of God." And you wait for one or two or three minutes. That's all. Then you accept the fact that this truth in your consciousness is a law and is a law unto every situation, and go about your business.

Whether or not you see immediate results from your treatment has nothing to do with the fact that you have done your work and that fruitage is taking place. Learn not to judge from appearances and that will give you courage to repeat it a second time, a third time, a fourth and fifth time if necessary, until eventually you do begin to see fruitage, until you do hear, "Well, I called on you and I went away refreshed," or "reborn," or "with renewed faith," or "the pain left," or "the swelling went down," or "I found a job immediately."

If Jesus were on earth today and you went to him, you would expect harmony merely from being in his presence. But remember, he said, "Go and do likewise." Yes, "Go out into this world and heal the sick. Do what I have taught you to do." Those who come to you have the same right to expect healing, happiness, peace, and supply, for you are building the same mind that was in Christ Jesus by embodying truth in your consciousness. "Ye shall know the truth, and the truth shall make you free," and all those who come to you.

Don't think when anyone comes to us for help that blind faith is going to help them or that we have some special God who is going to do something for us that he won't do for them. There is no such God. The benefit anyone gets from coming to us is in the degree of specific truth which we know, which is embodied in our consciousness, which we utter and declare. You are not going to accomplish any healing greater than your understanding of specific healing truth. You must consciously know the truth and the truth will make the rest of us free.

For tonight, I want you to see this: By living in this message you are touching individual lives. An Episcopal minister, who is a chaplain of a mental institute in Alabama, is now distributing several hundred copies of our writings to reach thousands of patients who are under his care. The truth entertained in one consciousness is so powerful. One with God is a majority, so think what happens when two or more are gathered together in this truth. You have no idea where the borders of your consciousness may be. A man in a mental institute receives it and a family outside the walls of the institute is blessed by it. You, on this little island of Maui, receive it and somebody in New York or Japan or Germany benefits by it. Your consciousness is as infinite as God because God constitutes your consciousness, and God is infinite. Therefore your consciousness is infinite, and all those who are embraced by your consciousness are embraced by the law of God, if so be you know the truth and consciously remember it.

God constitutes my consciousness. My consciousness is made up of truth, the word of God, scripture; and this word of God is quick, sharp, powerful, a law of good

~14~

unto all who come within range of my consciousness by virtue of the fact that "I and my Father are one." Through the word of truth God's grace reaches and touches all those who come into my consciousness. Do you see that? But if you are not giving yourself this treatment about the nature of your consciousness, your consciousness is limited to that of a human being, sometimes good, sometimes bad.

You invoke the power of truth by your conscious awareness and remembrance and declaration of truth. The word of God in the midst of you is power, but you must know the word of God and utter it. Declare it silently, secretly, sacredly, unless someone asks for an audible word. Then you speak it as it is given to you from within, but this cannot be done as rote or ritual. To go over this tape and hear it several times will be helpful. But to commit it to memory and then declare it is of no value. These treatments should be the spontaneous utterances with which you have filled yourselves over the years.

Always remember, you can be of no greater help to anyone than the activity of truth in your consciousness. Therefore, the first treatment is given to yourself. When you retire at night, realize: "I am not going to sleep as a human being, I am resting in the divine consciousness of truth which I have embodied these many years. I am going to rest, consciously aware of the word of God alive and alert in me whether asleep or awake." This is the conscious activity of truth in your consciousness and it changes the nature of your night's rest.

So it is these truths, consciously expressed before you leave in the morning, change the nature of your days. I've explained this to you before. A human being living as a human being is subject to chance, accident, change, every wind that blows. Whether infection, contagion, unemployment, lack, limitation, strikes, whatever it is that's in the air–zoom! The human being falls prey to it. Why? Because the human mind is like a vacuum and every thought that blows is picked up. Not so the spiritual student. Not so those who live and move and have their being in the word of God. Oh, no. The Master says in the 15th chapter of *John*: "If you abide in my word and let my word abide in you, you will bear fruit richly." Yes, but if you fail to "abide in my word and let my word abide in you, you are as a branch that is cut off from the tree and it withereth." Withereth! Subject to anybody and anything that comes along to smack you around.

God gave you dominion through the word of God, but you must accept it. You must accept it and express it. You cannot let your mind be a vacuum; you cannot let it be acted upon by every wind that blows. Oh, no. No. You were given dominion through the word of God, but not as a personal power. This is a universal gift. And if you abide in the word of truth, if you abide in these scriptural passages of truth and let them abide in your consciousness, you will bear fruit richly and be a blessing and a benediction. As Moses was able to lead his people out of slavery, as Jesus was able to lead his followers into a new dimension of consciousness, so do we lead those who come to us–out of sin, out of disease, lack, limitation, unhappiness–into spiritual grace, harmony, love, and peace.

You have heard me say this is not a lazy man's work. This is not an easy way of life. We don't believe there is some God sitting around just waiting to take pity on unfortunate mortals. We've seen too many unfortunate mortals and what happens to them, but we know that God has given us his word. We know that from the days of the Hebrews to the present time we have been told: "Put it on your forehead; wear it on your arm; put it at the entrance of your homes." And the Hebrews do. They wear scripture on their foreheads—the word of truth. They wear a band of scripture on their arms. They put it on before leaving their homes—the word of truth. At the entrance to every orthodox Jewish household there is a tiny metal case containing the Ten Commandments. They take that literally: Keep truth on your forehead; bind truth to your arm; post truth at the entrance to your household.

We do not take that practice so literally. We take it to mean: forehead—in your mind; on your arm—in consciousness where it becomes power; at the entrance of your household—at the entrance of your soul, or consciousness. Keep the word of God in your mind, in your soul, in your heart, at the entrance of your consciousness. "I will keep him in perfect peace whose mind is stayed on me." And, "If you abide in the word and let the word abide in you" consciously, you will be those who bestow satori, darshan. You will be those who give benediction and blessing, not of yourself, but by the grace of God through the truth you embody in your consciousness and which you will never forget.

And so, in the morning before you leave your home, when coming to our meetings, at night before you retire, the first step you now know—and the rest of the stairway leads all the way up to heaven!

~ 2 ~

A SPIRITUAL WAY OF LIVING

Good Evening.

"Except the Lord build the house, they labor in vain that build it." The major secret of spiritual living is contained in this and many other passages. "Thou will keep him in perfect peace, whose mind is stayed on thee . . . Acquaint now thyself with him and be at peace . . . Acknowledge him in all thy ways and lean not unto thine own understanding . . . If you abide in the word and let the word abide in you, you will bear fruit richly. If you do not abide in the word and the word does not abide in you, you will be as a branch of the tree that is cut off and withereth." Such passages as these are to be found in the Hebrew and Christian scriptures, as well as in every one of the Eastern scriptures. And the meaning is clear, since even the great Master could say, "I of my own self can do nothing; the Father within me, he doeth the works." How much more true must that be of us, that we can do nothing except God do it through us or in us or as us. "He that is within me is greater than he that is in the world . . . He performeth that which is given me to do."

These are confirmations of the great revelation of all time that we are as nothing except in so far as we are led by the spirit of God, guided by the mind, the intelligence of God, empowered by the love of God, and have God's grace on every step of our journey. "I go to prepare a place for you." That presence goes before us to make the crooked places straight, that presence walks beside us, it comes behind as a rear guard. These bring to light the secret of spiritual living, without which we cannot prosper spiritually.

Now, by human might and human will it is possible, if one is strong enough, to go out and battle the world to become a great success, without any assurance of course that it will last forever and that one may not be pulled down in the end. But for one to go through life joyously, fearlessly, successfully, and harmoniously, it is absolutely necessary to have that which is called the Father within, or the presence and power of God. This is only a first step toward spiritual living.

I want you to see that as human beings we exist very much as pendulums. Now a pendulum hanging right here cannot of itself move to the right or to the left. It must be acted upon before it will move—it has no control whatsoever. It must obey whatever energy moves it, swinging in whatever direction it is moved. So with ordinary human beings who awaken in the morning, get up, get dressed, eat, rush out to work, and then are moved by any influence that is in the air. If it is infection or contagion, they will come up with infection and contagion. If it is headlines of war or rumors of wars, they will come up with fears and anxieties. If there is a sign of a commercial layoff or strike, fear will strike their hearts. In times of prosperity the average man or woman prospers to some degree; in times of panic they suffer. In wartime, if they stay home they probably get rich, and if they go to war they get killed or wounded, or lose their ideals. This is not true of the those who embark on a spiritual path and who learn not merely to recite scripture, but to apply it as if it were really what it truly is: a principle of life, the book of life harmonious, the book of life eternal.

So let us go back to our beginning for a moment and agree that we have embarked on a spiritual way of living. Now this does not mean we will change our occupation or our family life or community life. It does mean that we will introduce a new note into our present life and that new note will be the application of certain scriptural principles of life. The first and most important principle that we must embody is that which Brother Lawrence called, "practicing the presence of God." In other words, we say to ourselves:

I am living and moving and having my being in the word of God, keeping the word of God alive in me, abiding in the word and letting the word abide in me. I know, when I arise in the morning, or even before rising, on first awakening in the morning, it becomes necessary to consciously remember this is God's day and God goes before me "to make the crooked places straight," God goes before me to bless, God will be with me every step of my way. Omnipresence guarantees that if I go up to heaven I will find God; if I make my bed in hell I will find God; if I walk through the valley of the shadow of death I will find God, and there will be no time during this day when I will be outside the realm of God. I will keep my mind stayed on God; I will acquaint myself now with him and acknowledge him in all my ways.

We rise out of bed, we start our physical preparations for the day, we sit down to breakfast, and here is a glorious opportunity to realize that without God there is no food. God is the very life of all that is. God gives us our daily bread. God has provided infinite abundance: the cattle on a thousand hills are there; the fields are ripe to harvest; the sun, moon, and stars bear witness to God's glory; the earth showeth forth his handiwork. Everything testifies to the presence of God, supplying us, blessing us.

In this age of fast automobiles and faster airplanes, it really becomes necessary to consciously remember that God's grace is with me in the car, on the road, up in the air, or down in the sea. "The place whereon I stand is holy ground." Why? Because where I am, God is. Omnipresence assures me that I cannot walk outside the kingdom of God as long as I abide in the word of God and let the word of God abide in me. In businesses there are business problems, and in our human life these business problems can be very serious. There is even a new illness now called vocational disease. But these problems do not come nigh the dwelling place of the individual who remembers:

He performeth that which is given me to do. He that is within me is greater than any problem that I can be faced with. I am not alone. If I walk through the waters, God is with me; if I go through the flames, God is with me. There is no place where I can be that God is not present where I am as long as I am where God is: in the word of God and that word in me. As long as I abide in him and he abides in me consciously, how can I step outside of God's grace?

Noontime brings another opportunity for gratitude. Whether we recite our thanks openly at the table in the form of grace, or whether we pray silently, sacredly, secretly within, is really our own choice, dependent on our background. Actually, if we were to take the words of Christ Jesus literally, we would say grace silently, secretly, sacredly, where no man could hear us and no man could observe us giving thanks and praise. In *Matthew* we are told, "When you pray, do not pray where you can be seen of men. Go into your sanctuary and pray secretly; and the Father that seeth in secret will reward thee openly." That does not exclude the opportunity to attend church, temple, synagogue, or meeting house to unite in prayer and thanksgiving. Oh no, that is carrying out "where two or three are gathered together in my name." But let us not believe that we must limit our prayers to those occasions. We must pray as Paul taught, without ceasing, and that means we should take more opportunity to pray silently, secretly, sacredly than even those opportunities for public worship.

While it has been said many times that to live the life of Christ is an impossibility in this modern age, any such statement is sacrilegious and untruthful. It is possible to live the Christ-life today. True, at first it may make us seem strange to others, but we need not make a public display of our life in Christ. We can let it be seen by its effects, just as every student of ours has been taught not to proselytize, not to boast, but rather to keep the fingers on the lips and let our lives bear witness to the principles we live by. Oh, I have heard students tell me how difficult it was when their friends smoked, but they didn't; their friends took a cocktail, but they didn't. I realize that. I realize how strange it is when our students first begin to withdraw from parties or conversations where off-color jokes are told. While it's a little strange, it's not impossible, and it's not even difficult. Very soon we find a miracle: the people who at first thought us strange now begin to honor us because we are not plagued with tobacco or alcohol or drugs and we are not indulging in the immoralities or obscenities that are part of the human world. We are more highly respected for those qualities.

In the same way it has been said that businessmen cannot follow the Golden Rule. One need only examine such businesses as J. C. Penney or the Golden Rule Tailors of Cincinnati to see how ridiculous that is, to see how possible it is to live by these principles. Oh, there are millions of people who have said they cannot tithe because ten percent of their income is too much to give to a spiritual activity. They have only to look at those who are now giving sixty, seventy, and eighty percent of their income and still have wealth left over every year to know that it's a fallacy to believe there is anyone on earth who cannot tithe if they can meet the requirements of tithing. Actually there is only one requirement: We have to feel gratitude for our spiritual activity. If we have gratitude, that ten percent becomes a very small amount out of a hundred percent. If our spiritual activity brings peace of heart, peace of mind, peace of soul, physical health, moral stamina, and even bodily comfort, ten percent is very little.

But let us not believe that we will be rewarded by giving that ten percent, for we cannot bargain with God. That ten percent is a free-will offering of gratitude with no strings attached. If we cannot give it in that sense, we should not give it. We should cut it down to five percent, four percent, three percent, or two percent, until such time as it begins to flow as gratitude. Then we find that gratitude is a quality of love, and love is God. The moment gratitude is flowing, God is flowing, love is flowing, and all the wheels of life are turning smoothly.

You must see that "except the Lord build the house, they labor in vain that build it." This statement must not be used as a cliché or an affirmation. It must be understood that it means before undertaking any activity, and this certainly means upon rising in the morning, do not expect too much of that day if you haven't had the actual experience of God contact and received the inner assurance, "I am on the field."

The God experience is not a mental one, not an intellectual one. All that we know mentally or intellectually is merely a footstep leading to the experience of God contact, or God realization, whatever word you wish to use for the actual experience of being in the presence of God and knowing it. You see, prayer in its true sense is a communion with God. It is not begging or beseeching God, it is not asking God. It is a communion with God. Even though at the start of the communion we may find it necessary to mentally rehearse, to remember consciously, some of these passages of scripture that help bring concentration to the mind to help quiet it, communion with God can only be experienced in silence. When this quiet does descend upon us, the experience of prayer or communion begins in which we feel, rather than say, "Speak Lord, for thy servant heareth. I am listening for that still small voice." Then, with a receptive heart, with a quiet mind, we are still—one minute, two minutes, maybe three—and eventually there comes that inner feeling of peace or release.

Often, the voice itself is heard with specific messages. Most often it is not the voice, but an awareness, a feeling, of a presence within, a gentle presence, a restful or peaceful influence. Sometimes it comes as a release, as if all of a sudden the weight is gone off our shoulders, and oh! then we know that we're in the presence of God and that presence goes before us to make the crooked places straight. That presence is with us and performs that which is given us to do. Now we can say, "The house will be built, the watching will take place, for God is on the field."

To pray without ceasing—and this is the sum and substance of the spiritual or mystical life—means that on every occasion of the day and night we permit ourselves to have conscious thoughts of God. It means that regardless of what we're doing, there is an area of consciousness always alive and alert in which we are receptive to whatever thought of God may come at any hour of the day or night. It really means that upon retiring at night, we dare not fall asleep without consciously realizing, "My Father worketh even when I'm asleep. I am receptive and responsive to the divine impulse, even while sleeping. I am never so deeply asleep that I cannot be quickly wakened by the Spirit if it has a message for me, a direction, a protection."

Some think to live the spiritual life it is necessary to leave the world and enter an ashram or a convent or monastery. Surely you realize that those who can go to a convent, a monastery, or an ashram and leave the world outside, experience a tremendous, tremendous benefit whether they go for a day, a week, a month, or as some few do, leave this world to live that life. That is why the retreats now being organized in the Protestant Churches, as they have been for so many years in the Roman Catholic Church, are of such tremendous importance to men and women, especially of the business world. Now they can go away from Friday night to Monday morning and live a life of meditation, prayer, and concentration on the things of God. But for those who cannot take advantage of that opportunity, there still exist twenty-four hours of every day in which they can retire into the sanctuary of their own being. These days more churches than ever are open for people to spend time in meditation and prayer. Offices have quiet washrooms; homes have washrooms or lanais. Everyone who truly is led of the Spirit will find dozens of opportunities during the day to retire to a quiet place where they can realize God's grace within. That, of course, is the goal.

When we arrive at that place in consciousness where we no longer live by might or by power, when the grace of God performs our tasks through us and within us, and is ever at hand to advise, to instruct, to lead, then we have reached the goal of our spiritual life. It is not necessary to leave the world, for the Master said, "I do not pray that my disciples be taken out of the world. Leave them in the world, but not of it." So at this time in our unfoldment, we who are on the spiritual or mystical path do not leave the world. We are needed in businesses, in schools, in politics, in courts, abiding always in the presence of God.

There are those who serve humanity outside the customary activity of this world and are a great blessing, for they are called to that way of life. But until we are called, we must remain in the world but not of it. We have lived through centuries when the religious work of the world was carried on by priests and rabbis, and the rest of the people were laymen. That day is fast fading away. Oh yes, there will still be priests and rabbis to serve as teachers, those who lead the way and are at the forefront. They will instruct and show the fruitage of spiritual living by their example. But if each of us does not become a priest, a minister, or a rabbi, we will fail in our mission, for it is intended that all shall live by grace. All shall be the kingdom of God. All shall be ministers in one form or another, not to serve as ministers of a church but to minister where they are: in business, in court, in the classroom, showing forth that same spiritual integrity they expect of their ministers, imparting the same spiritual light, exemplifying the same Christ-like qualities that transform this world into heaven.

As you know, the work of the Infinite Way dates from the time it was shown to me that the reason for the discords of the world is that God is present only where God is realized. The rest of the world can burn up, the rest of the world can go to war and be shot to pieces, the rest of the world can be bombed. No God is interfering in that. The prayers for peace that are being said all the time, if one may dignify them with that name, are ineffectual. Peace was prayed for long before the Master's day, and it was never achieved. The reason is, God is where God is realized. Where God is realized, the grace of God is in expression.

Wherever you find groups of people who have attained God-realization, you find peace, integrity, health, safety, and security. You find that these are not at the mercy or whim of men. It is literally true that you need not fear "man whose breath is in his nostrils," you need not fear "what mortal man can do to you," if you have attained this inner contact with the Father. Paul revealed much of this when he made it clear that you are not children of God except the spirit of God dwell in you. He made it so clear that a human being cannot please God and does not live under the law of God, but when that same human being receives the spirit of God, he becomes the son of God; he lives under God's grace.

Therefore, it behooves us not to go around prating about God, talking about God, but to attain God-realization by living and moving and having our being in this word until the Spirit itself takes over and begins to live our life. Here too, it was Paul who said, "I live, yet not I, Christ liveth my life." And the Master said, "I of my own self can do nothing. If I speak of myself I bear witness to a lie. It is the Father within me. . . ." So are we to abide in this word and let this word abide in us until the Father within us is no longer a quotation but an experience.

When the spirit of the Lord God is upon you then are you ordained, not only to heal the sick, but even to prevent sickness, to raise the dead, to preach the gospel, to feed the hungry. God must be to us a living experience, and the Bible must be to us a living book. You see, if we read the Old Testament and go back to the story of Moses, we find these Hebrew people who ostensibly were very religious, who were always sure that their God was doing something for them. What we don't realize is that they were in slavery, they were in sin, they were in disease, yet they had God on their lips all the time. But when Moses received God-realization, illumination, that one man was able to carry the whole nation out of their slavery. Not keep them out, oh no. He was in the same position as Jesus was centuries later, when he said "O Jerusalem, O Jerusalem, I would but ye would not." Moses wanted them to know and to obey the law, but they weren't ready for that experience and so they slipped back and they went forward, they slipped back and went forward again. But whenever a Hebrew prophet came, an individual who had attained God-realization, that one could lift the nation. In the time of Jesus, the Hebrews had a great temple and everything that went with it; they had lots of religion, lots of worship, lots of ceremonies, lots of sacrifices. They lacked only one thing–God. Then Christ Jesus came, a man ordained of God, filled with the spirit of God, and see what miracles were performed with God in the midst of him.

It is sometimes believed that only Jesus had spiritual gifts and spiritual powers. But for three hundred years after the Master, great spiritual works were done by those who came under that same grace, if not to the same extent, then in their measure. Spiritual works were performed on earth: spiritual healing, spiritual living, spiritual freedom, spiritual prosperity. For three hundred years the grace of God worked in and through those who attained and achieved some measure of God-realization.

Even before the time of Jesus and Moses, the story of Gautama the Buddha has been told. He was merely a rich man's son until he received his illumination, and then he became the head of a worldwide activity, showering spiritual blessings on so many. Then there was Paul in his missions, and John. I think of another, of the great light that the Hebrew Maimonides brought to his people at a time when they were in slavery to the Romans, who was persecuted, imprisoned, and killed. One man, spiritually inspired with the grace of God, changed the history of his people for centuries. Nanak, the great spiritual leader of the fifteenth century, created a religion of peace, of joy, of spiritual living, and for three generations his followers thrived as a people of peace. Only when they violated his teaching not to accumulate money, only when they violated that and accumulated great wealth did they also have to create armies to protect it. Then they who had been brought up in the same teaching as Jesus Christ to "resist not evil," became the Sikhs, the warrior race of India.

It has been my privilege and pleasure to travel the world meeting some of the great spiritual lights and mystics, some who are known and some who will never be publicly known. Always it is the same experience: having attained the grace of God, they are the leaders for the groups of devoted followers that surround them. In the past seventy-five years, we have seen that wherever the spirit of God enters the consciousness of individuals they are set free, at least to some extent, from the inequities of this world: the lacks, the limitations, the sins, the diseases, the desires. Even a grain of God-realization is sufficient to free us from most of the world's miseries. What two grains would do remains yet to be seen.

"Where the spirit of the Lord is, there is liberty." Do you think for a moment this is an idle statement? Do you think that this is merely a quotation or a cliché? This is a spiritual principle of life. "Where the spirit of the Lord is, there is liberty." Where is the spirit of the Lord? Where it is realized. You might say truthfully that it fills all space. Indeed, it does. But so did electricity before it was hooked up to provide electric power, electric lights, and all its other uses. God does fill all space, but the activity of God is only where God is realized in the consciousness of those who live in the word and let the word live in them. And we have authority for that: "If you do not abide in this word and do not let this word abide in you, you will be as a branch of the tree that is cut off and withereth." Let no one think the part of the human race that is not living in the word and letting the word live within isn't that branch that is cut off and withereth. Only in abiding in this spiritual realization are we connected with the vine and the tree.

The 15th chapter of *John* summarizes the entire mystical life of man; it contains the secret of man's harmonious, immortal, and eternal life, even on earth. "If you abide in this word; if you abide in me and let me abide in you, you will bear fruit richly for you are the branch, I am the vine, and God is the tree." If you do not keep the word of God on your forehead, on your arm, and at the entrance to your household, you will be as a branch of the tree that is cut off and withers. You will live a life of chance, a life that is called a statistic. Today, everyone has become a statistic. We all know where we can go to find out how much longer we are going to live or what our chances are of an accident. We are statistics. The spiritual man is not a statistic. The man who has the word of God abiding in him is not a statistic; he is a son of God living under the grace of God.

The Master has laid out a code of life which we can follow. It is not a code that is reserved for those in monasteries or convents; it is for those of us who walk this business world, who remain in the world but not of it. We can prosper in our business, in our professions, in our arts and in our sciences by the presence of God. We can be protected, fed, maintained and sustained by the presence of God. In whatever activity we engage, as long as that activity is not a violation of the Holy Spirit, the presence of God goes before us to make the crooked places straight and sometimes, when that activity is in violation of God's law and the prayer is sincere enough, we are lifted out of that occupation into another.

I had to meet that once when a man came to my office and said, "I need help desperately, but I know I can't get it. I represent a brewery and I can't believe that God will ever answer my prayer while I'm out selling alcohol to men, to befuddle them." My answer was, "'The place whereon thou standest is holy ground.' If you need help and truly are turning to God for it, your help will come. What its result on your work will be, I have no way of knowing. But I do know this: The mission of the Christ on earth was to forgive sinners, not to condemn them. He never sent them into outer darkness; he forgave them, whether the woman taken in adultery or the thief on the cross. 'Neither do I condemn thee, go and sin no more.' His whole mission was one of showing forth God's grace where you are and letting that grace lift you out of where you are. Peter had to learn that lesson when he tried to remain a Hebrew and refused to eat the meat of pigs, which later would have kept him from going to Cornelius, the unclean gentile. He had to learn to call nothing unclean which God had created, for 'God made all that was made.'" In the end, the man who came to my office did turn seriously to God and was lifted out of his occupation and into another one within two weeks.

Oh, yes. Where we are now in life is the result of the erroneous states of consciousness that have governed us.

But if in those erroneous states we return to the Father's house, we have the experience of the prodigal: right where he was in his banquet with the swine, he turned and was led out and back to his Father's house. There is no place where you can be, in heaven, in hell, in the valley of the shadow of death, where you cannot reach out to God and be lifted up. There's only one price: sincerity, integrity. Lip-service when we're in trouble brings few answers, if any. Too many say, "Oh, Lord! Lord!" when they're in deep trouble. They haven't yet reached that state of integrity to mean it, as is so often proven when they get out of trouble and then go back to sin again. The Master warned against that state of thought: "Neither do I condemn thee, but go and sin no more lest a worse thing come upon you." Some may, in their distress, seem to turn to God and either get no result, or at most, a temporary one, and then sink back. I say that at any given moment, whether you are on your death bed or in sin, if your turning to God is not merely to overcome the present evil, but really done in the sense of repentance, of realization, then it is possible to go from one extreme to the other. Look at Francis Thompson[1] who went from the gutter as a drug addict to become one of England's great mystics.

Let us never take the attitude of condemnation with ourselves or with those who come to us for comfort and

---

[1]Sir Francis Thompson, 1859-1907. English mystical poet. His well-known poem, *The Hound of Heaven*, depicts God as pursuing humanity midst its blind involvement in material living, drawing the soul back to himself. Available in *The Oxford Book of English Mystical Verse*, Chosen by D.H.S. Nicholson and A.H.E. Lee; first published in England, 1917, by Oxford University Press (reprinted 1997 by Acropolis Books, Inc., Lakewood, CO).

help, regardless of where they may be at any given moment. Let us accept them at face value and give them every bit of help we can. If we help them out and they don't hold it, that is their affair. If their own insincerity prevents their being helped, that is their affair. Our part is not to judge, criticize, or condemn, but to hold out that which we have. "Silver and gold have I none, but such as I have, give I unto thee." So whether someone is crippled mentally, physically, morally or financially, we do have our God-realization to offer those who seek us. How it changes their lives is something for them to ponder and to demonstrate.

In this work there are two parts to your prayer or meditation period. The first part is that you consciously remember these spiritual principles, spiritual promises, spiritual experiences of scripture. Bring them to con- scious thought, dwell on them, ponder them; if possible contemplate them, until some spiritual factor is revealed. Then comes a period of quiet for listening. This is the second part of your prayer or meditation in which the inner ear is opened as if to hear that voice of God, always remembering that "when God utters his voice, the earth melteth." If you receive a spiritual impulse within you, remember that the particular problem is melting, disappearing out of your life.

Never forget that it is an impossibility to attain even the blink of an eye of God-realization and not have some problem of human experience dissolve. And so it is, in the second part of our prayer or meditation, we are almost a vacuum; we are a transparency; we are a state of awareness as if expecting some inner unfoldment, or inner feeling, or inner experience. We dare not outline what it is because we do not know the nature of God's demonstration for us. We may think we need a home; we may think we need a trip; we may think we need employment, but we dare not pray for those things. We must always have the attitude in our prayer, "Not my will be done, but thine."

One thing to remember: No prayer must ever be advising God or seeking in any way to influence God. Don't let yourself be trapped into those side issues. You cannot influence God. God is the same yesterday, today, and forever. If you are not receiving God's grace, it is only because you are out of contact. Bring yourself back into contact and the grace will flow. God is the all-knowing mind; you cannot tell God what you need. You dare not ask for bread, or housing, or clothing, or employment, or health. God is the infinite intelligence of this universe, and "He knoweth your need before you do; it is his good pleasure to give you the kingdom," even before you ask.

Therefore, you must go to God a humble soul, an empty soul: "Fill me Lord. Be thou my grace." That's all. And when God-realization takes place, you'll find your needs will be fulfilled, for God is a law of fulfillment. God *is* fulfillment. Let us not believe that mortal man is wiser than God. Let us not believe that God will go out of his way to do for you what God is not doing for others. "God's rain falls on the just and the unjust."

, Make the contact and you will find God's grace flowing, and never will you have to tell God what you need or want. Never will you have to try to influence God on your behalf or on the behalf of another. If you open yourself so that God fills your consciousness, God fills the need of everyone who has been drawn into your consciousness, and you may not ever know in what way or to what degree. That is not your business, nor is it your business to know how God blesses, whom he blesses, and to what extent. When Jesus was healing multitudes, I am sure he did not concern himself with whether it was Jones, Brown, or Smith who got healed. Your part is to be a transparency for God, to rest in his word, to abide in him and let him abide in you.

~ 3 ~

TREATMENT: KNOWING THE TRUTH

Good evening.

The other evening we started by saying that as a human being you are a pendulum. You are acted upon, and whichever way thoughts fly in the air they move you. If there is pessimism or fear or danger in the air, you feel downhearted, discouraged, blue and fearful. If optimism, boom and prosperity are in the air, you feel inflated. If there is infection and contagion in the air, the first thing you know, you have flu or grippe. These things ought not to be because you were given dominion over everything between the sky and the bottom of the ocean—you were given dominion by the grace of God. But instead of exercising dominion, you wake up in the morning, get dressed, have breakfast, and run off to work leaving your minds a perfect blank for anybody to operate on or in, for anything to influence by whichever way the wind blows. This is why the human world experiences the things it does.

You know it has been demonstrated that those who are willing to take the driver's seat in their minds and govern their own thinking, who decide what they wish to think and for how long a time they wish to think it, those people have some dominion over their own lives. We have been taught how to do that. I'm going to give you a concrete illustration of how the power of thought acting on us influences us.

There is a minister who recently wrote a book on the effect of prayer on plants. He wrote this book after several years of conducting experiments that others had also tried through the years, and the results of his experiments and those of the others are always the same. He discovered this: If you take a plant, place it on a table, and have one, two, or three people sit in front of it and address it with what you might call prayer or treatment, in a few days the plant will grow at least four inches beyond the normal growth of that species. They love the plant, tell the plant that God created it, that it is a child of God, that it is fed and nourished and sustained by God, and that God loves it and wants it to be fruitful, to multiply and to show forth the beauty and glory of God—and it does. Soon it will have many times the leaves, buds, and eventually, blossoms.

But take another plant of the same species and have one, two, or three people sit before it, and treat it in the opposite way, "You hateful thing, you're ugly. Nobody wants you and nobody loves you. You just don't belong in this universe and you ought to die," and the plant will shrivel within one day and die within two. This man experimented with hundreds of plants of all different species and always the outcome was the same: If you have people sit before these plants thinking positive thoughts, they blossom; and if they think negative thoughts, they shrivel and die.

We have other examples of how the power of thought can work on individuals: In the experience of the Hawaiians, there were good kahunas and bad kahunas. The good kahunas were those who thought right

~40~

thoughts about you, and you prospered and were healed. You were blessed. The bad kahunas sent the wrong thoughts at you, and you got sick and even died. You may not believe it, but it happened. In Arabia they raise the very finest horses in the world. There is supposed to be nothing finer than the Arabian horse. What makes the Arabian horse the finest in the world? It is the only country in the world where a man of the mosque goes to the stables every single day when a mare is in foal and reads to the mare from the Holy Koran; he reads love, he reads truth, he reads life. That is why the Arabs bring forth the finest horses. In our work we have found that when women were pregnant and carrying their children, if they read spiritual literature and meditate and are immersed in this work, not only do they go through the period of their pregnancy with less trouble than ordinarily is the case, but they also bring harmony into the experience of their children, and in many cases carry their children all the way through childhood without the usual children's diseases.

The whole of what I'm saying is this: You govern your surroundings by the nature of what is taking place in your consciousness. You can make people love you very easily; you can make them dislike you even more easily. To be received joyfully, it is only necessary for you to live constantly in the realization that wherever you travel, and whomever you travel with are children of God; these are God's creations. God made them in his image and likeness, he planted himself in the midst of them; God gave them his mind, his life, his soul. Now, you are not saying this aloud to anybody. You are thinking this within your own heart, in your own mind, and not merely for five minutes. Your studies have brought you to this attitude. Always, you are seeing spiritual identity enthroned.

You may not believe this now, but you can experiment and prove for yourself that it won't take long until people are beginning to think you've changed, that you've become something other than who you were. They love you now. They didn't before, but they love you now. Oh, how you've changed! Yet only one change took place: You are seeing them as they are. You are not judging by appearances, you are judging righteous judgement. If you want to be well hated, all you have to do is take an inner mental attitude of criticism, judgement, and condemnation toward this world and the people in it and see if they do not react to what is going on in your consciousness.

I remember once when I was reading the Thanksgiving Day Christian Science service in a prison. The first service in the morning was the Catholic service, then the Protestant service, then the Jewish service, and the Christian Science service was last. On Thanksgiving Day, each one of these churches except Christian Science gave out candies, cigarettes, and fruit to all those who attended the service. When it came our turn, the guard went through announcing: "Eleven o'clock Christian Science service. No free gifts!" But the men were there, plenty of them. As a matter of fact, in eighteen months our attendance jumped from an average of eleven to a hundred and sixty-eight men.

What did it? Well, I'm telling you: Don't go into a prison and see a lot of prisoners who are bad men and hope to reform them, but go and realize that regardless of the human conduct of any individual, the seed of God, divinity itself, is within them. The kingdom of God is within them; the kingdom of love, the kingdom of life, the kingdom of truth is within them. The fact that they haven't awakened to it has nothing to do with it. "Know ye not that ye are the temple of God? Know ye not that your body is the temple of God?" That is addressed to mankind, but we don't always know it. We sometimes abuse the body, but it is the temple of God–and we certainly abuse each other every time we indulge in unnecessary judgement, criticism, and harshness.

Now, by realizing that man is actually the temple of God and that the kingdom of God dwells in him as a habitual state of thought, we are praying. We call it giving a treatment but really it is prayer. We are holding the truth of being in our consciousness, and that's what prayer is on its first level. On a higher level, we know that prayer is communion with God, but on its first level it is replacing beliefs with truth. We also call that treatment in metaphysics. It doesn't mean we are trying to heal or reform anyone of anything. It means that we are giving ourselves a treatment about the appearance. The appearance testifies to a sick mortal or a sinful mortal, but we are not to judge by appearances. Therefore our treatment is a recognition of the truth, not an attempt to change anyone. It is a recognition of the truth: "I know thee who thou art." Who? "The son of God." That's treatment.

If I continuously abide in that treatment about you, knowing you are the temple of God, that God dwells in his temple therefore God dwells in you, that the kingdom of God is within you, you respond by thinking, "Oh, I like that fella. I don't know why but there's something nice about him." You haven't the faintest idea in the world what it is, but it is this: You know as well as

I do that no matter how sick you may be or how much a sinner, there is a place in you which is awfully good and which nobody has recognized. You know there is a divine spot within you, and no matter how much the world condemns you and no matter what you may be doing to deserve that condemnation, you don't want to be doing it. You know it is in spite of yourself that you're doing it, and that actually if the world could only know it, you're a swell fella inside.

Do you see? I have recognized that without your telling me, and by my recognizing it you have the feeling, "Here is someone who understands me. Here is someone who knows me." But you don't know why you feel that way. Now in the same way, the moment you adopt that, you begin to have dominion over your human relationships. You are stopping people from hating you, you are stopping them from mistrusting you, and you are building up in them an affection for you, a trust of you, a confidence in you because you're the fellow who understands them. You're the fellow who has sought out and found their hidden spot, their divinity. So you see, by knowing the truth, by treating yourself with truth regarding man, you already begin to have dominion over your human relationships.

So it is with our own lives which heretofore we've thought of as occupying space from our head to the ground, thinking "this is me." Here I am in a world of four billion people, and I think, "Oh, here I am, one of four billion. I'm nothing. What chance have I got against so much competition? And who am I? Nobody! What's going to get me anyplace? How am I going to achieve anything? Me. Just an unknown against the world." That's the appearance. That's the way it looks in the mirror.

Now, let's see what a treatment will do for us. I look out of my window, I see a coconut tree, and I see a coconut on that tree. All of a sudden I'm reminded of Jesus' statement, "If you abide in the word and let the word abide in you, you will bear fruit richly. If you do not abide in the word and let the word abide in you, you will be as a branch of the tree that is cut off and withereth." Now you look at the coconut and think, "It's on the tree; it's connected with the tree." And, lo and behold, "That's right. It's a beautiful coconut, it's a healthy looking coconut. If I examine it I'll find that it has the hard shell and it has the soft meat and it has the liquid milk inside. That is because it's in its rightful place, hanging on a tree, connected with the tree." Why is the connection with the tree so important? Oh, because if it weren't connected with the tree, it would have only itself. But while it's connected with the tree, the life that's coming up through the roots and the trunk and the branches is flowing right into that coconut. That life is forming the shell, the meat, and the milk. We see the life of the tree forming itself as a coconut. It wouldn't be doing that if the coconut weren't attached to the tree; it never would get to be a complete coconut. In its attachment to that tree, the invisible life of the tree flowing through the tree flows out of the tree to become a coconut: it becomes the hard shell, it becomes the soft meat, and it becomes the liquid milk.

Now, we begin to see why we read in scripture, "Son, thou art ever with me and all that I have is thine." Why certainly. All of the life the tree has flows out to the coconut and the coconut has it all; it has it in the forms that it needs: the hard shell, the soft meat, and the liquid milk. And then we say, "Oh, the mirror does not testify truly; I am not just a something that goes from my head to the ground. There is an invisible bond between me and the tree of life which we call God, and from that life which is God flows the life that becomes me." Ah, now it's different. I'm not a little fella; I'm not a nobody. The life of God is my life; the mind of God is my mind; the soul of God is my soul. God even becomes my body, and my body is the temple of God. That life, that invisible life, flows out and forms heart, liver, lungs, and all there is to my body. It forms my character, it forms my intelligence, it forms my love. Oh, this is different now. "I and my Father are one" just as the coconut and the tree are one. The coconut is the manifested life of the tree, the coconut is the manifested form. God is the tree of life, therefore I am the form which it assumes in individual expression: I and you and he and she and it. Now, all of a sudden I'm a different being. Now I'm not this little insignificant person in four billion. Now the life of God is mine; the love, the mind, the intelligence, the wisdom, the guidance and the direction of God are mine. Now I can say, "I am a son of God. 'Now are we the sons of God.' "

Oh, what a different experience from what I saw in the mirror! You can call this prayer if you like; we call it treatment. We call it giving ourselves a treatment. We don't want to change anything. We are declaring that which is true but which was not evident to the five physical senses. "You shall know the truth and the truth shall make you free." What is the truth? Am I a lone mortal out in the world among four billion mortals? No. Am I an insignificant mentality? No. I have the mind of God. Am I a limited life that has to die? No. The life of God flows forth as my life. Ah yes, but once I separate myself from the tree of life, I wither and die. How do I separate myself from that tree of life, from the flow of life eternal? By shutting it out of my mind. My consciousness is the connecting link. What takes place in my consciousness gives me oneness with God. What does not take place in my consciousness constitutes the separation.

You must consciously know the truth, and the truth will make you free. If you walk around in a vacuum—getting up in the morning, dressing, and going out about your business with no thought of your contact with God, of your oneness with God, of your relationship with God—you might just as well be an orphan because the only contact there is between you and God must take place within your consciousness. If it doesn't take place there, it isn't taking place. Then you are like all the other human beings walking up and down the earth, wondering what minute you are going to be keeled over by an accident, a sin, a disease, a strike, or a depression, always pushed around by the whims of forces over which you seemingly have no control. You actually do have supreme control every minute if only you'll take possession of your own thinking. So you think, "Now it isn't thinking that makes it so. Ah, no. It's my relationship with God that makes it so." If you consciously bring that to remembrance, you establish your demonstration.

I've told this story before, of the time I had two savings accounts. I went to draw money out to buy a home but I left a hundred dollars in each one of the accounts to keep them open, thinking I'd build them up again later, which of course I didn't do. As the years passed and I moved from place to place, my bank books were misplaced, and so twenty years went by. In New

York State if an account stays open for twenty years without any activity, the money goes to the state, but the bank does make an effort to locate you before it turns your money over. They do this by publishing the number of the bankbook in the newspapers. Now there is an organization that makes a business of looking up those numbers every year in the newspaper and finding the people who own those lost bankbooks. Lo and behold, one day I received a letter telling me that this outfit knew where I had money and if I would give them half of it they'd tell me where the money was. Oh, of course I was glad to have half–that's better than none– and so I accepted their offer. My two hundred dollars had grown to four hundred, or nearly that, and so by giving them half I still had my two hundred. But my point is this: A short time before that I had really needed money, and two hundred dollars would have been a tremendous blessing to me. I didn't have two hundred dollars; but yes, I did. It didn't do me any good, though, because I didn't know it. I had it, and it could just as well have been two thousand dollars or two hundred thousand dollars, it still would have done me no good because I didn't know the money was there.

That's the secret I'm telling you about treatment. Treatment doesn't make you the son of God. That you are. Treatment doesn't bring God into your experience. It is already there, but it isn't doing you a bit of good because you don't know the truth. So when you know the truth, the truth can make you free. But you must know the truth–and we call that specific treatment. Why specific treatment? Well, in the instance I spoke of, establishing yourself in your community among your neighbors, you must specifically know the truth about your neighbors. You must know that they are the sons of God; that their bodies are the temple of God; that the kingdom of God is enthroned within them. This is a specific truth that you are knowing about your neighbors.

In the instance of your own life, you take the coconut tree and begin to realize that if you are a separate coconut, your life is very short and going to be shorter. But if you are at one with the tree, the life of that tree is maintaining and sustaining you even as it forms you. As a matter of fact, it doesn't form you, it forms itself as you. That's specific treatment about you, your mind and your body.

In the same way, suppose you were suffering from some bodily ill that had to do with organs or functions of the body, and suppose you were to realize that those organs or functions, separate and apart from God, wouldn't function and couldn't function since they can't move of themselves, they can't function of themselves. For example, this hand can't move; it can't give and it can't withhold of itself. It just has to stay here until I move it. Well, so it is with the heart, the liver, and the lungs. They're dead pieces of matter unless and until there is an I to move them. Then they can't resist. The heart can't say I won't beat, the digestive organs can't say we won't digest, if you are there and realize that you're governing the heart, liver, lungs, the digestive organs, the eliminative organs, and that God is the law unto your body. You'll change the picture which says that your body is a law unto you. If your stomach wants to get sick, it tells you it's sick and pains you; if the heart wants to get sick, it says to you, "You're sick." Ah, yes, but that's because you're letting the heart and liver and lungs talk back to you. When you become aware of spiritual truth, you look at this body and say, "Why, of yourself you are nothing. You can't be sick or well. I'm going to talk to you; I'm going to take possession of you; I'm going to take dominion over you. And don't forget this: The *I* that I'm talking about is my Father. The Father within has dominion over you; the Father within governs the organs and functions of this body and the muscles and the intelligence."

That's treatment; that's specific treatment that isn't aimed, remember, to change anything. It is treatment to know the truth so that you can have the benefit of the truth operating for you. We speak of diseases that are caused by weather or climate. If you let them, they will affect you. However, when you begin to know the truth, you'll find out that the weather and the climate are governed by God. They didn't create themselves. God created weather and God created climate. Therefore, God has dominion over weather and over climate and over your body, too. God never made weather or climate to be antagonistic to your body, and God didn't make your body to be antagonistic to the weather or the climate. God didn't give something else dominion over your body. God created your body, and God maintains your body and sustains it. So if you are letting weather and climate affect it, don't forget that you are letting it happen. You are giving it that power because you are not asserting your dominion by knowing the truth. God gave you a body and God gave you weather and climate, and God didn't make these antagonistic to each other.

It may be that we are dealing with infection and contagion. Did God create some form of life to be destructive to another form of life? No, no, no! The appearance testifies that by infection and contagion you can get a disease and die. But if you know the truth, you annihilate that appearance because the truth is that God did not make one form of life destructive to another. Therefore, whatever the germ-life may be, in the sight of God it is not destructive and God didn't empower it to be destructive. God has not empowered anything to be destructive. God's power is constructive. This is knowing specific truth, and this we call treatment. You are not treating anybody but yourself. Your treatment consists of knowing the truth about any given situation, and there is a spiritual truth about every specific situation. There isn't a situation that can come up in life—at least there never has been one yet—about which there isn't some specific spiritual truth. You don't have to find out what these truths are now. When the occasion comes up, turn within and the Father will give you the truth, and with the truth he will give you freedom.

Now, if you had a business you would have to know the truth about every department of that business or very soon it would run away with you. If you are teaching a subject and you don't know the subject, you aren't going to teach it very well and pretty soon the students will be running away with you. So it is with life. If you don't know the principles of life, you can't live it very well and life is going to be more or less accidental. The minute you know the principles of life and take them into your consciousness and remember them, every time there is an opposing belief or negative suggestion, you are knowing the truth and giving specific treatment.

Now, it would appear to us that as human beings out here among these four billion, we're always struggling to be successful, to get by, or to do as well as we should. If we succeed, we think we're pretty good, pretty smart, pretty strong. If we don't, we're apt to blame all the circumstances in the world except ourselves. It's always the other fellow's fault, or it's the government's fault, or it's capitalism's fault. It's never the fault of our not knowing the principles of life.

The other night, we took up a specific treatment that I call, "practicing the presence of God." You see, the appearance is that we are going through life, living our life and not having too much success. But the specific truth is that, "He that is within me is greater than he that is in the world"; that "He performeth that which is given me to do"; that there is a presence "that goes before me to make the crooked places straight." Ah. What a difference in my life when I bring those truths to conscious remembrance, and bringing those truths to conscious remembrance is specific treatment. That is specific treatment against the sense of separation which would make it appear that we ourselves have to make a success of our lives as if we didn't have a big partner, the Father within. Every time we remember there is a Father within, we are giving a specific treatment which corrects the belief that we are alone, one in four billion. Every time we remember a coconut tree with a coconut on it, we are giving a treatment for immortality and for intelligence and for support and supply.

You must have studied this work long enough to know by now that there is not some old-fangled or new-fangled God sitting around somewhere caring that something's happening to you. For all God is concerned, you could jump off the roof or into the ocean. People are doing it every day and no God is stopping them. Accidents are happening; children are kidnapped, raped, and murdered. Where is this God? Every day youth are being destroyed in wars. Where is this God? There is a God. But don't you see that it is not operating in our experience until we can specifically let it into our consciousness? By opening our consciousness to it, by learning the truths of life, and by putting those truths into operation through conscious awareness, we take dominion through truth; not that I of my own self am anything; not that I of my own self can be anything; not that I of my own self can do anything. But by virtue of these truths entertained in my consciousness, I am set free. Of what? Of limitation, disease, death, or sin. There is no other way, at least no other way that has been discovered yet.

The only way known is the way the Master (and some of the Hebrew prophets before him) taught: "Thou will keep him in perfect peace whose mind is stayed on thee . . . Lean not unto thine own understanding . . . Acknowledge him in all thy ways and he will give you peace . . . Abide in the word and let the word abide in you . . . Dwell in the secret place of the most High." Do you not see that all of these scriptures take conscious thought, conscious knowing of the truth, conscious application to the problems that confront us? Do you not know that when you get in your car to drive, if you don't want to be a statistic on the road you had better consciously realize that God is not only your mind at the wheel, but that God is the mind of every individual on the road? You've got to pray before you get into your car, when you are in it, and when you get out of it: "Thank you, Father, for thy presence at this wheel and at the wheel of every car on the road." Do you see that? By consciously bringing the truth to bear, you not only keep yourself alert and awake at the wheel, but you ensure that everyone else is going to stay awake and alert; and if there is someone drunk out there, they are going to sober up pretty quickly if you are knowing that God is at their wheel, too. God means intelligence, alertness, aliveness, and love.

Every business deal in the human world is undertaken by someone because of the benefit they are going to get from it, and that is not the truth about business. To believe that would be as sinful as to believe that when patients go into a doctor's office, the doctor thinks they are coming there to enrich him. A doctor doesn't feel that way. When he sees people coming to his office, he says, "Thank you, Father, for the opportunity you are giving me to help these people." If he makes money by it, that's incidental. Heaven help the doctor who is in his office, or the lawyer, or the minister, thinking, "I'm here to get rich and you are coming here to make me rich." Oh, no. "You are coming here to give me the opportunity to help you with my knowledge." Why isn't business that way? When I go into a department store, why isn't the thought, "Thank you for coming in here and giving us the opportunity to provide what you need? Of course we are going to make money, but that's incidental to the fact that we have met your need; we have served you, we are here for that purpose. You needn't go to New York to buy a shirt; we're here to see that we have it for you. That's our service and that's what we're in business for, to serve you. By this service we do make money, but only in proportion as our service to you."

Do you see that, spiritually speaking, every business transaction is performed for the benefit of the other fellow? That's why it's performed. When people sell us a book, it isn't that they should make money; it is because they are serving our need for that book and making money is incidental to the service. And so, whether it's an article of clothing or whether it's a book, whatever it is, our object in the business world is to serve the needs of the other fellow and say when he comes into our shop, "Thank you for giving me this opportunity of blessing you." A business need never worry about going broke while holding this attitude.

If a man were in business, this would have to be a specific treatment on his part. Almost every day he would have to remember, "I'm not going downtown to my shop to get rich; I'm not going down there to make money. I'm going down there to serve the community. Therefore, I must have a clean window and a clean door and a clean shop and make my shop a pleasant place for my customers to be in." We have firms like J. C. Penney that were built on those principles. We have the owner of a well-known machine building firm who, when he was bankrupt, tried to figure out why and finally realized, "I have everything in my business but God. That will never happen again. Now, when I go back into business I will take God as my partner. And the first thing I'm going to do is declare him in for ten percent without any thought of return." You know the rest of the story: Today he gives eighty percent of his profits to charity; he keeps twenty percent for himself (and last year we were told that his twenty percent amounted to two million dollars).

Yes, business is not cold or cruel; business is not mercenary unless the individual running the business has not learned the principles of life. Then it becomes necessary for him to remind himself of those principles—and we call that treatment. We give ourselves a treatment, just as I told you about this room. Do you think that I could come to one of these meetings without consciously remembering that whoever enters this room is entering my consciousness? Therefore I must meditate in order to have the presence of God here for them to meet when they enter my consciousness, and my consciousness must be clean and my consciousness must be friendly. What kind of reception do you think people would get if I had a little fight with my wife before I came here? (You know the answer to that: that's her protection. She can't have a fight with me because I can't afford to fight. See?) I have to keep a loving and friendly consciousness because nobody comes into this room to see the room and nobody comes into this room to see me sitting here. I don't look like Clark Gable or Frank Sinatra or Alan Ladd, so they don't come here to see me. But they come, and why? Because in coming, they enter the consciousness of God that they find here. For hours I have meditated or read or dictated mail—everything that keeps me in the consciousness of God. Then when they come in, they feel it if they're at all receptive, if they're at all sensitive; they feel that peace. See that?

Business is governed by the same principle. Every business person, every teacher, should make it a practice to meditate before going into their business or their school, so that everybody who comes into their consciousness comes in and finds God waiting to greet them, love waiting to greet them. That is treatment. That is consciously knowing the truth.

Now, major treatment, major healing work—spiritual healing work—can be successfully done only through the consciousness of a person who knows there are not two powers in the world, good and evil, and who is not eternally trying to get one power to do something to another power. This is major treatment, major healing work, and this takes training. It takes a lot of treatment, self-treatment, because, mark this! every single person who comes to you for help for a sick body or a sick mind instantly rouses in you the desire to want to do something to that disease. You want a power to overcome it or destroy it; you want a power to remove it. And you lose. You can't win if you take up the sword. You'll die. If you want to do spiritual healing, you have to maintain yourself in the consciousness which is always saying to Pilate, "Thou couldest have no power over me." And whether Pilate is an individual or Pilate is a sin or Pilate is a disease or Pilate is unemployment, you have to be the consciousness that says, "Thou couldest have no power over me, because there's only one power—that's God." And then rest and rest and rest in that. Do you see how much treatment you have to give yourself to be able to live in the conviction that there is only one power, and you don't use God, you don't use truth, to overcome or destroy? You realize truth to be the only power.

I was reading a paper written by a doctor and given by him at a very large meeting last week. He made the statement that a great tragedy has come upon the world in the form of antibiotics. He stated that whereas they actually did do their work of overcoming germs and killing infection as they were meant to, now more and more people are dying from them than from the diseases they cured. He's asked the doctors to stop using them or to find some way of overcoming the harm they're doing because the deaths from these remedies are greater than deaths from the diseases. Can you imagine that? That's a lesson for us in taking up the sword: one power to overcome another power. In our work we don't do that, at least not if we are sufficiently drilled and trained in the principles of life. We know there is only one power, but we don't know it well enough to ever stop giving ourselves treatments.

The pressure of the world is so great and the fear is so great that every time someone comes to us with a serious sin or a serious disease, we quickly turn to see if we can't find a God to help us do something to it—and we don't succeed. In spiritual healing we succeed only as we can attain an inner conviction that God is the only power, life is the only creative, maintaining and sustaining power, and God has no opposite and no opposition so we are not using God to heal a disease. Now this is difficult. It is difficult because theology has taught us that we can go out and find a God to do something for us. All material law tells us of two powers: good and evil. Every mental law is made up of both good and evil, just as the minister proved that with good thoughts you can grow a plant and with bad thoughts you can kill it. There are two powers in the physical and mental realms, but not in the spiritual. Once you reach the spiritual realm, there are not two powers; there is only one. How do you reach that spiritual power? You keep knowing the truth specifically—and this is treatment. Treatment is whatever I have to tell myself to keep reminding myself of the truth that already is. Do you see the importance of treatment?

Now, when you go back to my writings, notice that without telling you I was giving you treatments, you were receiving treatments on every page. Notice that while I didn't use the term, I was doing it. Why didn't I use the term? Because in the beginning it misleads students. They're apt to think that those treatments create new conditions; they're apt to think that those treatments are something you hold to so as to make something come true. I try to teach treatment without saying it is treatment as much as possible except when it comes to classes; and by that time students are prepared to know that a treatment isn't a treatment to do something to somebody. A treatment is something I give myself, first of all to enlighten myself about the truth of being and secondly, to keep calling to my conscious awareness the reminder of this truth forever and forever and forever. If I went one hour without the reminder, the very next hour I'd be trying to get God to do something for one of my friends. I'd be trying to influence God—sometimes I'd even be trying to tell God. And so, I have to remind myself: No! No! No! God is. God already knows. "It is God's good pleasure to give us the kingdom." God alone is. That is treatment, that is knowing the truth—and it is knowing the truth that sets you free from appearances.

Thank you, because this is a big treatment! And whatever's left, we'll have tomorrow morning at eleven o'clock.

~ 4 ~

TREATMENT:
ITS MEANING AND PURPOSE

Good Morning.

Sunday morning on Maui—one of those beautiful days Maui knows how to make!

We have done an important work this week. If these tapes are properly studied they can prove to be the most important work you have undertaken in the message of the Infinite Way, but this depends on what you put into it. You won't get more out of these tapes than you put in because all these tapes have are words, and the words only take on importance as they become imbued in your consciousness and their meaning is realized. You may have to listen to these tapes many, many times before you begin to get the meaning that I put into them. That meaning is the direct result of thirty years of this work. They are important, that I'll tell you—and why? Because they deal with the subject of treatment. Why is the subject of treatment important, when it is a word that is never heard in the religious world? To understand that, you have to understand the purpose of treatment. The purpose of treatment, metaphysically understood, is the development of spiritual consciousness. Treatment isn't aimed at healing diseases or at getting supply; treatment isn't aimed at making better relationships. Treatment has one specific purpose, and that is developing spiritual consciousness.

Now let me illustrate exactly how this is accomplished. In the material state of consciousness into which we were born, the greatest reality is matter and material force. That's what we fear the most and that's what we love the most. We love it most in forms of money, jewelry, property, and investments, and we fear it most in the forms of bullets, poisons, and germs. Matter in one form or another is the subject of our love, of our hate, and of our fear. In another sense, matter is something we use in the form of material force, whether it is water power or electrical power, to attain good in one way or another. But we also use material force for destructive purposes, to kill or to injure. And so, to those of us who live in material consciousness, matter and material force make up most of our lives, and we're very busy either loving them, hating them, or fearing them.

Spiritual consciousness is the opposite of that. Spiritual consciousness neither loves matter nor its forms, nor does it hate it or fear it. When we go back to money, jewelry, property, and investments, we can say we don't love them, but in our human experience we need them and we use them. There are legitimate functions for those things in our lives, and we have every right to an abundance of them, but not to love, hate, or fear them—just to use them for their legitimate purposes.

Therefore, we have to make the transition from loving those things to developing a state of consciousness in which we enjoy them, use them, and share them. That's coming into spiritual consciousness. On the other side, we have to make the conscious transition of not hating or fearing the matter that we've come to hate or fear from the human standpoint in the form of germs, poisons, or bullets, because they have no power. They cannot of themselves do anything to us, except by our consent. Now, that's not easy. We were born and brought up to fear germs; we were born and brought up to fear bullets and bombs; we were born and brought up to fear or to hate many forms of matter and material force. And we were born and brought up to depend on other forms of matter such as medicines, lights, electrical energy, and so forth. To make the transition to where we're no longer dependent on these—well, it's an impossibility unless you have help.

If you were an individual like Jesus Christ, and the spirit of the Lord God were upon you, then your problem would be solved. By virtue of the descent of the Holy Ghost into your consciousness, you would no longer love money or jewelry or property or investments, but you would make use of them—nor would you fear germs or diseases or Pilates because you would say: "What did hinder you? Pick up your bed and walk. Thou couldest have no power over me." In other words, it would be so deeply ingrained in your consciousness that matter isn't a power that at every appearance of it you would just smile. But since there are so few who have received that act of grace from God, the rest of us have to develop a spiritual consciousness. It can be accomplished by anybody with the will—but not just anybody, not those who sit around and say, "I hope lightning strikes me" (spiritual lightning). But anybody with a drive, anybody with a desire, anybody with an inner impulsion can accomplish it. The way of it is in that word *treatment.*

Now we have to remember this statement: *There is a spiritual truth with which to meet every problem of human existence.* The greatest problem in human existence is existing in a world of four billion human beings. That's the greatest problem because we have no way to get along; we have no way to even keep up with the crowd, much more pass them. We are, all of us, whether we know it or not, in the same position as Jesus Christ who said, "I of my own self can do nothing." Most humans don't realize that they of themselves can do nothing, so they try, and sometimes they get into difficult places from which they ultimately crash. But if a human being realizes, "I'm really getting no place in life. I wake up in the morning, I fill my job, I go to sleep at night, but there's no progress, no satisfaction, no joy of living, nothing to eagerly wake up to in the morning," he is ready for the next step. That is because, in one way or another, he learns that "man shall not live by bread alone," not by human activities, by human thoughts, even by studies, "but by every word that proceedeth out of the mouth of God."

Now, one of the first treatments for a sense of insufficiency in any way, would be that remembrance: "Man shall not live by bread alone, but by every word that proceedeth out of the mouth of God." And this immediately gives us a desire to look into the Bible and find out what some of those words are. Well, I suppose the average person turning to the Bible might have the same difficulty that I had. Either you always open it to where it says, "begat, begat, begat, begat" and nothing happens, or else you read some stories that leave you with no sense of their meaning. For people like us—and for how many years I was one of those, I can't tell you—there are Bible texts, such as *The Runner's Bible,*[1] little books of that

---

[1] *The Runner's Bible,* Compiled and Annotated by Nora Holm (Atlanta, GA: Acropolis Books, Inc., 1998).

kind, which are readily available in religious bookstores. They have Bible passages covering every subject of human life. If one needs comfort, there are passages offering comfort; if one needs supply, there are passages offering help on supply; there are passages offering help if one needs health, happiness; oh! every need of human existence is covered in these texts.

A person could do no better than to use one of these books like *The Runner's Bible,* to turn to the heading they're seeking that addresses specific needs until they have made those Bible passages a conscious part of their living being. Then when they have a problem, they have the word of God, and they don't have to run around outside looking for bread or for a bottle of medicine or a loan from the bank. They can get their spiritual meat, wine, and water, their spiritual healing, their spiritual comfort and grace, by taking those passages into their consciousness and pondering them, thinking about them, cogitating and meditating on them until an inner grace takes over and says, "This is what it means. *I* am with you."

You will find in those passages the teaching of "practicing the presence." Now, anyone who practices the presence of God through taking into their consciousness these particular passages, soon finds they are no longer one of the four billion, no longer just a wave on the sea; they are now the whole ocean–but if they are a wave, a part of the ocean, at least they've got all the rest of the ocean to support them and maintain them and sustain them, and push them on to their destiny.

Now we learn that we are not a helpless person in the world but an individual son of God, joint-heir with Christ. You'll only learn you are that through understanding those passages. You are not a mortal "if so be the spirit of God dwell in you"; you are not a mortal "if you abide in the word and let the word abide in you." You are an heir, joint-heir with Christ in God, to all the heavenly riches. Now you have the feeling of being somebody, not of yourself, but because of the grace of God. That is treatment. By using those passages of scripture, you've treated yourself out of material human consciousness into the consciousness of spiritual sonship. You've done it by knowing the truth that makes you free of your materialism, free of your humanhood, free of your mortality, and it releases you into your spiritual nature.

There are other problems: We don't think we have enough brains or enough education to really accomplish what we want in life. Yes, but if we sit down to give ourselves a treatment on that subject and recall the coconut tree and the coconut on it, we remember that surely the coconut of itself doesn't have enough of anything except by virtue of its contact with the tree. The invisible life of the tree is pouring itself into the coconut as it becomes the hard shell, the soft meat, and the liquid milk. Oh, the coconut could say, "As my own self I am nothing." Ah, yes, but the truth is, "I abide in this tree and all that the tree has is mine." And there again, our shoulders go up, and we have given ourselves a treatment about the sense of separation from the source of all good. So we now find that God is the intelligence of this universe and "I and my Father are one." Then the God-intelligence pours itself into expression as my individual intelligence, just as the life of the coconut tree is pouring itself into the coconut as its milk, its meat, and its shell.

Now do we see that by obeying the 15th chapter of *John,* abiding in the word and letting the word abide in us, the mind of God flows as our mind, becomes our mind? "Have that mind in you which was also in Christ Jesus." How do you have it? By your contact with the mind of God. How do you have contact with the mind of God? By knowing the truth. And the truth is, the mind of God is my mind, the life of God is my life; and because the mind of God is my mind, if I didn't have any education I'd still have all the intelligence in the world and it will tell me everything I need to know.

Because the life of God is my life, I am eternal, and because I am eternal I shall live out my life on this earth fulfilling myself. Then, when this life is finished, I shall drop this experience and advance to whatever the next higher plane may be because it isn't given in the nature of things for anything to remain static. Anything that stands still must die. But we don't stand still. The mind of God fills us, the life of God fills us. From an infant we become a youth, from a youth we become a young man or woman, and from that we become mature. Do you think we stop at any given point and say, "This is fulfillment?" No. We go on to the fullness of years.

I hope you realize that the greatest loss that has come to our country has not come through the depletion of our treasury. I hope you know that the greatest loss that has come into our whole nation is because we retire men and women at sixty-five, just when they are attaining their full maturity. We cut off the supreme intelligence of the nation because all of the great wisdom is in the men and women of sixty and over. Up to that time they are being educated, trained, and given experience. But from fifty-five or sixty on, they begin to attain maturity. The young man wants to fight his way through life, he's so full of energy. But when men and women reach their fifty-fives and sixties and sixty-fives, they begin to settle the problems of life with their intellects and their intelligence, not with their fists, not with strikes, not with wars. They've seen the folly of all that and they say, "Come, let us reason together." But what have we done in this age? We've cut off that intelligence, that experience, that maturity, and we take men and women of sixty and sixty-five and throw them on the scrap heap, put 'em out to play golf, and in a few years die. That's the greatest loss that has happened to our entire nation. You can get over financial loss, but you can never survive the choking off of intelligence, experience, and maturity. These are the greatest assets of a nation.

If you want greater intelligence, greater experience, greater maturity, turn within and realize your conscious oneness with God. Understand that the invisible mind and invisible life, which is God, is now forming itself as your mind and your life. Then you, too, will find that you're not cut off. You don't wither at sixty or sixty-five; you begin to mature at that time. Like our great composers and authors who did their best works at eighty and eighty-two, so will you as you mature, or what the world calls "age," because you have turned to your spiritual center for it. Now, to do this consciously constitutes treatment, but you experience the result of that treatment, and that treatment kept up over a period of time automatically turns from treatment to realization.

So it is with the organs and functions of the body: either they won't work at all, or they work too fast or work too slow. There is a spiritual treatment, a spiritual realization, that meets these conditions: It is the realization that mind is the substance of matter, mind is the substance of all physical form. Mind constitutes the body. Mind is invisible activity, but it appears visibly as body, as form, as organs, and as functions of the body. That's why my hand, which is mind, responds to directions given by the mind: up, down, left, right. The hand does that. Why? Is the hand intelligent? No. The hand has intelligence. Every single cell of flesh, of blood, of muscle, and of bone, has a center of intelligence in it, and it responds to me. I say, "Give," and it gives; I say, "Hold," and it holds; I say, "Pet," and it pets; I say, "Punch," and it punches. Why? Because the hand is responding to my instructions.

What is the difference between my hand and my heart, liver, and lungs? All different parts of one body, all responsive to my instructions. Therefore, I say, "Heart, liver, lungs, you can't tell me how to act; I'm telling you how to act. Act in accordance with the way God meant for you to act when he created you. God made you in his own image and likeness. God gave you qualities and functions. Now perform them. Don't talk back. I say to you, 'Arise'; I say to you, 'Come forth from that tomb'; I say to you, 'Heart, liver, lungs, or any other part of the body, be about your Father's business; do that which was given you to do. Let me have no back-talk from you!' " This is a treatment. But do you see that if you continue this practice when the occasion requires, ultimately you will go beyond treatment? All of a sudden something inside you will say, "You don't have to do that. I'm here to do that for you. I'll take over." Then you go about your business; you have now risen from treatment to realization.

You go out on the road, driving. Of course, the human picture is that you're a good driver, but not the other fellow. He's either a bad driver, or a careless driver, or he's fallen asleep, or he's drunk. And, today being Sunday, the police department can tell us right this minute how many accidents there are going to be on the Island between now and twelve o'clock tonight. Does it have to be that way? No, not unless you just go out on the road and hope that nothing is going to hit you. But if you give yourself sufficient treatment and realize:

"Here, let's make this clear: The mind of God governs me and every driver on the road. At other times, in other ways, I've said that the mind of God is my mind, but do I have a monopoly on that? Am I some favored pet? No. This must be a universal truth. These people on the road do not have minds of their own, or wills of their own. They, too, are under the guidance of the same mind that I am, the mind of God. Divine mind sits behind the wheel of every car on the road; divine intelligence governs every being."

This is praying for your friends and for your enemies.

God is the intelligence of every man, of every machine. Even machinery is subject unto the activity of infinite intelligence. When you sufficiently treat yourself, your treatment becomes a law of safety and security unto the entire road. You do that every single time you step into your car, and the day comes when, as you step into your car, a smile comes to your face and you say:

"That I know. I don't have to go through the treatment anymore because now the treatment is giving itself to me. It is reminding me that I need not fear for I have gone before you to make the crooked places straight; I have gone before you to prepare mansions of safety and security, of peace and joy and harmony for your well-being."

So as you search in those Bible indexes, or in *The Runner's Bible,* you will find passages that cover every phase of human experience and then eventually you won't need those; you'll know where to go in your own Bible. And eventually you won't need that; all of these passages and all of these stories that are in scripture will be in your own consciousness.

Do you remember how many times you have read in my writings the story of Moses leading the Hebrews out of Egypt because he had received spiritual illumination? One man, conscious of his oneness with God, could lead a nation out of slavery. Do you remember how many times you've read in my writings the story of Elijah? Even though he was persecuted and driven into the wilderness, the consciousness of God which he entertained in his consciousness never let him go without a meal, whether a poor widow had to give it to him or whether ravens had to give it to him or whether he had to find a miracle had taken place and cakes appeared baked on the stones. Do you remember how many times you have read in my writings that when Jesus Christ needed food it appeared for the multitudes with twelve baskets full left over, and when he had to still the storm at sea, it stilled? All because he had the consciousness of God ever with him. "I will never leave you nor forsake you" was always being sung inside his being. "As I was with Moses, so I will be with you. I go before you to make the crooked places straight; I go before you to prepare these many mansions." The word *I* must have sung itself in him over and over and over so that he always knew he wasn't alone; he always knew he had a spiritual checkbook with him, and he had a spiritual prescription blank with him, so that he could draw on any amount of supply he needed and any amount of healing he needed. Do you see that? That is because he had the consciousness of the presence of God, and he continuously lived with it.

This is treatment—when you constantly and consciously live with the truth that there is a divine presence within you that never leaves you nor forsakes you, that goes before you, that uplifts you, supplies you, supports you, sustains you, knowing you are never alone in the world because you are heir of God, joint-heir with Christ in God. When you live in that constant consciousness of truth, you're in a constant state of treatment, and that constant state of treatment reverses itself and brings about the very thing you're treating.

Do you see why I said last night that as human beings we live as a pendulum? Do you understand that better this morning? With every wind that blows, that's the way we twist and turn. That ought not to be. It should be that you have dominion. But you'll never have it if you don't assume it; you'll never have it if you don't declare it; you'll never have it if you don't exert it.

Have you ever stopped to think, really, why there are evil men in control of so many phases of our national and international life? Have you ever stopped to think why it is that some dictator can make us tremble so that we have to do everything he says and watch our every step so that we don't offend him? And what about leaders who misuse power in our own government?

Don't you see, if you want liberty and freedom you have got to deserve it. You are not going to get it by depending on leaders. You are going to have to put leaders there that you feel are dedicated to freedom, to liberty and justice. That isn't going to come about by sitting idly and doing nothing. And so it is, that if you don't want diseased bodies and you don't want sinful minds, make up your mind that you will take dominion of your bodies and your minds. You cannot sit back waiting for a mysterious God to act for you because a mysterious God won't do it.

Just as in pre-Revolutionary War days it took rabble-rousers like Patrick Henry and others to rouse the people to want freedom until the people followed saying, "Yes, yes, give us liberty or give us death!" somebody, somewhere must say, "Take possession of your own mind and your own body, and bring the light of God, the glory of God into your experience."

I only use these examples as illustrations. Be assured of this: There have been civilizations before us that have gone down for the same reasons that this one is going down, because people allowed the Caesars to take control and eventually they paid the penalty. Whether or not this particular civilization goes that way is a matter of opinion. Some great thinkers are convinced that there is no more hope to save this civilization, that eventually we will all come to where other civilizations have been. Men like Arnold Toynbee are convinced that it is too late to save humanity because nobody has come along with a human solution that can help and nobody can promise any help. Toynbee and others like him say there is a spiritual power that could save us if we could grasp it.

We are saying the same thing: You, individually, do not have to be a victim of the sins or the diseases of this world if you want to take possession of your body and mind and think things through. Give yourself treatments, pray metaphysically, until such time as spiritual inspiration comes and replaces the need for treatment. It may not be that your spiritual power will enable you to save this world, but at least it will make you one of the remnants of those who will start the foundation of the next civilization. Always remember: With every civilization that has been destroyed, there has been left a remnant that started the next civilization. And always, the next civilization has been a little bit better than the last. Remember that this present civilization is about the best that's ever been known.

In this civilization we have risen higher in the understanding of brotherhood, of loving thy neighbor. You see, in all other generations, like the Caesars', there were slaves. In later generations there were kings and queens and dukes and earls, and then there were peasants. And in the next generation, there were the industrialists and there were the laborers. But in the last century in England, there began a newer, higher civilization of realizing that men are neighbors and must love each other as neighbors. In the manufacturing towns of England, where there was extreme poverty and extreme wealth, men began to dream of utopias where everybody would really be equal—not necessarily equal in the amount of their money, but equal in the opportunity to earn money, to enjoy it, to at least live decently. This was not possible in England. Those ideas of utopia spread to the United States where utopian communities started with a sense of absolute equality.

Now, the idea of an absolute equality of that kind is fantastic and never can be, because there are always those who have inventive skill. They will invent the things we need, thereby earning more money than we do by just manufacturing them. There will always be the artists who eventually will turn out creative works which will entitle them to more income. There will always be business executives, always be employers, who will have more money than we will have, but they will not deny us the right to earn enough.

So we pass from that unrealistic utopian stage, which had a germ of the new generation leading us into what we call the new capitalism. The old capitalism took place up to 1900–1910, and, just as they had their lords and ladies in Europe and the peasants underneath, the capitalism of those days had multi-millionaires and multi-billionaires. Everybody else was slave to them or not even earning enough to get by.

After 1900–1910, we came into a higher form of capitalism in which employers tried to see that employees always earned enough. As the scale of living went up they tried to provide for hospitalization; they tried to provide the churches that were necessary; they tried to provide educational facilities, and they did support the colleges and universities. Capitalism began to accept its responsibility as keeper of the rest of us who couldn't ever hope to be businessmen and women, because our lives did not lie in that direction. That's the higher form of capitalism, where the employers are not in business solely to make money, but to care for those who are with them.

Now, it isn't only in that direction that we have advanced in civilization. We've advanced now to the place where the inventor, the artist, the researcher, can receive support from either the state or private wealth; we find these, too, are given opportunities for development. So this civilization really is demonstrating within the structure of capitalism a love-thy-neighbor attitude.

We're in a higher civilization than the old society that said "the public be damned," or the old society that called out the militia to shoot down the men and women who wanted a dollar-and-a-half per day wage. That's gone. Not only that, we're not in a civilization anymore where we live only for our nation. Our government is giving away more money for the good of other nations, and it isn't our government that's doing it. It's we who are doing it. They're merely writing the checks, but we're filling the checkbooks. We are recognizing our duties to other nations, the have-not nations, to a greater extent than ever before. That's high civilization. So you see, this is a higher civilization than has ever before been known.

There are more educated people today than have ever been known in the history of the world. We have more art galleries to go to; we have more museums to go to—all provided for us. That's high civilization. Now, when this civilization cracks, as it seems inevitably it must, there will be a remnant left who will begin to teach the coming generations: Don't settle your arguments by strikes, don't settle them by wars, and don't even settle them by lawsuits. Sit at the table, discuss them, and don't think that you have to solve them in a week. Let it take a month, let it take a year, but let's remain peaceful while ultimately we solve every problem.

That is going to be the civilization of the future. There will be no mental institutes because there will be nothing to drive people crazy. They are only being driven crazy by their worries, by the problems of human existence, by the drinks and drugs they have to resort to, to hide from their problems. There will be no mental institutes, and there will not be as many prisons. But there will have to be a remnant to teach that, and the remnant will be those who have discovered there is a fourth-dimension to life in which you do not live by might or by power, but by the spirit of God.

You do not live by bread alone; you do not live by money alone; you do not live by physical strength alone; you do not live by cunning alone. There is a fourth-dimension of consciousness to which you can turn. That is called the Father within, divine consciousness, the realm of God, the kingdom of God. It's the fourth-dimension, and it exists within you. Therefore, you can turn within and you will find that it will appear outwardly as the very form of good you need, whatever that form may be.

As you know, I quote our Eastern friend[2] so often: that if you have only two coppers, use one of them to buy a loaf of bread but buy hyacinths with the other, hyacinths for the soul. So with us. If you have only one dollar, spend what you think you need for your physical needs, but be sure that you spend something for the benefit of your soul, because you'll never live just by filling your physical needs. You'll only live the animal life, but you won't be feeding your cultural life.

From the time I came to these Islands, I felt that the University of Hawaii was meant to play a special role in this world. I made the acquaintance of some of the professors and saw how few of them realized that the University of Hawaii had been set apart from all the rest of the world to perform a special function. Once, the University came to a place where they couldn't raise five hundred dollars to keep their philosophy magazine on the press and so were about to let it go under. Then

---

[2]Gulistan of Moslih Eddin Saad.

some of our students provided that five hundred dollars to keep their magazine, *East-West,* on the press until the University could raise funds to keep it going. Think how close it came to disappearing. Is that magazine so important? In and of itself it has no importance; it's made up of a lot of human philosophy. But it's a bridge; it's a bridge between Eastern philosophy and Western philosophy and the culture of the world. That is what, ultimately, keeps individuals coming together and will break down Kipling's statement that "East is East, and West is West; and never the twain shall meet." There has to be a bridge, and the philosophy department and the comparative religions department of the University of Hawaii are two of the most important girders in that bridge. Too, the language department, the international nature of the student body, and the location half way between East and West, make the University of Hawaii a unique institution, the only one of its kind in the world and destined ultimately to play a very important role.

I receive many letters from senators and representatives thanking me for bringing to their attention the importance of the University of Hawaii, because all of these ideas were part of the basis for statehood. And this was one of the best reasons: it was the hyacinth for our souls. Industry can give the state sugar, and industry can give it pineapples, and industry can give it shipping, and industry can give it cement and tourism; but only the art museum, the Bishop Museum, the symphony orchestra, and the University of Hawaii can give hyacinths for the soul, the cultural gifts that lift us above being an animal.

It is only when culture, when love for mankind, enters the heart and the soul that you rise above being an animal and can say, "I am a son of God." You have to have love; you have to have brotherhood; you have to have philosophy; you have to have religion. Do you see that? You have to have art and you have to have music. Then you are no longer an animal, you are the child of God.

So it is with every contribution we make in our communities, seeing to it that there is a good orchestra, that there is an art gallery, that there is a museum, and that there is such a university. Every such contribution is a contribution of hyacinths to lift mankind out of being the animal that fights for its living, strikes for its living, wars for its living. You won't find those animals after hyacinths have entered the soul. When you have a touch of music and art, of brotherly love, you can't come down to that level anymore, and you don't permit those around you to come down to that level.

But behind all of this is what you put into your Bible and then draw out; what you put into your spiritual studies and then draw out. You must do something about it; you must not be a pendulum; you must not allow yourself to be acted upon by every belief that is going through the air; you must have command of your mind and your body; and you must insist that if half your time is needed for providing bread, the other half of your time must be for providing for your soul. Feed your body with bread, but feed your soul with truth, and do that through consciously knowing specific truths. And we call this treatment. We also call this prayer. And then, ultimately, these will lift us into an atmosphere of inner communion with God.

Thank you! Above all things, thank you for everything that has taken place here. Thank you for your generous spirits; thank you for your love; and, well, just thank you for being on Maui so that we could come together.

PART II

INTRODUCING THE HEALING PRINCIPLES

"For the word of God is quick, and powerful, and sharper than any two-edged sword, piercing to . . . the joints and marrow, and is a discerner of the thoughts and intents of the heart."

Hebrews 4:12

1959 Hawaiian Village Open Class

~ 5 ~

A TRANSITION IN CONSCIOUSNESS

Good Evening.

We have just had our usual meditation, but in this particular meditation we began by placing ourselves as superior to mind and body, which is our natural birthright. That is, we took the word I[1], which I am: I, Joel; I, Mary; I, William. Whatever your name may be, you identify yourself with the word I. That I of course is your being, the being which you are. Your mind is something you possess and your body is something you possess. The mind is not you; the body is not you. I am you, and I was given a mind and a body through which to perform your functions on earth. The mind is that instrument which you use for thinking purposes, reasoning purposes, or any purpose of awareness. Through your mind you become aware, through your mind you know, through your mind you think, through your mind you receive decisions or make judgements.

The body is a physical instrument and it takes its orders from you through the mind. I say to this hand, "Up," and the mind communicates that to the hand and the hand obeys the mind, which in turn obeys me. I have dominion over the mind and over the body. But

---

[1] The word "I," italicized, refers to God.

suppose I do not exercise that dominion which was given to me by God in the beginning, and suppose I turn to the mind for its judgements or to the body for its conduct. I would soon be in all kinds of trouble, just as those who have not learned to accept their dominion over mind and body are in trouble much of the time. The mind was given to you, the body was given to you.

When you sit down to meditate, the mind does not wish to come under control, not because it has a wish or will of its own, but only because you haven't assumed dominion and it is accustomed to doing what it wants. I'm afraid it's much like the horses I've ridden: they don't acknowledge my control a bit, they just take me where they want to go. That's because I don't know how to assume dominion over a horse, and so he has his fun with me. So it is, the mind has its fun with us only because we have not learned to take dominion over it. In some ways, the body behaves better than the mind. At least the hands won't steal if we don't direct them to and they will cooperate and share and give if we direct them to. The mind doesn't always obey that readily, but the body can be as unruly as the mind. It tries to determine for us when we are well and when we are sick as if we had no dominion over health. Rightly understood, we have as much dominion over health as we have over morals or as we have over the thinking mind. When we do not seem to have dominion, it is because we have not assumed dominion.

Since our work teaches us that we must not use force, we must not take up the sword, we must not punish our mind or body, we have recourse only to discipline, but not the harsh discipline of an unthinking parent over a wayward child. Rather, we exercise loving dominion that a wise parent exercises: a discipline with love, a discipline with gentleness, a discipline with peace and patience. And so we learn to gently take dominion over the mind so that we can meditate the way we did in this meditation:

I say unto thee, peace be still, fear not. Fear not—not all the armies of the aliens, for God in the midst of thee is mighty. God's peace give I unto thee, God's grace give I unto thee—peace. In quietness and in confidence shalt thou meditate. In stillness and in joy shalt thou receive God's grace. Peace be unto thee—peace. My peace, give I unto thee. You need not battle; you need take no thought for what you shall eat or what you shall drink or wherewithal you shall be clothed. God's grace clothes thee. God's grace feeds thee. Be still, be still, and receive God's communion. Be still and hear the still small voice. You need not battle, you need not take thought. Be at peace, be still. Nothing shall enter the mind that defileth or maketh a lie. No weapon that is formed against thee shall prosper, for where the spirit of the Lord is, there is liberty, there is peace, there is harmony, quietness, calmness, assurance. In God's presence is fullness of joy, fullness of life, abundance of good. Here where I am, thou art. I need not fear what mortal man can do to me and no weapon that is formed against me shall prosper. They have only the arm of flesh. We have the Lord God almighty.

So you see, in this meditation you have taken possession of your mind and body, and you have acknowledged that all of this comes, not by virtue of any qualities of your own, but because of the presence of God. But the main thing you accomplished was that you realized your own identity as separate from the mind and body, as having jurisdiction over the mind and body, and you assumed that dominion. In ordinary human life, people do not realize there is somebody called *I;* the mind and body seem to constitute all there is to them, and no one is there having dominion. In our work it becomes necessary to know there is someone called *I,* Joel; *I,* Bill; *I,* Mary; born of God, created in his image and likeness, governed, maintained, and sustained by God and by the grace of God. *I* have a mind and *I* have a body, and these are the instruments given to me for specific purposes on earth.

The value of this is that when you are faced with a problem, whether your own or one concerning someone who has turned to you for help, you come to the subject of treatment. As you know, for many years we have taught that treatment and prayer were synonymous. This is not wholly true; it is only true in the sense that treatment is a form of prayer–let's call it a much lower form of prayer. Actually, treatment is preparation for prayer. Why is this? Well, prayer itself is a spiritual activity. Prayer is communion with God. As a matter of fact, prayer in its highest sense is God's impartation of himself to us. Whether we take it from the standpoint of communion with God or God's impartation of himself to us, either of these is prayer that takes place within us, without words or thoughts. Therefore, we, more especially we of the Western world, cannot easily rise to the highest form of prayer. But we can rise to it through that which we in metaphysics call treatment, or that which in orthodox religious circles may be called their form of prayer–that is, using words and thoughts.

Most in orthodox religions still use pagan forms of prayer which came to them when their churches were first founded and their own forms of prayer had not developed: They used the prayer of petition: "O God, send us rain for our crops"; or, "O God, take away the rain; there's too much"; or, "O God, save my child." This form of prayer wouldn't be good without that "my" in there because we're not interested in our neighbor, especially if our neighbor lives over the hill, out of sight.

These ancient paganistic forms of prayer were the only forms of prayer the church had to work with, and it is only now that many in the orthodox churches are realizing a higher form of prayer is necessary. They are beginning to accept teachings that have been discovered and taught for the past hundred years in the metaphysical world and which have always been known in the mystical world. There is nothing wrong with these forms of prayer any more than there is anything wrong with our forms of treatment. Remember, it isn't a question of right or wrong, it is a question of the degree of consciousness. Because we are in a human state of consciousness at the moment, it is necessary that we start our prayer work with words and thoughts. In the metaphysical world these are called treatments; in the mystical world they are called realizations.

The attainment of harmony is never accomplished by words or thoughts. Going back to the churches, although prayers of petition have been uttered for thousands of years, there is no more harmony on earth today with all of their prayers than there was in the days of the Hebrews. They cannot bring spiritual harmony into this world through their petitions, their praise or adoration, or anything else that is expressed in words or thoughts. But neither can metaphysicians bring spiritual harmony into their experience through the words and thoughts of a treatment because they are but the introductions, the aids, given to bring us into an atmosphere where words and thoughts are no longer necessary to lift us to an inner communion through which God's grace reaches us.

Now I would like to explain right here that there are mental sciences which do bring harmony into peoples' experience through affirmations and denials and consciously knowing the truth. But this has no relationship to God or to spiritual healing except in the cases of those who, through prayer or treatment, rise above the treatment into the atmosphere of God. This happens to metaphysical workers in mental sciences just as frequently as it does to those in spiritual sciences. The reason is that when individuals rise so high in consciousness as to give themselves to a ministry, it automatically follows that regardless of what method they use, they do attain spiritual consciousness. This explains why some practitioners in the mental sciences do not succeed and it also explains why some in the spiritual sciences do not succeed. In both cases it is because those individuals remain on the level of their treatment without rising into the atmosphere of God-consciousness.

So remember, I have no word to say of right or wrong about the prayers of churches or treatments in mental or spiritual science. I do say that whoever rises into the atmosphere of God-consciousness in whatever manner it is attained—and be assured of this: I know of ministers and priests and at least two rabbis in orthodox churches who attained as much God-consciousness as anyone I have met outside of the churches—rises above the beginning stages of their religious development and outgrows their baby stage of mouthing prayers. It is the same in the mental or spiritual sciences where we must rise above the mouthing of treatments into the atmosphere of God-consciousness. The point I am making now, and will for the balance of this year in my travels, is that you cannot eliminate that stage, that baby stage if you will, of treatment any more than the church could have eliminated its orthodox prayers—although those of you who will be here fifty years from now will witness such a transformation in the orthodox churches as will make you wonder whatever happened. It is already apparent that within many of these churches there are groups learning how to outgrow their present mode of worship.

Our students of the Infinite Way must not forget this: You will only rise into the true atmosphere of prayer and God-consciousness by a thorough understanding and practice of the subject of treatment. Treatment means consciously knowing the truth; treatment means applying principles of truth in your mind. In order to do this, you must first establish yourself as *I*, having dominion over mind and body, for until you do that you cannot give or receive a treatment correctly.

Let us assume for the moment that we have a problem of supply, not that you have this problem, but that someone has brought it to your attention. We are taking that problem because it is a common one even in these days of prosperity. So we will take the subject of supply and assume that you may have some other metaphysical background than the Infinite Way. If that is true, what I'm going to say to you will make it necessary for you to forget what you were taught because we are not in agreement with any of the metaphysical movements on the subject of treatment. Therefore, if you are having satisfactory results in some other work, be satisfied. Do not attempt to combine it with our work in the Infinite Way, for you will not succeed and you may find yourself worse off than you are now.

To begin with, we never, under any circumstance, take patients into our treatment. We never take their name into our thought. As a matter of fact, if they don't tell us their name, we don't ask it. We are not interested in their name or their identity for our work has nothing to do with them, although they will receive the fruitage of it. How, you may ask, do they receive the fruitage of it instead of everybody else? Because they have brought themselves to our consciousness and made themselves a part of it by asking for our help. "It is thy faith that has made thee whole. Do you believe that I can do this thing?"

You are the prime factor in your experience, and to whom you submit yourself, that person will you obey and from that person will you receive. And so if you say to me, "Give me help," you have made the necessary contact with me even if I don't know your name, what you look like, or your identity. So it is, in our work you must remember that the person does not enter the treatment or you have spoiled the treatment; you have made that a barrier against the success of your treatment. You must not under any circumstance take the person into your thought.

With that in mind, you have just been asked for help on the subject of supply. Now we take the next step, which is that you must not take the claim into your meditation either. You cannot take lack or limitation, nor can you work on the subject of lack or limitation or abundance, nor can you in any way handle that problem by taking it into your treatment. There is only one thing that you do now that you have been asked for help on a problem of supply. You turn from that person and from that problem, and you immediately begin to consciously know the truth. What truth? Well, your consciousness has just been given a terrible temptation. You have just had a miserable appearance presented to you and so you must know the truth, but not about the problem. There isn't any truth about a problem, but there is a truth about the Truth. That truth must be the first thing to reach your consciousness, not necessarily in these words but in some similar passages of scripture, or metaphysical or mystical language. The first thing that must enter your thought is:

The earth is the Lord's and the fullness thereof. God constitutes the fulfillment of all being. God is the only supply. God doesn't belong to anyone, the earth doesn't belong to anyone. There isn't anyone who can get supply. This earth is God's footstool, and all that is therein. God constitutes this universe, God's presence fills this universe. God is the only life and the only law unto this universe.

Then, as you begin to dwell consciously on truth, you begin to remember other passages: six, ten, twenty, thirty—all that bear out the fact that God alone is and that "I am the bread of life . . . I am the meat, I am the wine, I am the water." Where is there an abundance of *I?* Where is there an absence of God? *I* fills all space. *I* am here and *I* am there. Do you see where your treatment is? It is with statements of truth—yes. It is with passages of scripture—yes. But it is not on the level of supply or lack or limitation, it is on the level of spiritual truth. You are consciously knowing the truth about God—the fullness of God, the omnipresence of God, the omnipotence of God—and what constitutes supply. "Man shall not live by bread alone, but by every word that proceedeth out of the mouth of God."

Where is there an absence of God's word? I'll tell you where: with those who do not abide in the word and let the word abide in them; with those who do not dwell in the secret place of the most High. That's where their absence of supply is: cutting themselves off from the only supply there is—the word of God, the bread, the meat, the wine, the water, the word itself—the realization of God's presence. "I have never seen the righteous begging bread." Ah, yes, but you have probably come to the theological conclusion that if you are obeying the Ten Commandments you are righteous. That doesn't constitute righteousness. That merely constitutes good humanhood. Righteousness has to do with spiritual awareness. Certainly the Pharisees and the Sadducees were not righteous. Humanly they obeyed the law, but they were not righteous. Oh, no. No. The only sect that was righteous were the Essenes. The others were law-abiding; the others were good Jews; the others were obedient, but they weren't righteous. The only righteous sect were the Essenes. Why? Because they were righteous in spiritual realization.

If you keep your spiritual treatment up there in scriptural (or metaphysical or mystical) passages—away from your patients and away from their problems but on the truth of being—you will eventually run out of thoughts and words. Then you settle back for the second half of your treatment. Here, too, is where we are unique in our work in that we do not consider a treatment of any value in and of itself. It is only a stepping stone to the second part of the treatment, that period in which we are through with words and thoughts and our remembrance of spiritual passages. Now we say, "It's your turn, God. 'Speak, Lord, for thy servant heareth.'" And then there follows a period of listening, of waiting, for by the time you have gone through your passages, consciously knowing the spiritual truth of these passages, you are ready for the moment of waiting, of expectation. Then comes that inner peace, that click, that something that enables you to know that God is on the field—not mentally declared, but spiritually realized, inwardly felt. Then you go about your business. Your treatment is complete.

Your patient may be obstinate, or more especially he may happen to be one who believes that he can just go on being an ordinary human being and add to himself God's grace. I'm sorry to say, too many metaphysicians really believe that all they have to do is say the right words or do the right thing and the blessings of God will come to the patient. That's far from truth. The patient himself has to yield to God. There has to be a transformation of consciousness in the patient, there has to be a spiritual regeneration in the patient, there has to be a yielding of the mortal sense in order to make room for spiritual awareness. It doesn't always follow that this transformation comes before the first or second healing. That is the reason so many students do have one, two, three, four, or five wonderful demonstrations or healings, and then later find that it doesn't work anymore. In other words, the patient has benefitted by the practitioner's state of consciousness, and now, not having yielded himself, he comes to the end of where it will work.

The Master gave us this principle when he said, "Neither do I condemn thee, but go and sin no more lest a worse thing come upon you." In other words, it is possible for the practitioner through his own dedicated life to free you from many of your trials and tribulations, lacks, limitations, sins, diseases. Heaven help you, though, if you go on in the same old human way for very long, because then you will find not only is it true that it doesn't work, but sometimes worse things come upon you that make you wish you were back in the original error. You see, Paul taught, "If so be the spirit of God dwell in you, then are you the sons of God." Jesus gave it to us in another way: "Pray for your enemies that you may be children of God." Not pray for your friends, not pray for your relatives; pray for your enemies.

The principle is this: If you have come to a place in consciousness where you can seriously and honestly pray that your enemies be forgiven, that they be re-leased from the punishment of their sins, that the spirit of God enter their souls and minds and beings, that they be given release from these mortal claims, you are no longer a mortal. A mortal can best be described as Jesus described the ancient Hebrews: "Ye have heard it said of old, an eye for an eye and a tooth for a tooth." You see, if you are in that state of consciousness where you still want revenge or you still think that sinners should be hung or given solitary confinement or put away for life, if you are still in that state of consciousness where you believe that so-and-so had it coming to him, you are back in that "ye have heard it said of old" state of consciousness.

When you make the transition to Christhood, you are able to say with the Master, and mean it, "But I say unto you, forgive seventy times seven. I say unto you, resist not evil; turn the other cheek." When you have been brought up to a level of consciousness of that nature, you have yielded your humanhood, you have yielded your will, your opinion, your convictions, and you have accepted the grace of God, the consciousness of the Christ. Then the spirit of God does dwell in you, for the spirit of God does not dwell in a person filled with envy, jealousy, malice, hate, or revenge. If you feel yourself yielding in these directions, if you really feel that your negative human emotions are yielding, you can know you are now in an atmosphere that is not only receptive and responsive to spiritual healing, but that you are now approaching the consciousness which can do healing work.

You surely know there are many, many people who go into healing work in the metaphysical world who are totally unprepared for it. They go merely because they believe they are qualified by right of having a title or a degree or an authorization. But that does not make a healer, and that is why we have so many failures in that work. A healer is one who actually has yielded up much of his humanhood, much of the "ye have heard it said of old" state of consciousness and has, at least in a measure, attained some of the "but I say unto you" state of consciousness—the ability to forgive seventy times seven, the ability to pray for one's enemies, the ability to resist not evil, the ability to put up the sword of antagonisms, hates, envies, jealousies, maliciousness. When an individual has yielded and the Christ has taken over their consciousness, filling it full of the forgive-thine-enemies state of being, then they are prepared to be healed spiritually and to heal. And you will find, as I have found it in every one of the metaphysical and spiritual movements, that there are practitioners who have attained enough of the measure of Christhood, or Christ-consciousness, to be able to heal. It doesn't make any difference which approach they come through. What counts is the degree of spiritual consciousness they attain. That is what determines their healing ability. Not whether they belong to the Infinite Way or to Christian Science, or Unity, or New Thought, but what degree of spiritual consciousness they have attained with whatever teaching they are working through.

So, too, you will find the next case that will come to you will probably be a physical one: the organs or the functions of the body are not doing their job, or the muscles, or the bones, or the blood system. But remember, before you sit down to your treatment, you have wiped out the patient's identity. You no longer have them in thought because your treatment has nothing to do with a patient. Your treatment has to do with knowing the truth, and there is no truth about any patient or there wouldn't be a patient. So you are going to know the truth, and you are going to forget what you were told about their body. Since you are not a physician, it really makes no difference to you whether it's the heart, liver, or lungs, because you don't know the difference. As a matter of fact, you don't even believe that it's the heart, liver, or lungs.

I don't mind telling you, just between us, about a lady who has been writing to me for over twelve years. She had a terrible cancer then and she still has a terrible cancer, but she doesn't miss a week of her singing job, she doesn't miss a week of her activities. She's been remarried in the last few years and has made trips here, there, and other places all around the globe, but she still enjoys her cancer. Of course, she didn't have it then and she hasn't got it now. But neither can she surrender it. She knows I'm a wonderful practitioner because she can keep on enjoying life in spite of this terrible thing. Well, you know better than that.

Actually, many of the people who come to us with cancers and heart disease haven't any more of those claims than she has. A little pain comes up in the chest and immediately it's heart failure. Then they perpetuate it by holding it in their thought. So for you to sit down and work on heart failure or heart disease every time someone tells you they have a heart condition would be as nonsensical as if a physician did it. No. You are to forget the claim as fast as it is unloaded on you, and you are to forget the identity of that patient. That is one of the reasons why there are no books or records in my office of who came and who called. The only time a name appears on my office pad is when I have an appointment and have to make a notation of the day or the hour. But there are no other names for lists of treatment, no other names for lists of bills to be sent, no record of names, and certainly no record of claims.

So let's go back: You have been asked for help with a physical problem, and you are sitting down to give your treatment. Immediately you are forgetting who asked for help and what they asked for, although of course you can't forget that it was a physical problem. That stays in your consciousness. It would be all right if you could forget it, but you can't. And so, when you sit down, probably your first thought is: "The body in and of itself can't be sick." That word, *sick*, just rang a bell with me. Sick: There is no sickness in the whole kingdom of God! Well, that wiped that out right away. Now I can forget even the word sick. Just as fast as the word sick touched me, the response came: "There is not a trace of sickness in the entire kingdom of God." If there were, there would be no immortality, there would be no eternality, because sickness eventually leads to death. So there can't be sickness in the whole kingdom of God. The only place sickness can be is in the mind of man, and the mind of man isn't a creator. It's the mind of God that creates, not man. Therefore, man can't even create a disease. The best he can do is create the belief that he has one. That ends that. There is no sickness in the entire kingdom of God.

What is the kingdom of God? To begin with, "The kingdom of God is neither lo here nor lo there," so I couldn't possibly attempt to describe it. I can't even locate it, but at least I do know that the kingdom of God is made up of immortality, of eternality, of life, of love. Why, the whole ministry of Jesus Christ is one of love. Therefore, the kingdom of God must be a kingdom of love, and if there's a kingdom of love, the Master's whole ministry was saying, "What did hinder you? Pick up your bed and walk. Neither do I condemn thee. Lazarus, come forth; thou are not dead; thou sleepest." We are all asleep in so far as we believe in conditions of mortality. The kingdom of God is a state of grace. Ah, now this comes to me: Under Moses we had the law, but under Jesus Christ we have grace. Therefore, the kingdom of God is a kingdom of grace, not of law. There can't be laws of matter or laws of mind, there can't be laws of weather or laws of climate or laws of food. There can't be laws of limitation because the whole kingdom of God is a state of grace. "You have come out from under the law. You have become separate; come out from among them. You are no longer under the law, you are under grace."

Oh, do you see where you are now? Not once has your mind gone to that person or his claim. You have tabernacled with God. You have kept your conversation in heaven and now you can sit back and say, "It's your turn, Father. Speak, Lord, thy servant heareth." Remember that old hymn, "I Will Listen For Thy Voice, I Will Listen For Thy Voice"? That is not a hymn, it is the truth. It is a spiritual state of being. "I will listen for thy voice. Speak, Lord, thy servant heareth." And you will find that in a few moments of that quiet, of that peace, something will come to you within: some feeling, some word, some message, some light. And you'll know that God is on the field and a smile will come to your face.

Someone else comes to you and asks for help, and this time while they're talking to you or you're reading something they've written to you, your mind tells you there is a power operating, a negative power, an evil power, a sinful power, or a disease power operating in their experience. So you turn from them and their claim. That word, *power.* Hmm. This is an easy one really, because we wouldn't even be this far along the path if we didn't believe in God. Probably I shouldn't have said that. Everybody thinks they believe in God, but I didn't mean in that sense. I mean by the time we have come to the metaphysical or spiritual way of life, we've gone beyond a belief in God. We've come to a conviction, if not the very experience itself, that God is. Of course, our treatment is going to be a very short one because if God is, there isn't any power but God. That can be the only meaning of God: infinite power, omnipotence. That rules out the possibility of there being a material power or a mental power. There can't be a power of the human mind, there can't be a power of matter. Don't misunderstand me: In the human picture you are always being presented with the power of the human mind and the power of matter. It is only when you come to the kingdom of God and have risen above the pairs of opposites that you can say with inner conviction, "Since there is a God, there are no material or mental powers unless these are instruments for God, and then they are good. Surely now we know there is no evil or destructive power—that's it."

Is there a God? Does God exist? What is the nature of God? If God isn't infinity, if God isn't immortality, if God isn't omnipotence, and if God isn't omniscience, God isn't God. But if God is these things, there is no such thing as a destructive, harmful, injurious, negative power. Ah, when you've established that within yourself, God is and there is no other power, you have given your treatment. Now you are ready. "'Speak Lord, thy servant heareth.' I'm listening, I'm receptive and responsive. Just place the seal on this treatment." And then it comes, that click, that inner assurance, and you are through with that.

Now, what I've tried to illustrate tonight are the two points. First of all, there must be a you, there must be a me, there must be an *I* with complete dominion over mind and body so that we can sit down and give an intelligent treatment. That is, we can consciously know the truth and not let the mind or the body keep us from our duty, our obligation, which in the end is our privilege and pleasure. And, how do we come to know these truths that we must consciously declare? You must live in the word and let the word live in you. You must study these writings; you must study scripture. You must study these Infinite Way writings because it is in these books that these particular principles are given, revealed, taught, and repeated and iterated and reiterated over and over and over again in a thousand different ways so that if you study these books and practice them, you will have at your mental fingertips every one of these passages of truth so that you too can sit down and give a conscientious, intelligent treatment.

~6~

ONE POWER

Good Evening.

We read the other day about the governor of Ohio, who, many years ago, was responsible for a law imposing the death penalty in his state for certain crimes. Last month he went before the same legislature that had passed this law, to have this law repealed. When asked why this change of heart, he answered, "I have matured." As you read further, you see that he meant he had matured from the ancient Judaic belief of an eye for an eye and a tooth for a tooth, and had seen the vision of the Christ: not only love thy neighbor but pray for thine enemies.

In these ancient Judaic teachings we witness the birth of all the world's troubles. All the evils that were apparent on earth were set into one word, *devil* or *satan*. It made no difference whether a person broke the First, Second, Third, Fourth, Fifth, Sixth, Seventh, Eighth, Ninth, or Tenth Commandment, all these evils were ascribed to the devil or satan. Satan was the cause, the source, of all of this. Then, the entire Old Testament was devoted to warfare against the forces of evil, utilizing the power of good to destroy the enemy, and it has been a continuous warfare.

It is only when we come to the New Testament that we learn we are to put up the sword, we are to forgive seventy times seven, pray for the enemy, not sue the man who cheats us. It is in this Christian dispensation we learn that the greatest secret ever revealed to mankind in the entire history of the world is that you can sum up all the evils of the world and acknowledge their source to be devil or satan. But you have no right to war with satan or fight the devil or resist evil, for there is no power in evil. The Hebrew world to which this message was addressed was not ready to accept this. They couldn't understand such a message because it was too much. It was too contrary to everything the Hebrews had been taught for several thousand years. It was too radical to be accepted.

In his three years of ministry the Master realized what was taking place. His sad words indicate this: "O Jerusalem, O Jerusalem, I would. I would take you under my wing. I would teach you these things. I would comfort you and save you; but ye would not." Not quite ye would not: ye *could* not. You could not accept the fact that evil of any name or any nature is not a power, and that is the reason it isn't to be fought. It is only a power in the mind and in the experience of those who accept it as such and who then begin to battle it, to war with it.

Even before Jesus, some of the wise and spiritually illumined Hebrew leaders saw this point, although nowhere in the Old Testament is it really taught as a specific principle as the Master taught it. But you do remember there was one to whom the Hebrews came and said, "The enemy is coming against us, and they outnumber us many times. Their weapons are better than ours; their power is greater." And their master told them the enemy had only temporal weapons, the arm of flesh, and were not to be feared. These are strange words! The enemy is stronger than we are, has many powerful weapons, but these weapons are called the arm of flesh, not to be feared—temporal power. Then we are told, "They rested in his word." Another tremendous experience! They rested in his word. Evidently they rested from fear, they rested from anxiety and concern. Then the miracle happened: "The enemy began to fight among themselves and destroyed each other," and all the Hebrews had to do was go out and gather up the spoils for themselves.

This is virtually what the Master taught when he said, "Put up thy sword . . . Resist not evil"; when he said, "Return good for evil"; when he said to Pilate, "Thou couldest have no power over me, lest it come from the Father." He was revealing the principle of the First Commandment: "Thou shalt have no other gods before me"; thou shalt not acknowledge any other power, whether you call it devil or satan, or mortal mind or carnal mind; whether you call it temporal weapons, whether you call it enmity, jealousy, hate, or malice. Thou shalt not acknowledge anything as having power, or anybody, or any groups of anybodies, or any amount of temporal weapons. Thou shalt acknowledge no other power, no other god, no other presence, but Me, the One.

As long as we are looking out from human eyes, this will be as difficult for us to believe, to accept and prove, as it was for most of those Hebrews of old. As long as we are as materialistic as they were and put our faith in material form, material weapons, material-mindedness, we will be in the self-same position as they were. We will lose the demonstration, even as Jesus saw his people losing it by their inability to accept that there are only two commandments with which we need concern ourselves. The first one is: There is but one power, one presence, and you must have no other, acknowledge no other, fear no other, but rest in this word. And then, "Love thy neighbor as thyself."

We of course know we live in one of the most materialistic ages of all times. We know the human world accepts all forms of mental and material power as if these were greater than God-power. We know we fear material force and mental power much more than we trust the one power. The reason is, we think of material and mental power as power opposed to God. There is where we lose our entire vision. We think of material power and mental power as if these were power, but they are only power in the absence of God. If you were to see this universe separate and apart from God, you would have to acknowledge that material and mental power are real power and the more material power or force you had, the better off you would be, or the greater your mental power, the better off you would be. And all this would be true if you were operating solely in the realm of a human universe, separate and apart from God.

The moment you bring yourself into even a tiny measure of God-realization, you come to a realm of life in which neither mental power nor material power is power. In other words, the mind becomes an avenue of awareness, not a force, and so do all of these things we speak of as a material universe: they become instruments for good. It is only when you begin to think in terms of good and evil that you can use a flower for the purpose of beauty, decoration, perfume, and yet still think of producing a poison with it. It is only when you think in terms of two powers that you can think of injury, destruction, theft, and all of these other things that come under the remaining commandments.

Many of the aboriginal races knew the power of the mind for good and the power of the mind for evil. In Hawaii there was the activity of the good kahuna that blessed and healed, and the bad kahuna that cursed and killed. In Central America, South America, Africa, and Australia, too, the power of the mind was used for both good and evil. In the earliest days of mental science in the United States we found the power of mind was originally used for good, and for healing. Then we found that some of the very earliest students discovered that the mind could be used for evil purposes.

In these last few years, when the subject of propaganda and advertising has become such a major influence in American life, it was discovered that the power of the mind could be used to sell and to put over a project, but the power of mind could also be used to influence erroneously, even in the business world. And so we had the spectacle last week of a legislature trying to pass a bill forbidding the use of subliminal suggestion for advertising on the radio and television, with one organization blocking it because it would interfere with their activity. In other words, some businesses had made the determination to use the human mind to control masses of individuals for personal profit and personal gain, not content with merely offering you an article and leaving you free to choose whether or not you believed the advertising, or whether or not you needed the article or wished to purchase it. Oh, no. They felt the human mind must be used to compel you to buy whether or not you wanted, needed, or could afford it.

Now you have what would ordinarily appear as the end of the world, because if it is possible for an individual or a group of individuals to control the masses and make them do their bidding, then you no longer need a Russian dictatorship with armies. You only need a little group of men sitting in a studio with a television or radio to control your world. The answer to that is this: Don't fear it; don't fear it, it will never come to pass. And the reason is, the mind isn't such a power and the mind cannot be used for such a power once it is recognized that God is the only power. It is impossible to be controlled by anyone or any circumstance when you know that God is the only power.

Let us understand for a moment what we mean when we use this word, *God.* Try for a minute to think of God: God who is neither Jew nor Christian; God who is neither Moslem nor Hindu. Think of a God that has no denominational connotation. Try to think of God as absolutely independent, above and beyond any form of religious belief. Now take another step: Try to understand God as above and beyond every form of worship, a God that cannot be reached by human beings regardless of what manner, what way, what form they may use to reach that God to influence, to sway, to move him. Try right here and now to think of a God who governs you. Try to think of a God who thinks as much of the white race as the black, brown, and yellow races. Try to think of a God who has no awareness of your name, color, or identity, a God who is a complete state of free being that man cannot touch or reach, cannot influence or sway. Think! Try to envision a God who at this very moment is the reason the sun, moon, and stars are moving in their orbits; a God who is the only reason apples always come from apple trees, and pineapples from pineapple plants, and papayas from papaya trees. Think! Think of the God you cannot influence to put apples on an orange tree, you cannot influence to move the stars out of their courses or the tides from the seashore. Think of a God entirely beyond your reach, and then reverse the position in which we have always thought of God.

Now see God as the governing influence of this whole universe, the only law unto this universe, the creative principle, the maintaining principle, the sustaining principle, the life of all being performing its function the same yesterday, today, and forever. Think of this God whom even the multitudes can't sway, even the millions of allies praying for victory, or the millions of the enemy praying for victory. Think of not one word of those prayers ever reaching God's ear. Think of a God who has never been influenced by the billions of prayers to save my side or your side or his side or her side or their side, or my child or your child. Then you will begin to realize that no harm, no evil, can come nigh your dwelling place, for God never empowered anyone or any power to injure or destroy his creation.

Only by disregarding the true nature of God can you be made to fear temporal power, whether in the forms of weapons or the malpractice of minds. Only by understanding the nature of God as law, the only law—thou shalt have no other law but me—only in this realization can you understand that at this second you are God-governed. You are no more outside of God's government than the stars, the sun, the moon, the tides, the fish swimming in the sea or the birds flying in the air. Relax into the awareness that there is a creative, a maintaining and sustaining principle of life, and it is holding this world in its grasp. Then you will be able to smile at the intrigues of men who believe they have power to set aside the laws of God, to destroy the life of God or the freedom and harmony of God, or interfere with the operation of God.

There is the thought: Can you conceive of anything that can interfere with the operation of God? Then, when you wonder at the evils you have witnessed on earth, you will know it has been our ignorance of this truth that has brought these catastrophes upon us. We have not understood that God is not influenced by man, but rather that God governs man and all creation. God alone governs, and God does not share his government with man whose "breath is in his nostrils," for he isn't even to be accounted of.

There can be no fear of this infinite, universal God. When you study scripture and see how the Hebrews lived their lives in fear of God's punishment, and then turn to the New Testament and realize that the Master gave as one of his reasons for being on earth, the forgiveness of sin and sinners, you know there is no reason under the sun for continuing to fear punishment for your sins of omission or commission. As a matter of fact, even if some of those sins should be continuing into our present experience, even if we have not reached the spiritual elevation in which all sin has departed from us—and who has?—even then we are to know we are not under the law of punishment but under the law of grace, under forgiveness, under God's grace, which not only wipes out the penalty for sin but wipes out the capacity for sin. Sometimes sin lingers on even after the penalty has been wiped out, but it isn't any different from the chicken that runs around after its head is cut off. It's just fooling us for a little while; it's dead but it doesn't know it. So, too, our past is dead, even if some sins are temporarily being continued in the present. Why is our past dead? Because we acknowledge there are not two powers operating. There is only one.

You will find, then, that some of these ancient beliefs are religious beliefs and some are medical beliefs. I recall in my younger days that we were given two major reasons why insane asylums were filled. Neither one of these reasons is given or believed today. *Materia medica* has dropped both of those beliefs as causing insanity. Now we know that those people were not confined for the conditions claimed for them, but for the mental malpractice, the ignorant beliefs of materia medica, accepted in those days. So it is with us today. We are suffering from the mental suggestions which are eternally thrown at us as if they were authority, as if they were law. They aren't if we will accept God as the only power, as the only law. There isn't a single law of matter or mind that can stand up as law in the experience of one who can begin to understand the universal nature of God governing its own universe and not permitting any interference with its government. Think of trying to interfere with God's government of this universe and we know it cannot be done. Therefore, when we suffer, we are suffering only from these mental images that have been thrown at us which we in our ignorance have accepted.

There are thousands of theological laws, medical laws, food laws, legal laws, and many other types of laws that aren't law any more than a scrap of paper. But they will remain as law in our experience until we come to the realization that there can be no such thing as a law contradicting or contrary to the law of God. There cannot be a law that isn't good; there cannot be a law of any name or nature that isn't a blessing. And every law that claims to be such must be understood as theory, belief, mental imposition, which in our ignorance we have accepted.

You have read, I am sure, of the way circus elephants are trained. Iron bracelets are placed on their feet and attached to a chain ten or twelve feet in length, and they are left that way for several months, until the elephant knows it can walk only ten or twelve feet and then must stop. By the time the elephant knows that, even when the bracelets and chains are taken away, it goes only ten or twelve feet and stops. It's been mentally conditioned to accept that limitation even though the limitation isn't there anymore. We, too have accepted laws–some of them mental, some of them material–that limit and bind us. That is only because we have not acknowledged that the God who creates, maintains, sustains, and manifests itself as this universe must be an eternal and an infinite law of good, and that there can be no other law. There can be no law of limitation, no law of destruction, no law of sin, no law of disease, no law of death. There can be no such laws. There cannot even be a law of age.

Again and again I write to students: "Please stop accepting the Judaic law of three-score years and ten. God never made it. Man made that law, and we are being malpracticed into accepting it. It cannot be a law because God cannot at the same time give life and destroy it. God cannot provide for life and for its destruction. That cannot be. Yes, I know, in insurance policies the little print tells us about acts of God that are destructive. But man made insurance policies, not God. The law of God doesn't contain any clauses providing for the destruction of God's handiwork. "The heavens declare the glory of God, the earth showeth forth his handiwork." And ye are the sons of God. Where do you find provision in that for a law of age, infirmity, a law of disease, a law of death?

In our metaphysical and spiritual approaches to life, we call this knowing the truth–treatment. It is sometimes used as a synonym for prayer. But one thing is certain: If we are to escape from the limitations of ordinary human existence, if we are to escape from the laws of matter and the laws of mind, we are only going to do it through learning some form of treatment such as this, and by reminding ourselves each day that God is the only law-giver and God is Spirit. The only laws are spiritual laws, and these govern my being and your being; these govern all being; these govern friend and foe; these govern all mankind.

What of material laws and mental laws? These cannot be laws if God is law. God is Spirit, therefore his law is spiritual. Then what we have termed law is recognized, not as law, but as an imposition, a universal malpractice that has been passed down to us, one we have accepted and demonstrated and which we must now consciously reject. We have to recognize frequently that we are not under the law of punishment but under the law of forgiveness. We have to remember every single day that we are not under law, we are under grace. We were under the law when we were under Moses. We came under grace when we came under Christ Jesus. But this grace cannot act except through our recognition and acceptance of it.

The ways of God are exactly the ways of all God's work. There could be no automobiles and airplanes until the laws governing these were discovered, recognized, and then applied. So with the law of God. The law of God fills all space. It is here and now available to us, but only in proportion to our recognition of it, acceptance of it, and consciously bringing it into our experience—practicing it, really practicing it with every contrary appearance and suggestion that comes into our lives. Consciously realize that you are not under the law, you are under grace. Realize this cannot be a law since only God is law; and then always rest in the word, settle back in the realization of what you can feel God to be.

You cannot really know God with the mind. That would be bringing the infinite into finiteness. But you can at least realize that God does not respond to the will of man, that man responds to the will of God. You can, instead of trying to use God or make God your servant, submit yourself to God; be God's child, God's instrument through which God's glory is made manifest on earth. Then, let God's glory flow through you. It will never be your glory, regardless of how beautiful you are or become, or how worthy or worthwhile. It will never redound to your credit for it will always be God's glory, God's freedom, God's health, God's understanding. Scripture tells us his understanding is infinite. Therefore, no one can ever boast of his wisdom, no one can ever boast of his knowledge, no one can ever boast of his power, for all power is of God and we are the instruments through and as which God's glory appears on earth. But we have to submit ourselves to it and not try to use it on our behalf. And above all, we do not try to use it against evil, for evil has no power. The very idea of trying to set God against the devil will defeat your purpose, for in the eyes of God, in the consciousness of God, there is no evil, no devil, no satan. These are man-made images.

It is the most glorious thing in all of this world to be able to realize that no one on the face of this globe has the power to do evil to anyone. No one on the face of this globe has the power to be evil. God is the only power, and God's power is a universal spiritual power of eternal and immortal life. No one can thwart the will of God. There is no way to thwart the will of God, for there is no will but the will of God. When man tries to set up his puny will and power against good, he might just as well be sending his armies against the Hebrew prophet who had the wisdom to say, "They have only the arm of flesh," nothingness, no power. "Stand ye still; ye need not fight." Regardless of the appearance of evil in your life or in the lives of those in your family, your friends—or if you're active in this work, your patients or your students—it lies within your power to realize that God has never given his power to anyone, to any group, to any condition. There is no power on earth but God.

The vision of this only comes to you as you can forget whatever you may have learned in your younger days about God, whatever sectarian beliefs you may have learned about God. Lift your vision to the God that existed before there was religion or a religious teaching. Try to visualize that just truth, just God, existed before ever a religious doctrine or theory was formulated, and that the nature of God then is the same as the nature of God now. God is the same God today, yesterday, and forever. God is God in every quarter of this globe and of all the other globes that exist. And there is no power, there will never be a power, to thwart the will of God, the law of God, the life of God, the way of God, unless we continue to accept the mental impositions of limitations, unless we accept a power apart from God.

Some of you might wonder whether these things have been proven. Heavens, yes! They have been proven in one way or another, in one degree or another, for the past seventy-five years. They have been proven in the demonstration of harmony in individual lives: physically, mentally, morally, and financially. They have been demonstrated in business activity, in agricultural activity, in every form of economic and government activity. They haven't yet been tried on a wide enough scale to be nationally or internationally accepted, but they have been tried and proven in the experience of individuals and groups. Oh, yes! To prove this in even a tiny measure is to prove it in the greatest degree. To be able to heal a simple cold with the understanding of one power is to prove the entire principle. The rest only has to be worked out through experience and continuous practice.

We have pitted one power against another. We have used, or tried to use, the power of God against the power of the devil. The world hasn't won out with it; the world hasn't been able to prove that God is greater than evil because there is more evil in our experience on earth than good. Success cannot come by trying to use one power against another power, but by giving up power and accepting God as one power, by submitting one's self to one power, by never attempting to destroy evil power, just recognizing its nature as nothingness.

Every form of error that would touch you must touch you through the mind. If you don't accept it in your mind, it can't have any effect on your body or your pocketbook. The only approach there is to you is through your mind. The body itself has no intelligence, therefore it cannot do anything or be anything of itself except through your mind. Therefore, you are the determining factor in your life's experience because you can reject that which you do not wish to demonstrate, and it is only difficult in the first few weeks or months of practice if one practices faithfully. In other words, every time a suggestion of any kind tries to come into your mind as an erroneous condition, circumstance, or influence, it is only necessary to remind yourself there is only one power, there is only one law, there is only one life, there is only one substance, there is only one cause—and rest in that word. It is only necessary to remember that if it is of an evil connotation, it cannot be of God. Therefore, it cannot be endowed with power, "for thou shalt have no other powers but me."

Ah yes, but if you are not alert to reject these subliminal perceptions or malpractice, then you are accepting in your mind that which will ultimately appear in your body, your pocketbook, or your human relationships. We were given dominion. Right from the start, we were given dominion. But wherein lies our dominion? In our ability to accept or reject. Are there two powers, good and evil? Then God is not infinite, God is not omnipotent, God is not omnipresent; and it is just foolishness to go around thinking you believe in God. You cannot actually understand God and accept the reality of two powers. Your dominion lies in your ability to reject whatever erroneous thought, condition, or appearance comes to you.

There can be but one law and that law is spiritual. There can be but one power and that power is spiritual.

It isn't a question of dynamite over atomic force; it isn't a matter of missiles over bombers; it's a matter of "there is no power but God." All power must be spiritual since God is spirit, and if power is spiritual, we need not fear the powers of matter or of mind. It is true that "if you do not abide in this word and let this word abide in you", you will be "as a branch of a tree that is cut off and withereth." It is true that if you do not abide in this realization of one power, if you do not reject consciously all of these mental impositions that are flung at you, you will suffer as the world is suffering. But if you do abide in this word of truth, if you do live in the secret place of the most high where there is only one presence, one power, one cause, one law, one being, none of these evils that destroy "a thousand at your left and ten thousand at your right" will come nigh your dwelling place.

This doesn't mean that we cold-bloodedly leave our neighbors on the outside. It means this: that the truth is here for all of us and that those of us who cling most steadfastly to it will benefit the most, those who try a little bit each day will benefit in some degree, and the others not at all. Dominion was given us but we must exercise it; truth is available, we first must learn it, recognize it, respond to it and then practice it. It is not a force that is hanging up here in the air. It is not a force that is either up in the heavens or within you that will operate by itself. It operates as an activity of your consciousness, and it operates in proportion to your acceptance and practice. Truth is—of that you may be sure. It is—that you cannot doubt. The experience of God in our lives is entirely dependent on our ability to open ourselves to it, to maintain it in these forms of what we call treatment, or knowing the truth, or prayer.

In our work we like to use a form of contemplative meditation in which we are sitting alone quietly, peacefully—or sometimes gathered together—and then contemplate as I have been speaking to you tonight, which is really an inner contemplation, outwardly expressed. But it represents what often happens in my experience when I am sitting alone, or sometimes even with others, and I contemplate the nature of God. What kind of a God is that? What is the nature of God? Is it possible to lead a God-governed life, or must we be eternally fighting each other and the world? And as we contemplate this nature of God, many scriptural passages come to thought, and then we're reminded that God is infinite. That God is closer to us than breathing, and we find our peace.

Thank you.

~ 7 ~

THE NATURE OF GOD

Good Evening.

These experiences that we have of classwork in all parts of the world are very exciting experiences. We had one of these periods two years ago in 1957 when students came from all over and we had a most glorious time here. Many of you who are present remember it and it has made for a wonderful relationship with students who travel because they meet in all different parts of the world and have this bond in common. Of course we have had these classes all over the mainland of the United States and Canada, England, Holland, Sweden, this year we're adding Switzerland, and we've had them in South Africa and Australia; next trip we will be adding New Zealand.

This week contracts were signed for the publication of *The Art of Meditation*[1] in German and that will be the second book published in Germany; and an option has been taken on *Living The Infinite Way*[2]– that will be the third book as soon as it is translated. In this way, you

---

[1] *The Art of Meditation,* © 1956 by Joel S. Goldsmith (New York: Harper & Row, 1965, paperback edition, 1990).

[2] *Living The Infinite Way,* © 1961 by Joel S. Goldsmith (New York: Harper & Row, 1961; Harper Collins, paperback edition, 1993).

can see how the message is traveling the world: England now publishes fourteen Infinite Way writings in British editions in addition to all of our American editions. There is a reason for this, and that's what I wish to make clear in this series that we have been having and in this class that is to come: The Infinite Way is not traveling the world with any organization, with any movement, with any financing, with any promotion or advertising. It is traveling this world on its own merit all by word of mouth. Again, there must be a reason for it, and there is. The reason lies in the principle which governs our healing work.

Mysticism in and of itself is the same wherever it may be found. All mystical teachings are exactly alike in that the basis of all of them is conscious union with God, realized oneness with God—the actual experience. There could not be a mystical teaching unless there was a mystic to have the experience of conscious union with God. Everyone who has had the experience has had the same experience and receives the same message. You can follow this in the mystical messages of the entire world. But neither a mystical message nor even the mystical experience results in what we know as healing work.

Rarely is a mystic a healer unless he is an exception. One of the first exceptions of which we have any record is Gautama the Buddha. He attained the mystical experience and with it experienced the healing consciousness. Jesus, another who attained the very heights of mystical experience, lived most of his years in conscious union with God and always consciously knew that God was his real identity. That part of him which appeared to our eyesight, whom we call Jesus, was nothing, could do nothing. But there was this inner selfhood which had been realized, attained, and consciously lived. This was his mystical selfhood which brought him the healing gift.

History records hundreds of mystics, men and women who attained their spiritual experience, but only a few received the healing gift. Most of the mystics lived in conscious union with God but lived separate and apart from their human experience so that even when they were in their humanhood, they were not able to bring out the spiritual grace which results in health, harmony, and abundance. That is why many of the mystics were sick and penniless. They lived in the atmosphere of God but could not bring the fruitage of that atmosphere into their daily experience of human life. They could not bring success into their human lives. They were successful on the inner plane; they were happy, they were joyous, they had enough to eat and a place to sleep, but they had nothing of this world's benefits. Jesus was one of the outstanding examples of a mystic through whom the word became flesh so that the tremendous spiritual light which he experienced became food for the hungry, sight for the blind, hearing for the deaf, health for the sick, and regeneration for the sinner. There have been only a few who have attained that state of spiritual consciousness.

When my first religious experience took place, it brought the healing gift with it at the same time. I was called upon for healing within forty-eight hours after the experience, and the healing came through. That healing gift has remained with me, and has been the major part of my life's activity ever since. But the healing principle did not reveal itself to me at the time, and so I know why all mystics do not heal. Also, some, who temporarily do have a healing gift, lose it because they do not discover the principle which produces the healing work.

It is true that if everyone on earth could be brought to a spiritual experience, they probably wouldn't care too much whether they were healthy or sick, wealthy or poor, because the experience itself is enough without these added human things. But it is also true that very few people in any part of the world can actually seek the spiritual experience itself apart from what it will bring into their human experience. In other words, most of us seek the kingdom of God for a reason related to our human needs. We seek physical health, mental health, moral health, financial health, or better human relationships, so it is much easier to enter into the spiritual life through healings (through being healed or by healing others) or by seeking the kingdom in order to bring greater harmony into our human experience.

The healing ministry is an important one. It is important because when you experience a spiritual healing, it arouses some sort of feeling of emotion, something inside of you that makes you long to know more about the spiritual life, about God, to know if God can be found. And so it is that the healing activity of a movement or the healing ministry of an individual is important, not only because of the actual health or harmony it brings to individuals, but because it brings out in them a desire to go further than just being healed. It brings out the desire to know God, to live the spiritual life, and then to be able to help others.

In the earliest years of my healing work, I did not know the principle by which these healings took place, and as I studied metaphysical writings I realized there are different states and stages of consciousness and different principles that apply in these stages. There is not just one healing principle but many, and some are more on the mental side than the spiritual, yet they do produce healings. There are principles which combine the mental and the spiritual, and these too, when properly understood, produce healings. As my spiritual experience deepened, more and more healing experiences came. One particular principle became so evident to me that the book *The Infinite Way*[3] was written, and the Infinite Way work began.

This work was based on two principles that had not heretofore been used to any great extent and were little known. When I began teaching them I taught them as the nature of God and the nature of error. Many of our students didn't like the term the nature of error, and many wouldn't give their time to studying that subject. I can't blame them. It is really much more wonderful to think about God and if possible to sit on cloud nine. But when you sit on cloud nine a long time and suffer too, your demonstration is incomplete. So I have remained steadfast in teaching the two basic principles which are unique in the message of the Infinite Way. If you catch these two principles, you are not only led to the actual spiritual experience itself, you not only find it easier to be healed, but it will not take long until you yourself can do some measure of healing. From then on, the degree of healing depends on the intensity of your own desire because it takes further study and practice.

The first of our principles has to do with the nature of God. The nature of God! God is nothing at all like men

---

[3] *The Infinite Way*, © 1947, 1956 by Joel S. Goldsmith (reprinted 1997 by Acropolis Books, Inc., Lakewood, CO).

have been taught. As a matter of fact, there is no such God as the vast majority of mankind is worshiping. That is why there is so little fruitage from their prayers. You know that if there were such a God as men pray to, all the tens of millions and probably billions of prayers that have been uttered for peace would have been answered by now. I am sure that all the prayers that have been uttered for food for poverty stricken countries would have been answered. The prayers are sincere enough, the people who pray are certainly sincere and honest, but the sad thing is, they are praying to a non-existent God and so they cannot receive an answer. If they continue to pray as they have for the last five thousand years to this unknown God, there will be just as many wars in the future as there have been in the past, just as much poverty, just as much of man's inhumanity to man.

The world will have to know the true nature of God before it can know how to pray to God. And one thing is certain: Five thousand years of history have proven that praying to God for health, for supply, for wealth, for home, and for peace on earth is a profitless pastime. It's a thorough waste of time. There is no God answering such prayers. If men wish to know God, to receive answers from God, they will have to wipe out the past five thousand years of historical teaching about God and seek the answer that the vast majority of religions has not discovered. That is: What is God? What is the nature of God? How do you approach God? And how do you receive answers to prayer?

As you study the writings of the Infinite Way message, you will discover what has been revealed to me about the nature of God. Always remember, you are not asked to accept that; it is merely presented to you as that which has revealed itself to me. You can take this revelation: experiment with it, work with it, try it, and see if you cannot bring some response into your experience. You see, the fact that Jesus had his experience with God and received answers to his prayers hasn't helped the rest of the world because the rest of the world hasn't done likewise. Merely reading about his experience or hearing sermons about it will not accomplish it for the world. You must go and do likewise. Regardless of the nature of my experience with God, regardless of what that experience has done and is doing with my life and with the lives of so many students following this way, that will mean nothing to you except as you go and do likewise. In other words, if you experiment, if you follow the teachings as they have been outlined in our work until you find out for yourself whether or not they are true, then you can bring these experiences into your life.

One of the earliest revelations that came to me regarding the nature of God was that it's a waste of time to ask God for anything at any time because God isn't withholding it. If God were withholding it, then there might be some reason to go to God and say, "God, let loose! Give me my health; give me my supply; give me a home; give me peace on earth." But before you can ask that, you must actually believe God is withholding it. It became very clear to me that God is not withholding anything from this universe. He's not withholding sunshine in the daytime or moonlight at night. He's not withholding rain, or stars, or sun, or moon. He's not withholding the cattle on a thousand hills. He's not withholding crops in the ground. He's not withholding fish in the sea or birds in the air. He's not withholding the incoming and outgoing tides. He's not withholding days and nights.

Why is it that no one prays for these things? Because it is so well established that God is not withholding these things from the earth. Then why believe that God is withholding health or success or happiness or peace on earth from mankind? The answer is, God isn't! God isn't withholding these things, and therefore God doesn't have it within his power to answer such prayers. Oh, yes, your child may come to you and ask for a dollar, but that is only because you didn't know your child had the need. But it isn't that way with God. That isn't God. God is the same yesterday, today, and forever. God's rain falls on the just and the unjust. God is no respecter of persons. And God's hand is not shortened that it has lost its power. No. God is not withholding anything from anyone for any reason.

If this world had not been taught from the Hebrew scriptures, if all the churches on the face of the globe had accepted the message of Jesus Christ, the world would not be suffering from self-condemnation, from guilt complexes, from fear of God. That is one of the most common diseases on earth, the fear of God: fear of God's wrath, God's punishment, God's vengeance—all that God does to sinners. God doesn't condemn anyone. That teaching grew in the minds of the ancient Hebrews long before spiritual enlightenment came to their human consciousness, and it was wiped out when Jesus Christ gave his message to the world. His entire teaching was, "Neither do I condemn thee." He was talking in God's name. He took the thief on the cross right into paradise with him that night without waiting for any long periods of retribution, punishment, or vengeance. It didn't take him two seconds to forgive the woman taken in adultery. It didn't take him very long to forgive Judas Iscariot or

Peter who denied him three times or Thomas who doubted him. None of these were held in bondage to their sins by the Master. If he taught that we should forgive seventy times seven, and that we should pray for our enemies, what do you think his God did?

Everyone who suffers from guilt complexes, everyone who is fearing God's wrath, everyone who is fearing that God is now or may at some time in the future, in this world or the next world, punish them for some sin of omission or commission, has never accepted the teaching of Jesus Christ. They are still living back in the Hebrew testament with a God of wrath, a God of vengeance. Even those people who pray that the enemy be destroyed in times of war are back in the Hebrew testament. It is only the Jewish God who destroyed enemies, not the God of Jesus Christ. You could never imagine Jesus Christ praying, "Please destroy Judas Iscariot for me, and the Jewish Sanhedrin. They are doing these terrible things to me." Oh, no! "Father forgive them for they know not what they do. . . Put up thy sword; those who live by the sword will perish by the sword."

If we hope to achieve the actual experience of God-realization, the very first thing we have to do on the spiritual path is not to accept some ancient concept of God, but to realize that God that has been revealed as love. We must accept the God of love, the God that does not punish, and even if we deserve punishment, the God who would hasten to forgive us. "Your heavenly Father knoweth that you have need of these things, and it is his good pleasure to give them to you." That must include forgiveness.

So you see, unless you come to realize that just as God is pouring out the sun, moon, and stars, the tides, the times, and the weather, so God is pouring forth every good thing into expression, unless you grasp that as the nature of God you will not know how to pray. Your prayers will still have the nature of expecting something from God, of believing that God is withholding it, or fearing that God will withhold it as punishment. All of this must be eradicated from your thought before you can come into even the first stage of God-awareness. Until you can see the nature of God as purely good, you are not realizing the one God that really is.

Throughout the Infinite Way writings you will find references to this very subject: the nature of God. You will find God presented in a way that will contradict everything that has ever been taught in ancient Hebrew scripture, but it will not deviate one iota from the God revealed by Jesus Christ. You cannot imagine what must have happened to those back there on those Galilean shores and in Jerusalem when a man of their own church began to tell them how wrong they were in their understanding of the God they had been worshiping since Abraham, Isaac, Jacob, and Moses. He told them in plain English—no, in plain Aramaic, plain English to us—so that they understood, "God has no pleasure in sacrifices."

Have you ever stopped to think what it means in your own life: "God has no pleasure in sacrifices"? God doesn't ask anyone to sacrifice anything. God requires no sacrifices, no burnt offerings, not even tithes. Tithing is one of the greatest blessings on earth, but it has no relationship to any demand by God. God doesn't require it. Tithing's only value is in what it does for us: to share fruitage with some spiritual purpose that is going to reveal more of God to the world, or some benevolent purpose which is a service to God's children. There, too, you remember the Master said, "In as much as ye have done it unto the least of these my brethren, ye have done it unto me." So every time we share in some form of benevolence with the poor or the sick, or with spreading a spiritual message, we are doing it unto one of the "least of these my brethren" and therefore we are doing it unto God.

Jesus taught another thing that horrified them: "The sabbath was made for man and not man for the sabbath." Why, you know it is still being taught today that you are to keep the sabbath holy from the standpoint of not working or not doing anything but being lazy. Sometimes even cutting the grass disturbs your neighbor because it's Sunday and he doesn't think it's holy. You are back to the old Hebrew teachings but under a Christian name. Man wasn't made for sabbath; sabbath was made for man to utilize in accord with his life of that moment.

Begin now to change your concept of God and realize: There is no one day of the week which is holier than any other day. There are seven days in the week and they all belong to God, and you have to be just as holy on Monday as on Sunday and just as holy on Tuesday as on Saturday, for there is no such thing as relaxing from holiness. That gives you an entirely different concept of God, so you'll know that Sunday isn't the only day to say prayers or go to church, nor is Saturday. Not that you need stop going; just be sure that you're not limiting yourself to the belief that only Saturday or Sunday is God's day. Seven days a week are God's days for prayer. Seven days a week are God's days for living up to the Sermon on the Mount. Seven days a week are holy for living in accord with spiritual teachings. We have to change our concept of God from that Hebraic God who was so strict about his Saturdays, and who has become equally strict about Sundays, to the realization that none of these days is set aside for God separate and apart from any other day.

The nature of God is such that man cannot influence God. Once you perceive that God is an infinite intelligence, omniscience, you will know how useless it is to tell God what you need or what you think you need. Once you realize that God is omnipotence, all power, you will begin to realize how stupid it really is to try to move God to do something, God that is already all-power and is the same yesterday, today, and forever. The moment you realize God is omnipresence, you can't pray up into the sky; you can't pray in holy mountains nor yet in Jerusalem, for "the kingdom of God is neither lo here nor lo there," but within you, "closer than breathing, nearer than hands and feet."[4] The kingdom of God does not have to be sought, it merely has to be recognized.

Yes, there is an excuse for searching for God. In the days before Jesus Christ, God was supposed to be up in a place called heaven. That's a hard search. That's why he hasn't been found. But God isn't in holy temples to the exclusion of being anywhere else, nor is God in holy mountains to the exclusion of being anywhere else. God is in holy mountains and God is in temples, but that is only because God is omnipresent and God is wherever you are. "The place whereon thou standest is holy ground . . . If you make your bed in hell, God is there . . . If you walk through the valley of the shadow of death, God is

---

[4]Alfred, Lord Tennyson, 1809-1892, *The Higher Pantheism.*

there." And of course if you go to temple God is there, if you go to church God is there. Wherever you are, God is.

Begin to realize the nature of God as omniscience, omnipotence, and omnipresence. Then watch the miracle that happens when you sit down to pray and realize there is no use of your thinking any thoughts because whatever you might be thinking, the all-knowing God knows it before you think it. Whatever you may be expecting to get, the all-knowing God knows before you even know that you need it. Whatever you have in mind to go to God for, when you sit down to pray you laugh at yourself and soon you won't go to God for anything except the joy of communion, the joy of being in that presence which is already closer to you than breathing and nearer than hands and feet. That presence, which you now realize, knows your need before you do and it is its good pleasure to give you the kingdom, the allness, divine grace.

As you realize the nature of God you begin to know the nature of true prayer, the prayer that will bring God right into your experience, because you'll realize now that prayer does not necessarily have anything to do with words or thoughts. There isn't anything you have to tell God; there isn't anything you have to ask God for. There is only one function in prayer, and that is to be quietly, gently peaceful where God is, in the silence within your own being. You'll find that this is the highest form of prayer. Before you reach that, when you sit down to pray you will begin to rehearse some of those things we have heard here tonight. When you sit down to pray, you will remember: "Well, one thing I know, I'm not trying to influence God; I'm not going to God to get anything; I'm not here to tell God what's in my mind or what I think I would like him to do; I'm not here to influence God. In fact, I don't expect that I have any such power as to influence God to do my will. If the Master taught 'Not my will but thine be done,' how then can I be any better and expect God to do my will? And now that I know all these things, God, there's just no use of saying anything further."

Here I am and here thou art. The very place whereon I stand is holy ground. Here and now where I am, thou art. Thou knowest my need. It is thy good pleasure to give me the king-dom. Thine is the power and the glory. Thy grace is my sufficiency, and I am willing to rest in thy grace; I am willing to trust my life to thy care. I can surrender my personal wishes, desires, hopes, ambitions. I can accept that Jesus Christ spoke from a heart full of experience when he said the Father knoweth my need and it is his good pleasure to give me the kingdom. I am sure that Paul knew enough to know what he was saying when he said thy grace is my sufficiency in all things.

You will see for yourself the miracle that takes place when you begin to perceive the nature of God and the nature of prayer, how you have been limiting God, believing that you had to pray for something, you had to tell God something, you had to try to influence God. You weren't trusting the infinite invisible. Jesus knew much more about God than the Old Testament; so did John. In those Gospels of the New Testament you have a far, far greater teacher and teaching on the nature of God than if you permit yourself to be taken back into the Old Testament to try to get along with that God, a God that never really existed.

We, all of us, fall into this category. We attain more and more light on spiritual truth the longer we persist in spiritual living. This is why, when the Hebrews began their experience as slaves, they had very little spiritual light. They had evidently been well trained in obedience—they did observe holy days and they did observe dietetic laws—but this was merely obedience to man-made rules and it had nothing to do with God or with their relationship to God. And so their concepts of God couldn't possibly be as high, as deep, or as true as would come into their experience later when more and more had the opportunity to live freer lives with the greater possibility of attuning themselves to the truth.

With the coming of Jesus Christ, we have the greatest light on the subject of the nature of God that had been given up to that time. Jesus' Sermon on the Mount, revealing the nature of God, is one of the finest teachings ever given to the world. And John tells us of his visions which likewise reveal the nature of God. Then comes the period of your own experience (all Jesus could do was reveal his experience to us). All who have come since had to have their own individual experiences. Paul had his, John had his, and as I said before, all through history there have been hundreds of mystics who have come into the full experience of God, into the full light of spiritual vision. It is possible for everyone who feels that hunger within to attain God-realization. It may be that we attain it in different degrees, but it is possible to all of us. The first and greatest requisite is that we wipe out of our thought every concept of God that we have ever believed and begin to see the nature of God that Jesus revealed.

Watch it as it appears in the Infinite Way writings. Then put it into practice by this form of prayer, contemplation or meditation, until your mind is so freed of any desire to influence God or seek something from God that it settles down into a state of peace that cannot ever come until you have come to understand God as he really is. And when you attain that, your mind settles immediately. Your mind becomes calm and clear because there is no longer a reaching, no longer an activity, no longer a seeking. There is just a resting.

Because thou art, I am. Even if I walk through the valley of the shadow of death, I will not fear for thou art with me. Thou leadest me beside the still waters. Thou makest me to lie down in green pastures.

Oh, the mind is so still, so calm, so peaceful in those assurances. The mind is only stirred when it begins to reach up to God to get something, to want something, desire something, or fear something. Stop fearing God. If there are any of you who still fear God, stop it. Stop it. God knows more about love, care, forgiveness, in one second than the best mother that ever lived knew in a whole lifetime. And if mothers can love and forgive and care and be tender, try to imagine what the nature of God is.

God is love and nothing enters that consciousness that "defileth or maketh a lie." There is no punishment in it. We are punished for our sins but not by God. By our sins. That's the only punishment there is. God knows nothing of punishment or of sins. Sins arise in our own thought. That is why so many people are suffering from sins they never committed. They are only suffering from what the human race calls sins. Oh yes, there are people who have violated some church rule or other and believe they have sinned and are suffering from it. Don't suffer from your past sins, even if some of them persist into the present.

Don't let them make you suffer. Recognize that God is at hand every second, forgiving more often than you can sin. And in the end, the sin itself disappears along with the desire for it.

Never fear God because that indicates a lack of understanding of God. God is love, and in him there is no death, there is no vengeance, there is no hate, there is no punishment. Just think of the crimes men have committed against humanity. Then ask yourself if you really believe God would hold them in eternal damnation or punishment. Not one second longer than it would take them to realize their wrongs and ask forgiveness. Oh, no! No! Understand God as life, a life which can't end for any reason, not even for sin, or for accident, or for disease. Life can't end because God is life, and God is the life of you and the life of me. We fear disease because we fear that it will end in death, and it does because of our fears. We know that death comes because we fear it. If we understood the nature of God, we would know there is no power but God's power. And God's power knows no death. We live eternally. We would be immortal, and as a matter of fact we will be immortal in the moment we realize the nature of God.

God is life eternal. "God has no pleasure in your dying. Turn ye and live." God is the life of you and the life of me, and God doesn't destroy its own life whether it appears as you or whether it appears as me. Therefore, life never ends. Even those who go through the experience of what we call death quickly realize how mistaken they are and realize that their life is continuing. It never did end. It never can end. God is life, therefore life is immortal, life is eternal, life is omnipresent, and life is not at the mercy of any external condition because God is the only power.

~8~

THE NATURE OF ERROR

Good Evening.

You will remember last week we started on two major principles which are unique to the message of the Infinite Way and upon which the healing principles are established. As you know, the subject of healing is a broad one, and these days it includes not only spiritual healing but also mental healing, psychological healing, and faith healing. Today, all of these are embraced under the title of spiritual healing. This is natural because when metaphysical healing was introduced to the world, it was first introduced as "mind healing," which certainly signifies mental healing. Then, later on, the word *mind* became divine mind with a capital M, and it became a synonym for Spirit. And so, divine mind healing and spiritual healing are now one, yet really meaning mental healing and spiritual healing. Eventually mental healing and spiritual healing became so mixed that all metaphysical healing was a combination of mental and spiritual activity. There is no exact dividing line in metaphysical healing between the mental and the spiritual because you will find in the literature of healing work that the mental argument, the activity of the mind, enters into spiritual healing as does Spirit itself.

Later, when the idea of spiritual healing started to become popular, evangelical healers, who were known as faith healers, also adopted the term *spiritual healing* which was their right because they were working with the Bible and with prayer. So they were fully entitled to use the term spiritual healing. And then another form of healing sprang up which was called *spiritualistic healing*, that is, healing by mediums through contact with individuals who have passed on. There is a good deal of this practice in the United States, but even more in England. Then *spiritualistic* lost its suffix, and that practice became known as spiritual healing.

And so when you hear the term spiritual healing, do not jump to the conclusion that you know exactly what it means, because there is no way of knowing what it means except by knowing who says it. This was well illustrated in England when the Church of England set up a committee to investigate the subject of spiritual healing for five years and then to publish a report of its findings. Last July the report came out and in it was published the evidence given by faith healers, evangelical healers, spiritualistic healers, mental healers, Christian Science healers, and Unity healers. Strangely enough the entire report was published under one heading: Spiritual Healing.

Now, as you come to the message of the Infinite Way, you also hear that same term, spiritual healing. But we mean something far different than many of these other teachings because the spiritual healing we are speaking about is a healing based on certain specific principles, principles ascribed only to the Infinite Way. We have no more right to the term spiritual healing than these others, yet we do have the same right that they have. But don't be misled into believing that all metaphysical healing, or all healing that is not physical, is spiritual healing according to the principles of the Infinite Way. That is why we are having these classes for the next six months.

If you wish to avail yourselves of healing through the Infinite Way principles, it is necessary that you understand the principles upon which this work is based and not try to bring with you those principles which you may have learned in some other metaphysical teaching, because all you can do is bring confusion to yourself. Remember, this does not mean right or wrong. This is in no wise saying that the Infinite Way healing method is right and the others are wrong. But this is definitely saying the Infinite Way healing principles differ from those of any other metaphysical teaching. If you have not discerned that, and if you have not discerned what the specific Infinite Way principles are, this is a good time to start. Also those of our students who have been with us some years and who have not entirely separated themselves from other forms of healing can learn now why they are not getting the results they seek.

Truthfully, I had no idea at all that our students weren't completely aware of the fact that the Infinite Way healing principles differed from others, nor did I realize how many of our students do not know what these Infinite Way principles are. And it was through the unfoldment given to me after our return from Holland that I realized I was to spend these next months making this point clear.

Spiritual healing is quite different from spiritual living. Spiritual living is something that has been known to the mystics of all ages. There are European mystics,

Eastern mystics, mystics from many, many parts of the world who can reveal to you the secrets of spiritual living because they all agree there is no difference whatsoever in spiritual living. The basic principles are the same and that means this: The spiritual life is lived after one has made contact with, or come into conscious union with, God, the source of being. The spiritual life can be lived as a student, as a seeker, by following the rules laid down by mystics. But the life itself begins when conscious union has been attained. There is no difference of opinion on that score anywhere at all on the face of the globe.

The subject of healing is something entirely different. Probably throughout all time there have been people who have attained the mystical experience, that touch of the Christ or conscious union with God, and felt an influence working in them that healed. You have it all through the Bible. Moses did some healing work; Elijah did some healing work; Jesus, of course, was the greatest master of healing. In very few cases do you learn from any of the biblical characters the principle or principles by which they healed. The spirit of God had touched them for, as Jesus said, "I am ordained to heal the sick." Even after that time, and all through the years up to the present, there have been a few people who received this same healing gift of God. They did not necessarily know what the principle was and therefore they were unable to teach it. They could do beautiful healing work, but they were unable to leave any students to carry on that work or to teach that work.

Then in the middle of the last century, when meta-physical healing work began as a general practice, it became mental-suggestion healing: "You are well; you are spiritual; you are perfect; you are in the kingdom of God; you are about your Father's business": always somebody projecting ideas of health and harmony and good into your thoughts, until the mind yields and you feel better. And sometimes it is a complete healing, and sometimes it isn't. This is the form which metaphysical healing originally took, and as it spread into the wider field of New Thought, this was the pattern that was accepted and in most cases still is.

In Christian Science, Mary Baker Eddy[1] made great strides in spiritual understanding and eventually came into a tremendous spiritual experience that included spiritual healing, healing without mental argument, healing without using the mind. Probably this was the first introduction to the world of that form of spiritual healing which had a measure of principle behind it. The principle she taught was that God was the only cause and the only creator, therefore there could be no effect from any other cause. So, the basis of her spiritual healing was the absolute allness, the omnipresence, of God.

My entrance into spiritual healing work was also through a spiritual experience, and at a time when I knew nothing of any principle of healing or any method of healing. So I was in the healing work for quite a long time without knowing how it happened, or why, or why above all people I should have been given the healing gift. Study, prayer, and revelation brought principles into my experience that had been glimpsed here and there but were never brought together as specific healing

---

[1]Mary Baker Eddy, 1821–1910: Founder of the Christian Science Church.

principles. It is for this reason we have a message of the Infinite Way with specific healing principles, and of course with a sufficient degree of success to enable this message to go around the world and find acceptance without promotion, without advertising, without organization, and without any financing—merely by those people who have been healed or benefitted.

We have no organization, and as long as I sit on this platform we never will have one. And I do hope that all those who follow me will have the courage never to permit anyone else to form one, because unless individuals are absolutely free to take these principles into their own consciousness and work with them, they will lose them. The very moment this becomes organized—and God forbid it ever does—be assured that you are within twenty years of losing the healing principles. The reason is that in every organization there is an authority, and instead of going into your own consciousness, taking the books and the tapes into your own consciousness for guidance, it becomes so easy to ask someone else, "What about this?" or, "Give me some lessons." Then you get an interpretation that does not come from the source within you. That has happened before and it can happen again.

The first of these principles has to do with the nature of God. Last week our entire hour was devoted to that subject, and you will find it on the first side of the tape being made tonight. This tape will therefore embrace these two principles. Spiritual healing, which means healing that results from an activity of God, cannot come to an individual unless he or she knows enough about the nature of God to be able to relax and not ask God for anything or expect anything from God beyond what God is already doing. Certainly, spiritual healing can only come when individuals no longer attempt to influence God on anyone's behalf, even their own. All of this you have on the other side of this tape. Now we will go into the second part of this healing principle. If you know the first part, the second becomes the most important; but without understanding the first part, the second part isn't reasonable or intelligible.

This has to do with the subject we call the nature of error, or the nature of evil. In the Infinite Way you do not use truth to overcome error, you do not expect God to heal disease or to reform sin or to exchange lack for abundance. God, when you understand God, is already performing its functions. God is eternally bringing forth cattle on a thousand hills, crops in the ground, iron, gold, silver, copper, and oil, and all of the things that are not only needed today but which will ever be needed. Recently, one of our students showed me a passage in the Encyclopedia Britannica which spoke of a certain mountain in which there was an abundance of uranium, a "worthless" metal. That is the way it read: a worthless metal–uranium. As human beings we may have given no value to uranium and therefore might have wondered why an infinitely intelligent God wasted time forming an element called uranium. And you know there was a time when oil was thought to be useless and valueless. So we are going to learn that an abundance of everything has been provided, not only for us today, but for all those who are to come in the future, and that the process is a continuous one.

God does not stop the activity of the sun, the moon, the stars, the oceans, the tides, the birds in the air or the fish in the sea. Therefore, this activity of God must be understood as a permanent dispensation, omnipresent here and now throughout all time: the same yesterday, today, and forevermore. That relieves the mental strain of trying to get in touch with God for some reason. The mind can relax in the realization, "God is, and all that God is, is now, and all that God intends to be, is now." Let us not waste time trying to reach God for any purpose since God already is "closer to us than breathing, nearer than hands and feet,"[2] and our own Master has assured us, "He knoweth your need before you do, and it is his good pleasure to give you the kingdom." When we sit back, relax, and rest in that assurance, we are bringing spiritual good, spiritual harmony, into our experience, and that spiritual harmony appears in due order and in the form necessary to our experience.

Now, let us understand that by taking the principles and statements of truth out of their context, you can lose your demonstration. This is how many other healers have gone astray. Here is a commonly misunderstood quotation from the Master: "Therefore, I say unto you what things soever you desire when you pray believe you receive them, and ye shall have them." And the question arises: "Doesn't that mean one must use the mind to heal, that mind is the healer? Doesn't that conflict with the Infinite Way message?" Of course not. If you know only a few quotations taken helter-skelter out of the message, of course it's conflicting. But when you fully understand the message of the Infinite Way, you realize the Master is saying that in opening your consciousness to the presence of God, you will be fulfilled. And you know right well that God is Spirit, so there is no use opening yourself to anything except that

---

[2] Op. Cit., p. 130.

of a spiritual nature. You have already been told in the message "not to take thought for what ye shall eat or what ye shall drink or wherewithal ye shall be clothed." Then there is no conflict. In fact, that is the principle itself, when you sit quietly in peace, calmness, and assurance, realizing that God is forever pouring itself into visible manifestation. All you're doing then is asking, "Father, reveal thyself to me, reveal thy grace. Thy grace is my sufficiency." As long as you are resting in the assurance that this is already being done, you are not asking God to do it; you are not begging God to start a program today; you are relaxed. You are relaxed in the same way you would be if you wanted sunshine. You would go out-of-doors and just stretch yourself and find yourself flooded, bathed with sunshine. If you wanted to be wet, you could jump into the ocean or into your tub and immediately find yourself immersed in water. You don't have to ask, beg, plead. It's all here, and it's all present where you are, where I am: in your consciousness, closer than breathing, nearer than hands and feet. And in the realization of that, you begin to demonstrate it. This, I tell you, is spiritual living and it leads to actual conscious contact or union with God.

In that same way, once you understand the principle of God's omnipresence, omnipotence, omniscience, once you understand the principle of God as forever being, forever flowing, forever appearing, nothing is left except to relax in that grace. Now, in spiritual healing you have to go a step further and that is where the specific principles of the Infinite Way come into our expression, our activity, our manifestation or demonstration.

The churches used the word *devil* or *satan*, which is the impersonal source of evil. Most metaphysical teachings have used mortal mind, the impersonal source of evil. The mistake has been to accept devil or satan or mortal mind as a power in opposition to God, a power which God is always fighting and never defeats. That battle between God and devil goes on to this day in orthodox teachings, and so far the devil is winning—and there is very little possibility of God ever overcoming the devil. The reason for the failure is that although devil or satan is the impersonal source of all the evil that ever tempts man, it isn't a power. It never is more than a temptation, a suggestion, an appearance which we have been taught to fall for, to fight, and to argue with. It comes down to us from the Old Testament where the Hebrews appealed to this Jehovah-god to defeat their enemies. Always, always the Hebrews of old were turning to this great God of theirs to help them defeat the enemy, and sometimes God did and sometimes he didn't. And you know, we learn that often when God didn't defeat the enemy, the reason was the Hebrews had carelessly lost the Ark in which were kept their holy writings. If they ever lost those, they lost the battle or the war because God was not on their side when they lost that Ark.

That's superstition, of course, but remember we're talking about the days of ignorance, of illiteracy, when perhaps not one person in a thousand knew how to read or write. No wonder there was ignorance, no wonder there was superstition. When the Master came he changed that entire aspect of religion, but unfortunately the churches couldn't accept it. He brought to light the God of love, the God who never punishes, the God whom you can't implore to destroy your enemies. Not even when the Master himself was facing death did he ask God to destroy an enemy. Ah, no! He asked God to forgive the very enemy who killed him.

You see, the Hebrews didn't have the right concept of God. Jesus Christ came with it and it couldn't be accepted. So from that day to this, we still have the world praying to God to destroy our enemies; we are praying to God to destroy our diseases, which are also our enemies; we are praying to God to destroy our sins, also our enemies. Sin hasn't lessened, and I don't think disease has either. Some forms have, but then other new forms have come into existence.

Now, when we come to metaphysical teachings, it was first revealed that this mortal mind was not power. It wasn't a power, and if you recognized that any form of evil was just an activity or a substance of that mortal mind and then dropped it, the healing would follow. But that vision was lost very quickly because the term mortal mind became exactly what it did to Paul, who called it carnal mind. Just as Paul fought carnal mind until it killed him, so did metaphysicians begin to fight mortal mind. They would protect themselves from it and walk on the other side of the street whenever they recognized it in some form. So to this day, whenever you find metaphysicians fighting mortal mind, warring and battling against it, trying to overcome it or protecting themselves from it, you are witnessing metaphysicians who must fail.

In the same way, it was brought to light in the early days of metaphysical teachings that there are specific mental problems causing specific physical problems. Mrs. Eddy accepted that idea in her early days, and when she later realized there wasn't a word of truth in it, she eliminated it from her teaching the best she could.

But unfortunately one of those close to her refused to accept her new revelation and published a book containing a list of the mental causes for physical effects. Incidentally, that identical list has become the foundation of a new medical profession called psychosomatic medicine. Of course, their work is just as much a failure as the work of all metaphysicians who believe there is a specific mental cause for a specific physical disease. That is why some students who come to the Infinite Way and do not realize that none of that plays a part in the principles through which we work, lose the opportunity to benefit by the principles that have been revealed to me and have been found to be successful.

Now, take this next step with me: Regardless of the name or nature of the particular discord that confronts you or your patients or your family—whether it is some form of sin or disease, lack or limitation—remember, it has its basis in an impersonal source whether you call it carnal mind or mortal mind or devil or satan. Give it any name you like as long as you understand it to be an impersonal source. Then take the next step and realize that since God didn't create that source, it has no cause, no substance, no activity, no law to uphold it, no avenue or channel of expression. In other words, it is a nothingness; it is exactly what Hezekiah called it, "the arm of flesh."

This enables you to withdraw from the battle so that you do not fight evil, rather you come into the Sermon on the Mount: "Resist not evil. . . Turn the other cheek. . . Put up thy sword." The moment you can come into the presence of any form of evil with a relaxed mind, a mind that isn't going to just jump right up and start battling it and denying it, you are ready to see evil dissolve into its nothingness. But if you raise your mental sword and try to deny, to argue, to overcome, you're lost. The minute you try to think of a truth with which to meet it, you're lost. The way to approach any and every form of evil is with the realization that it is causeless, an appearance from an impersonal source that has no power.

Then you will find that you are working with this healing principle of the Infinite Way message. We do not have a truth that overcomes your errors; we do not have a God that will reform you or heal you; we do not have a God that will support you or supply you. The God of the Infinite Way is already maintaining and sustaining your spiritual perfection. All you have to do is to awaken from the belief in two powers of good and evil and begin to honor God by respecting the First Commandment, "Thou shall have no other God," thou shall acknowledge no other power. How can you fear an evil power if there is only one power and that one power is God? It is only in honoring the First Commandment that you can begin to perceive the healing principle of the Infinite Way. And of course the Second Commandment of the Master's is equally important: "Love thy neighbor as thyself."

That doesn't take away your human understanding that some individuals are not fully showing forth that which they are. That is why you make a choice of your religious teachings or your religious teacher. You even make a choice of candidates when you go to the polls, not because you are malpracticing anyone, but because you know the truth about them. There is not now and has never been an individual on the face of the globe who wasn't the pure manifestation of God. But you also know that there are those who have no interest in accepting that estimate of themselves. And so, when you're choosing your friends, or when you're choosing your teachers, or when you're choosing your elected officers you have the right to be led to those who most nearly represent your spiritual ideal, and when not that, at least your human ideal.

But in your spiritual living, in your healing work, and in being healed yourself, you must never malpractice another, even as you would not be malpracticed. It is a direct malpractice to see in another anything other than the qualities of God. That is their true identity, even when to human sense they're not manifesting it, even when they don't want to manifest it. Nevertheless, as far as you are concerned, God is their true identity. Now, even when you behold forms of error appearing as human beings, whether in the form of sickness, or sin, or lack, always remember this: In order to be helpful (and this is expected of you whether or not they ask for help), recognize the erroneous nature of what they're manifest-ing. Know that its seat is not in them, but in the imper-sonal mortal mind, impersonal carnal mind, impersonal devil, impersonal satan, any word you like as long as you recognize it to be an impersonal source having nothing whatsoever to do with the individual manifest-ing it at any particular moment.

If you make the mistake of going back to some other form of metaphysical work or treatment to try to remove the error from your patient or from your relative, you won't succeed. You won't succeed any more now than you did before you found the Infinite Way teachings because there's no more benefit to being in the Infinite Way than there is to being in any other teaching. The only benefit there is from the Infinite Way is the practice you make of its principles. That's why it would do no good to create an organization and take all of you in as members. It wouldn't do a thing for you except take from you some of your inherent individuality. You'd be trying to live up to the standards of the organization which may be depending on your membership, depending on your regular attendance, or depending on your regular contributions. And be assured, none of that counts one single bit. One thing alone counts, both in spiritual living and in spiritual healing, and that is: What truth do you know and how true is that truth and how steadfast are you in its application? That's all there is to it.

When you are healed by another, by a practitioner or a teacher, remember you have only had a temporary benefit from the developed consciousness of another person. You will still have to develop your own consciousness in order to make health a permanent dispensation and in order that you may help others. Try to believe me when I tell you that no one in all this world ever receives a spiritual blessing or benefit for their own sake. Never. Any spiritual blessing that is ever given to us by the grace of God is for the benefit it will be to this universe. Of those to whom much is given, much will be expected and demanded. Nobody is ever given the grace of God and then given permission to go up on a mountain and hide somewhere with it. No, no. The more realization we have, the more activity is given to us through which we put to work our understanding and our development for the benefit of this world.

It is just like the sun that never shines just for your garden. Your garden is incidental to the whole picture. The sun shines for this entire globe, and the rain falls on this globe, and God's love is given to the entire world, to saint and sinner, to the just and the unjust. And so it is that when we are given one grain of spiritual understanding or grace, it is only that we might be a transparency or an instrument through which it must be given to others. It doesn't mean that we should have another generation of practitioners sitting in their offices; it means that everyone who receives God's grace should be prepared to help, in a spiritual way, all those who come within the range of their consciousness.

Now if you've been studying these teachings and have not found the answers to your problems, you can see a probable reason in just this one tape. Somewhere you have not understood the nature of God and therefore have been wasting a lot of time trying to influence God. Or, you have not correctly understood the nature of error. You have been battling error, fighting it, trying to overcome it, or trying to use the power of God against it, and that won't work—that won't work. You won't find it easy, but you must bring yourself to a place in consciousness where you can agree that, "the Lord is my shepherd and therefore I shall not want." You must actually know and understand that is the way and you don't have to pray, plead, implore, or affirm. "The Lord is my shepherd, I shall not want," and that's it, period. At some time you must come to the consciousness that "he maketh me to lie down in green pastures; he leadeth me beside the still waters...." And even if I do "walk through the valley of the shadow of death, I shall fear no evil."

Some time or other, as Infinite Way students, you must come to the full and complete demonstration of the Twenty-third Psalm. (Our booklet on the Twenty-Third

Psalm gives it in a form with which you can easily relax and rest.)[3] Then you have to be able to look at the world and even if you see Judas Iscariot, say, "Father forgive him, for he knows not what he does." Even if you are looking at disease you have to be able to do as Jesus did: "What did hinder you? What power is there in that disease? Rise, pick up your bed, and walk." You have to be able to see the nothingness, the non-power, of that which appearance says is terrifying.

In other words, it is a complete change of consciousness. It is a surrendering of the Adam-man who believes in two powers, the power of good and the power of evil, who has to earn his living by the sweat of his brow or has to get healed the hard way. The true understanding of that first Adam was that God alone is power, that whatever is appearing as sin, disease, death, lack, limitation—any of these and the infinite forms and varieties of them—belongs in that impersonal source. Since it isn't God-created or God-ordained, there is no law of God to support it and you walk away from it.

As you persist in this teaching, you will develop that state of consciousness which is included in the Master's two commandments, "Love the Lord thy God" to such an extent that you don't believe God ever empowered evil. Acknowledge God as such an infinite power of good that no other power could have existence. Then take the next step. Realize that your neighbor is the full and complete embodiment of the Christ, has only the Christ qualities, and any other appearance belongs to that impersonal source, devil, or carnal mind, which we

---

[3] Joel S. Goldsmith, *The Secret of the Twenty-Third Psalm.* Reprinted through Mystics of the World, Box 164, Eliot, Maine 03903.

are continuously nothingizing. This, you see, is the entire story of our healing work.

Part III

Living the Healing Principles

"Let the word of Christ dwell in you richly in all wisdom
. . . singing with grace in your hearts. . . ."

Colossians 3:16

1959 Hawaiian Village Closed Class

~9~

METAPHYSICS AND MYSTICISM:
THE INFINITE WAY PATH

Many of you who have been in class work with me know that at no time in my life did I dream of there being such a work as the message of the Infinite Way or that I would ever be connected in any way with a spiritual teaching. My work was in the business world, and while I was never interested in any organized religion, I did have that longing to know what made the wheels of truth go 'round, especially after I began traveling in Europe in 1909. There, for the first time, I was awakened to man's inhumanity to man: I was awakened to the fights, the discords, the inharmonies that take place, and to the dens of iniquity that existed. I didn't know they existed in the United States too, but I learned later we also had our own San Francisco and New Orleans, and these things puzzled me because there were so many religions that claimed there is a God. So it was, I turned my attention to learning more about God. My only purpose was to find out for myself what lies behind this world, so I asked why this thing called God, or man called God, or whatever this being is, wasn't doing something about the sins of the world, the wars, the discords, the causes of strife.

I was only a youngster in New York when the first ladies' ready-to-wear strike took place where men and women were killed, beaten up, and injured in the name of business. I remember when the steel workers in Pennsylvania were striking for a dollar-and-a-half a day and the militia was called out to shoot them down. I wondered about these things. I was in London in 1909 when the German and English fleets were lined up against each other in the North Sea, the World War ready to start. It was man's inhumanity to man that brought me to the search for truth but with no other object or motive than to learn for myself why, if there truly were a God he would permit this inhumanity.

Many years later, when my first religious experience took place, it brought with it the healing gift, and healings began immediately. For a while it seemed as if there were no other purpose in my life and no other motive than being a healer. But the inner unfoldment continued; one religious experience followed another, and each brought with it new revelations, new unfoldments, new discoveries. At the same time I discovered books on mysticism, books which I'd never heard of until then, and these revealed the great mysteries that had been discovered by mystics of all countries, all nations, all races. Time passed, then in 1940 an inner revelation told me that I must learn about the impersonal Christ and about impersonal healing. In 1941 I began an automobile trip around the United States, going as far north as Banff and Lake Louise, then south to New Orleans and Florida, from the East Coast to the West Coast, traveling nineteen thousand miles. The most important revelation came in the early part of the trip when it was revealed to me that all forms of metaphysics which teach that error in individual thought is responsible for illness and inharmony are erroneous. Every teaching that says your wrong thinking is responsible for your ills is incorrect. Any teaching that says jealousy causes rheumatism or cancer, or resentment causes headaches, and so forth, is wrong. And remember, this was very much a part of the Christian Science teachings of which I was then a practitioner.

Now, at the same time it was revealed to me that these teachings were wrong, it was also revealed that all evil, all error, has its source in the universal mind, or universal carnal mind, or mortal mind, and that as individuals, we suffer only to the degree that we admit these mental impositions into our thought. And this we do ignorantly. In other words, by virtue of having been born into this world, we are victims of a universal source of error or evil. Naturally in my healing practice from that time on, I worked from the standpoint that individuals were not responsible for the sins, the diseases, the lacks, or limitations from which they suffered except in the sense that they were responsible because they were human beings who had not been taught how to protect themselves from these universal beliefs.

Not long after that, a whole series of spiritual experiences began, culminating in an experience that lasted two months. These experiences led to the unfoldment from which came the book, *The Infinite Way,*[1] and all this work that followed. Even then, there was no thought in my mind that this would ever amount to anything other than my own individual experience, and so when we began our work in California with a few friends, it was only with the idea that those who came to me for healing might also be interested in the healing principles. It was

---

[1] Op. Cit., p. 119.

for this reason that when *The Infinite Way* was published, only two thousand copies were printed. Actually, one thousand were sent to storage because I never believed we would need that second thousand.

You know the history of the work, how it has developed and how it has spread–Australia, New Zealand, the United States, both coasts of Canada, England, and South America–how these unfoldments have continued to come into my experience, and always with signs following. It has been a great privilege for us because these experiences are a tribute to the power of the Word. This really has been a testimony to what the message does for students, not only under the direct guidance of a teacher or practitioner, but also when students have only the books or tapes available as teachers.

At the very start of our public work in the Infinite Way, I was told that my function would be to do that which was given me to do and that I would have no responsibility. That is, the Presence would always go before me to accomplish the work. And this quickly proved to be true. As money was needed for publication of the writings, money was there. Invitations came to lecture in New Thought temples, in Religious Science churches and institutes, in Unity, in metaphysical libraries and in all places where, by every standard, I had no right to be invited. I knew nothing of those places or of their teachings and writings. In fact, I knew nothing about any of the metaphysical writings outside of Christian Science, and yet these doors were open with invitations, even invitations to write articles for their magazines. You see, no man or woman could do this of themselves. There had to be a Presence going before to bring those invitations to my doorstep, to bring about this work.

Every step has been taken in that same way. Sitting at my desk one day here in Honolulu where I had the apartment on the Ala Wai, the voice said, "Go to New York, wait the first few days of December, and then go on to London." The voice was just that clear, yet there wasn't a reason in the world to go to London that I knew about. As far as I knew there were only twelve people over there who had copies of *The Infinite Way*–at least that's all I had ever heard from–and you wouldn't go to London to call on twelve people who hadn't sent for you. But I went to London in obedience to that voice, sat down in the hotel room and said, "Well, you said to come and I'm here, but I have nothing to do!" The voice told me each step to take. By the time I left London, two of my books were in publication, lectures and a class had been arranged, and contact had been made with Mr. Hamblin.[2] The work in England has flourished to the extent that today two publishing houses are printing all of the Infinite Way writings and the British edition of the *Monthly Letter* is being sent out from London. From England the work expanded into Germany where *The Infinite Way* was translated into German. And you have seen the growth since.

Another such experience happened when a man I'd been corresponding with in South Africa wrote me a letter. I had also been hearing from three or four other people in Johannesburg. This man wrote, "When you're traveling, why don't you come to South Africa?" Of course, you see how ridiculous that would be with only

---

[2] Henry Thomas Hamblin, 1870-1960. English New Thought writer and editor, founder/publisher of *Science of Thought* (also called *Science of Thought Review*).

three or four people there interested in the work. But the next week I was in the airline office making arrangements for my trip to Europe. Without thinking about it, I asked the travel agent, "Couldn't I come back by way of South Africa?" He said, "Certainly." "And how much would the additional cost be?" It was a very small sum. Well, I said, "Why not give me a ticket returning that way?" And so I wrote the South African gentleman that I would be there.

By the time I reached New York City, my book department had written asking what we should do about an order from a South African book store for two hundred copies of each of the writings. Of course I wrote back: "Send them twenty copies. They must think I'm Billy Graham coming down there." But when I got to London I received a telephone call from South Africa: They wanted to know if their money wasn't good. They had ordered two hundred copies of each book. When I asked why, they told me there were two hundred people waiting for class instruction. Actually, when I got there, there were eight hundred!

You see, a human being couldn't know that, and a human being couldn't plan that, and a human being couldn't do that. Something had gone before to make the crooked places straight, and every event of the Infinite Way work has taken place in that same way.

In one of my spiritual experiences during those early days, the voice said, "My consciousness is your consciousness, and my consciousness is doing the work as you. Never seek a student, but never refuse a student who is sent to you—for they are being sent to you." This has been our policy ever since. Never have we advertised or sought or solicited, and never have we refused anyone who showed any eagerness at all for this message.

We know there is such a consciousness. What is called Christ-consciousness in Christian mysticism, and Buddha-consciousness in Eastern mysticism has been known throughout all times, but it is the same consciousness, the consciousness of enlightenment. I could tell you about many, many of these experiences. One day a woman in San Francisco came to me and said, "The students want copies of the lectures you are giving. Please give us permission to record them and print them." My answer was, "Oh, no, I'm not saying anything important enough for that. Nobody would want these lectures printed." "Oh, yes," she said, "the students do want to have these lectures." I eventually permitted her to record a lecture one evening just to see if it were true. Well, it was true, and that's how the *First, Second,* and *Third San Francisco Lectures*[3] got into print and how *Metaphysical Notes,*[4] *Consciousness Unfolding,*[5] and *The Master Speaks*[6] got into print. Just by having been taken down on a recorder and then mimeographed.

You see, it wasn't human will; it wasn't a human desire that those lectures be printed, they were pushed out. But when the idea to have tape recordings was

---

[3] *The San Francisco Lecture Series,* © 1954 by Joel S. Goldsmith. Now published as *Rising In Consciousness,* Joel S. Goldsmith (Atlanta, GA: Acropolis Books, Inc., 1997).

[4] *Metaphysical Notes,* © 1947 by Joel S. Goldsmith. Now published as *Consciousness In Transition,* Joel S. Goldsmith (Atlanta, GA: Acropolis Books, Inc., 1997).

[5] *Consciousness Unfolding,* © 1962, 1990 by Joel S. Goldsmith (reprinted 1998, Acropolis Books, Inc., Atlanta, GA).

[6] *The Master Speaks:* © 1962, 1990 by Joel S. Goldsmith (Atlanta, GA: Acropolis Books, Inc.).

presented to me, you will never know how I resisted it. Nor will you know how the first two attempts failed. Then all of a sudden, on a trip to Hawaii, the work began to grow, and it's been growing ever since. It never has stopped. Everything connected with the Infinite Way has gone in just that manner. It is not only as if there were a divine being, a presence or power, doing it, but there actually *is* a divine being, presence, or power that is doing all of this—and I am its instrument. I am just an instrument awaiting orders and then going out and obeying them. It is as if I were a messenger for something far greater than anyone or anything could be on the human plane. I've recognized that always. I've recognized that the message coming through our manuscripts, through our books, through our letters, could not come from the mind of man because the mind of man doesn't know God. Many of these teachings have never appeared before in literature, and if they have, it would have made no difference to me, for I wouldn't have known it. Therefore, these teachings come from an infinite source.

The question that came to my mind early in the work was how do these teachings come through? How can they be brought through? How can they be taught? How can I convey this spiritual message, this guidance, this protection, this direction from within? The answer given to me was meditation. Meditation was known in the East, but it was not taught in the Western world. There was very little written on this subject, and in those days when I looked around for more information, the only publication I found in occidental writings was a tiny pamphlet issued by Unity. Of course this was far from the teaching of meditation itself, although it contained wonderful thoughts on the subject. Some of the writings on Eastern meditation were published by Englishmen, but none of them were teaching it; none of them knew how it was practiced; none of them showed how contact is made with the infinite source.

And then began the experience of trying, for eight months, to make contact with that source which I knew to be within—not only I knew, but what everyone else in the world must have known since there were so many tens of millions of Bibles, all saying, "The kingdom of God is within you. It is neither lo here nor lo there, it is within you. It is not in holy mountains nor is it in temples in Jerusalem, or any place else, it is within you." Therefore, if the kingdom of God is to be contacted, it must be contacted within. It was for that reason I could stick with it night and day for eight months in the attempt to prove this was true. And I proved it. Then began instruction in meditation, which really came to fruition in the first San Francisco lecture. This was my first writing on the subject of meditation. From then until now it has been one of the major activities of the Infinite Way, one of the major teachings, one of the major parts of the work, and for this reason: It really makes no difference how much truth you know intellectually; if you know it only with your mind you will not bring forth spiritual fruitage.

Now here is a strange thing: If you really know the truth of being, even intellectually, and are willing to work with it, you can do healing work. But that will have no connection at all with making contact with the kingdom of God; it will only have to do with a mental activity of knowing the truth. It is possible to do healing work without actually making contact with the Spirit, but it is healing based on the letter of truth, on knowing the truth, on being willing to be one-pointed enough so as to be consistent and persistent. But if you are persistent and consistent, the miracle is that you will break through to the kingdom of God by that very practice. That practice of healing through the letter of truth is one of the ways to break through into the kingdom of God, the spirit of truth, the consciousness of truth. There are many who avoid that step and believe that merely by meditating they will get there. Some do, but many do not. Many do not break through just by meditation, and if—and this has been my experience—you practice this letter of truth, if you combine meditation with consciously knowing the truth, you will definitely break through to the kingdom of God.

Tonight I'm going to bring to light a few things that would not be clear to you without this background. These have been very difficult for me to say except to very small groups of students who were receiving personal instruction or were actively engaged in healing work. That is: There is no God in the human world. That is why the human world is full of sin, disease, death, lack, and limitation. That is why the cream of our youth get killed in war. There is no God to stop it. And that is why we can have road accidents every weekend and every holiday, because there is no God there to stop it. These horrible things couldn't happen in the presence of God. In the presence of God there is liberty. In the presence of God there is freedom. In the presence of God there is life eternal. "To know him aright is life eternal." To know him aright would save us from the sins, diseases, deaths, accidents, the lacks and limitations of this life. Therefore, the human world as it is exists is completely cut off from God.

Whenever you find an individual who in one way or another makes contact with God, that individual is experiencing God and the fruitage of God right here in this world. During the war, you heard about many of our boys in dangerous and hopeless situations where there was no human way out. In their desperation they turned to God, found contact with him, and had miraculous escapes and miraculous experiences. So it is that whenever any individual makes contact with God, they become immune to the ills of their circumstances. The Master phrased it this way: "I have overcome the world." He also said, "My kingdom is not of this world." No! You have to rise above this world to reach *my* kingdom, the Christ kingdom, and therefore this world which he says is not *my* kingdom has none of God or the Christ in it. Every individual on earth who breaks through, who makes contact, has also overcome this world and is now "in this world but not of it," no longer living under the law but under grace. Paul told us the same thing very plainly. But the world doesn't like bad news. Therefore it glosses over his statement that we as human beings "are not under the law of God, indeed cannot please God, are not under the protection of God, and do not receive the grace of God." Then he continues, "If so be the spirit of God dwells in you, then do you become the sons of God."

Yes, if the spirit of God has touched you, if you have made contact with your spiritual source, then your life is no longer lived under the law but under grace. Then you find that scriptural promises such as, "The presence goes before you to make the crooked places straight," or "I will never leave thee nor forsake thee," to be absolute truth. You find that they're demonstrable, but not until this contact has been made. The world has overlooked this scriptural truth and has believed that by using the mind or the lips and praying to some unknown god, it is going to find answers. And it doesn't. It doesn't realize it is praying to an unknown god, to a non-existent god. It is praying with the mind through which one cannot reach God and therefore it doesn't get outside the limitations of the second chapter of Genesis. In that second chapter of Genesis you are cut off from God, you have to earn your living by the sweat of your brow, and bring forth children in pain. In other words, life is a hardship. And it is, and it continues to be until, "If so be the spirit of God dwells in you, then do you become the sons of God."

Throughout all ages there have been mystics who have had the conscious experience of God, conscious union with God, and yet have not been able to overcome the dangers, the pitfalls, the sins, the diseases of humanhood. That has always been a great mystery. Why is it that some of the greatest known mystics, including religious leaders, have suffered horrible afflictions, terrible diseases? The Master, Christ Jesus' experience did not come to him through ignorance of the law but came to him because he took it upon himself, most likely, to prove something. We cannot always speak with authority about some of the things that concerned the Master because some of the literature about his ministry and even about his message has not been available. Some manuscripts that have been discovered have been hidden from the world so that the world cannot have access to them. It really isn't possible to know whether Jesus believed that by the crucifixion he was going to prove to the world that life was immortal, and therefore his message was true, or whether he paid the penalty for being what he was. Perhaps the Hebrew church had to get him out of the way, and crucifixion was the way to do it. That seems more likely to me than his believing he would prove anything to the world by going through the crucifixion. At his stage of unfoldment, I'm sure he knew that the human mind could never grasp the significance of his experience, even if it could witness it.

In this same way, if you were to witness a miraculous healing you would know it, you would recognize it, and you would acknowledge it as a miracle. Something within you would tell you what you had seen and the nature of it. But you do not know how many of these miracles have been witnessed by people who have said, "Oh, we can't account for it, but it sometimes happens that way." It takes depth of spiritual vision, not only to bring miracles about, but to recognize them.

If a person you knew to be of spiritual vision, of spiritual stature, were to pass on, I would not be surprised if most of you would see that individual rise out of the body. I think most of you are far enough along to not be fooled by the appearance but would be able to witness the resurrection from the tomb of this body and then the ascension. Yes, but don't go and tell the masses you saw a resurrection or an ascension, for this cannot be accepted by the human mind. Even if you told them you'd seen it, those without spiritual discernment would never see it, know it or believe it. That is why we are told, "Go and tell no man what things ye have seen," or "Go and show it to the priests."

All revelation is an individual experience. You acknowledge, I'm sure, that there are people of all faiths–Protestants, Catholics, Hebrews, Moslems, Hindus, Buddhists–of deep, deep spiritual consciousness, deeply religious, who have wonderful visions and understanding of reality. The vision of God is available to all who can open themselves regardless of what church they may be in and even regardless of the fact that some may not be in any church (but being in or of a church is not a barrier either). At the same time the world has wondered why there are many, many people in all religious faiths who are unable to free themselves from the inequalities, the injustices, the diseases of human existence.

This is the reason the Infinite Way message, of its own accord, is spreading and doing the work it is, because it has solved that riddle. The revelations that have been given to us in this message reveal the life of mysticism, the way to attain it, and at the same time have given us the metaphysical principles by which the laws of human existence are nullified and life under grace is achieved. This is really a two-fold message: it consists of the mysticism of the Infinite Way and the metaphysics of the Infinite Way, and it has been that way from the beginning.

In all of the writings, you will notice passages that tell you the correct letter of truth. That is the metaphysics of the message. Then you find other passages which go from meditation to the actual experience of illumination. That is the mysticism of the message. Through this message, you can attain the mystical contact, or conscious union with God. Through this message you can learn and practice the laws of metaphysics which bring about harmony in human experience. One helps you to achieve the other: more especially, knowledge of the letter of truth and its practice will lead to the mystical experience whereas the mystical experience itself will not always lead to the correct letter or metaphysics of truth.

I explained before that when I began healing work, I knew nothing of the letter of truth, knew nothing of how healings were accomplished or why—I only knew that it was so. But you see, others have had the same experience and lost the gift because eventually they came up against the one thing that will make everybody lose their demonstration of harmonious life. That is, faith in some kind of God, faith that God is healing disease, or faith that God will heal disease. Eventually all those who have a natural gift of healing come to a place where it doesn't work any longer, where they have to change the nature of their work, because the healings do not continue to come through as they did in the beginning. Always that is for the same reason: they somehow come to believe that God is healing disease through them, and that's enough to destroy their entire demonstration, because God is too pure to behold iniquity. If God ever knew there was a disease on earth, God wouldn't be God anymore. If God ever healed a disease, God wouldn't be God anymore because God would be sharing its power with disease. God would be permitting something else to exist, some other power than itself. Oh, no, that just cannot be! In the entire kingdom of God there is no such thing as a disease or a cure for disease.

In my experience, I was fortunate enough, through revelation, to begin to perceive this letter of truth, to begin to understand what was happening. Ultimately I made the discovery that God is not a power that heals disease and that God is not operating in me or through me. The secret? There is no law of disease. Disease is man-made, man-created, and it is only perpetuated in the mind of man as long as he believes it is a power, that it has a power, that it has a law to maintain or sustain it. In other words, fighting the disease is what perpetuates it. Fighting the disease is what prevents its cure. Praying for it to be healed is enough to keep it going forever because it is an acknowledgment of it as a something. But you've got to destroy your God before you can admit that there is a something called evil power, deathly power, destructive power. You can't have a God of infinity, eternality, immortality, omnipotence and then acknowledge that in some way or other this little pipsqueak power came into being, and now you're going to get God to do something about it. Oh, no. No. You will not get it that way. It is that type of blind faith that eventually makes us lose our demonstration.

You must understand this: God is. Behind this universe is an invisible, incorporeal, infinite Being which is eternality, immortality, omnipotence, omnipresence, and omniscience. It maintains and sustains its creation perfectly unto eternity, from everlasting to everlasting. Nothing of an evil nature has ever touched God, or the kingdom of God, or the son of God, or the world of God's creating. Once you understand that, you have to account for all of these things we witness on earth. Here is the revelation which makes this the Infinite Way: at the time of that experience called "eating of the tree of the knowledge of good and evil," the sense of separation took place in which life was lived in the mind of man instead of in the mind of God. Man has made the conditions of life; man has even made his god. Everyone who has an idea of what God is entertains only a man-made god, a man-made concept of god. In the earliest days, the god which men made—oh, it wasn't a god, it was gods—was one you could pray to for rain, one you could pray to for fertility, one you could pray to for something else. Gods for everything. Then, when all of these gods were condensed into one god—and we refer now to the period of Abraham, Isaac, and Jacob, when the idea of the one God was formulated—it was only a god that embraced the capacities of all those multitudinous gods. So instead of praying to twelve different gods for twelve different things, now we were taught to pray to one god for the same twelve things. That one god was just as much a myth as the twelve gods had been.

Every mystic, saint, or savior broke through the limitations of the human mind and made contact with that infinite consciousness we call God: Abraham did it; Isaac did it; Jacob did it; Moses did it; Elijah did it; Elisha did it; Isaiah, Jesus, Paul, John, and hundreds of others. Yet even though they received illumination to the extent that they were able to do great things for their people, they could never give them a freedom that could be maintained.

We have every reason to believe that Jesus was not only one of the most illumined, but probably the most illumined of all time. He could do miracles for his people and impart enough of that consciousness to his disciples so that they could continue with his unfoldment for a period of nearly three hundred years. Then the unfoldment disappeared from the face of the earth again. And so you find in every age that the revelation of mysticism has come to earth, but it has been lost because every leader can only bring a certain number of people to spiritual awakening, and they in turn a certain number, and then it eventually drops away. Then it has to be done all over again by another light that comes in a later day.

At no time throughout the history of the world have any of these leaders been able to teach their people the principles upon which their own demonstration was made, and the demonstration they made for their followers. Now we face the question: Since we not only know the attainment of mysticism, but also the principles upon which these demonstrations were made and are being made now, will our students learn them? Will they be willing to practice them so that this time they remain on earth and continue to unfold until that day comes when the entire universe will be illumined with the one infinite consciousness?

~ 10 ~

METAPHYSICS OF THE INFINITE WAY: KNOWING GOD IS

For many, many centuries of human history there seems to have been very little thought about the subject of freedom and equality. The world lived under systems of government and the rule of individuals and groups, but the masses have always been to some extent slaves and peasants. The Hebrews dreamed of being free from Pharaoh, but probably not with any true sense of freedom because it is doubtful if they could even visualize what true freedom was. They imagined what it would be like to be free from slavery under Pharaoh, but true freedom—the real sense of freedom, the real desire for freedom, and the real ability to enjoy freedom—evidently came from the Greeks. As you know, France had its day for finding freedom, the United States had its day, England had its Magna Carta, but nowhere have any people been able to maintain their freedom for any great length of time.

Freedom never remains with a people. A few centuries seem to be about the limit that anyone can hold on to a free system of government, one that guarantees freedom and equality and justice. Eventually nations lose their freedom, either to a political dictatorship or a religious dictatorship. One or the other always swallows up the freedom of the people. Unless we come into some spiritual experience in the near future, that same condition is going to continue: country after country will lose its freedom, including this one. In fact, the day isn't far off when this one will lose its freedom; it is due in less than twenty years. Then the struggle to get free will begin again, and in a century or two or three, freedom will come again.

No country is ever going to make the demonstration of freedom through human means. It cannot be done and there are two very good reasons for this. The first, and probably most important, is mental inertia. People just do not care about the subject of freedom while they've got it. As long as their human needs are being met, let them earn enough to get by, keep them reasonably occupied with baseball, football, wrestling, television, radio, or some other external amusements, and you own them body and soul. You can do anything you want with them—manipulate them politically or religiously—and they have no complaints about it. They're perfectly happy. Of course they wouldn't be if you interfered with an automobile outing, or their radio or television show, or the movies, or sports. Then you'd have a revolution. But as long as you don't touch those things, you can own the masses body and soul and do with them as you wish.

Don't say you don't believe it. You were told here yesterday, by a man who hopes to be president, that one of the biggest criminals in the country is bigger than the law and can't be reached by the law, that he has control of political and economic situations. That same candidate who didn't have the courage to tell you that you have the same thing going on here because that criminal is his political ally. You are asleep. You pay no attention to the fact that your liberties are menaced, that your economic well-being is menaced, because nobody is interfering with your pleasures at the moment. Nobody is interfering with your profit at the moment. So you let these things go by. And it isn't only you sitting here; this is you all over the world, and this is what goes on until the population wakes up when it's too late.

In one guise or another, this has always happened, and is happening here. Whether or not these things will be changed in the next ten or twenty years is something yet to be seen. But for our purpose, the fact is the entire world is threatened, threatened not only from Russia, threatened not only from church rule, threatened not only from labor bosses, but threatened most of all by ourselves and our own unwillingness to think. Mental inertia. It is so easy to read a picture magazine because no one has to think when they're looking at pictures. It has been pointed out many times, that only between five and six percent of the newspaper reading public read the editorial page on which the real news of the world is published. Of course you can read on the front page about murders, divorces, and rapes, and you can read advertising on all the other pages, but you can only read the news as it affects your life on the editorial page. Still, only five to six percent of newspaper readers in the Unites States read that page. That's what I mean by mental inertia.

I'm only using this as an example to bring up the subject of spiritual freedom. You, as an individual, are under very strict physical, mental, and material laws of this world until you come into some form of metaphysical teaching. In the beginning it makes no difference which teaching. There is enough truth in any of them to actually start individuals on the way toward freedom from physical, mental, and financial limitations. Unfortunately, all of these movements are losing their followers, and the reason is the same: people complain that they cannot make their demonstrations. Nine-tenths of the responsibility for this is theirs. They won't work with the material they're given; they won't put into practice the principles they've been taught. They take the attitude: "Well, God will do it," or "I can trust God to do it," or "God is omnipotent, God is all-power. Oh, there's no other power but God." By relying on God in this way, they lose their demonstration.

Now we come to the message of the Infinite Way. I have no hesitation in telling you that the principles of life have been revealed in this message, and with understanding and practice we can free ourselves of nearly all, if not all, of the limitations of this world. The only reason we may not free ourselves from all of them is that our intensity does not reach to that degree. But certainly we can be free of seventy, eighty, or ninety percent of the discords of this world if we work with the principles given to us in the message.

From the beginning of the work, I've received letters from students telling me, "Oh, I thought there was no other power but God, so I don't have to do anything." It is true there is no power but God, but that isn't saving the world from sin, disease, death, lack, and limitation, wars and still more wars. The allness of God, spiritual reality, has no relationship to the human world until each of us, as individuals, lift ourselves up and out of humanhood to where we too can say, at least in some measure, "I have overcome this world." This is an individual demonstration.

We know that practitioners and teachers, those who have worked with the principles a little more than the rest of the world, can free young students. They can bring healing, supply, happiness, and joy to some extent, but they cannot maintain that state of consciousness for the student forever. They cannot bring about the highest degree of consciousness that each student would like. There just isn't that much time for a practitioner or teacher to devote to any one student. But those who do break through mental inertia to the extent that they learn and practice these principles, attain a measure of spiritual consciousness and can do healing work. Of course students benefit from that.

But you know, it has been said that Jesus raised Lazarus from the dead yet Lazarus died later anyhow. Jesus healed the multitudes of sickness, but watch their histories. Probably all became sick again later and even died. In other words, no one can make a permanent demonstration for anyone else but themselves. Every bit of help you get from a practitioner or teacher is really to bear witness to what these principles can do. But if it were possible for practitioners or teachers to save everyone from the sufferings of this world, then all the rich people would have to do is to hire us! Wouldn't that be sweet? All the rich people could give us a good income to live on, just to keep them from sin, disease, and death, accidents, and limitations. You don't believe it could be done, do you? You don't believe there is that much money in the world that would enable them to hire somebody else to keep them spiritually, physically, mentally, morally, and financially free? You know better than that. You know it couldn't be done. If it could, all the practitioners would have been snapped up long ago by big corporations; they might even have been put on government payrolls to keep governments in power.

The spiritual life is an individual life for this reason: The spiritual life is an individual experience, experienced within, and then expressed outwardly—secretly, silently, sacredly. That is why it can only thrive among a free people. You cannot have a communal spiritual life. You cannot have a communal spiritual source from which each can share their demonstration. That can only be achieved according to each individual's ability to break through. Remember, there is only one barrier to a perfect spiritual life, and that's mental inertia. That's all. There's no other reason that students of metaphysics go on year in and year out under the evil conditions of this world. They will not, or cannot, break through long enough to sit down and consciously learn the correct letter of truth and then put it into practice.

The great miracle is this, and it is a miracle: There is no use for you or me or anyone else in this world to sit around waiting to be favored with a spiritual experience, because in the vast majority of cases it isn't going to happen. The miracle is that it will happen to any individual who can break through mental inertia to the extent that they will not merely read books of truth, but will study them to learn the principles and then begin to apply them in their lives, facing the specific problems that arise. Through this practice, the spiritual lives of individuals are finally opened, and usually quickly, if they work faithfully with the principles.

Just as we have learned that it isn't enough to go to church and let the minister pray for us—because that doesn't bring us salvation—we eventually learn that we cannot hire practitioners and teachers to bring about our own salvation either. We learn that it becomes a matter of individual activity to put these principles into practice.

"Ye shall know the truth and the truth will make you free," and as these principles are put into practice as specific problems arise, our own spiritual life unfolds.

Let me show you exactly how this works. I said to you previously that even those who do have some spiritual light may lose it through not knowing the correct letter of truth. Here's what I mean: God, being omnipotent, is the only power, the only truth there is. That is contrary to the belief in human experience that we have material power and mental power, material force and mental force. These material powers result in disease and eventually death. Mental powers more likely result in sin, because our false appetites, our sinful thoughts, our evil suggestions, have their rise, not in our bodies but in our minds. It is through the mind that we admit sin into our experience, and through the mind we also admit disease, both of which appear as though they were material power, material force.

The ordinary human has no protection against material or mental force and therefore fights fire with fire, fights material force with more material force. We fought bows and arrows with javelins. We fought javelins with pistols, pistols with rifles, and eventually rifles with cannons; and then we developed atomic bombs. So it is that some years ago, someone made a great discovery and used a drop of penicillin to overcome a lot of infection; and gradually they had to double the dose of penicillin, and then quadruple it. Now we have to use hundreds of times the dosage to do what was originally done with that one drop. In other words, we are always using a greater force to overcome a lesser force and then must develop a still greater force, and then a still greater force.

So it is with mental power. Before mental power was known, people were victims without knowing they were victims. Then, when Mesmer[1] discovered mesmerism, or hypnotism, some people at least discovered they were suffering from the activity of other peoples' thoughts. As metaphysics began to unfold in the middle of the nineteenth century, the power of both good thoughts and evil thoughts was discovered so that those who used good thoughts could do healing work, and those who used bad thoughts could bring about evil influences and events. From that time to this, we do know that on the human plane you can, by thinking good thoughts, produce good results; by thinking evil thoughts you can produce evil results. We know that, but the world itself doesn't quite realize that, and neither does it realize how it can be mentally manipulated by a small group of individuals who do know the power of the mind.

You saw an example of that a couple years ago when experiments with subliminal perception proved you could be made to get up out of your seat in a movie theater and go downstairs to buy popcorn and Coca Cola, even if you didn't want it. Of course, you didn't know you were being compelled to do it by somebody manipulating your mind, directing you to do this. So, more and more it is known that there is such a thing as mental power, there is such a thing as good thoughts producing healings and evil thoughts, being destructive in nature, producing ills.

Throughout this entire experience on the mental level, you find what formerly was known about the

---

[1]Friedrich Anton Mesmer, 1734–1815. Austrian physician considered the forerunner of the practice of hypnotism.

material level: a stronger power overcomes a weaker power; a little more material strength overcomes a less material strength; a stronger prize-fighter defeats a weaker prize-fighter. We all know this on the material plane. Now we're beginning to discover it on the mental plane. Those who have the strongest power of mental concentration can do good if good is their nature, and they can do evil if evil is their nature. So we have two powers warring with each other, one on the material level and one on the mental level. Ah, yes! but now we come to the revelation as given in this message and which we have been proving: that in the world of God there are not two powers–there are not *any* powers. Material force isn't a power and mental force isn't a power because when spiritual contact is made, the laws of both matter and mind disappear. This has been proven in the healing of physical disease and mental disease. The moment you introduce the new dimension–Spirit–you nullify material force and mental force.

The first step on the metaphysical path is to concern yourself with, "What is the truth with which I am to work?" Remember, you do not have to concern yourself at this moment with whether or not you're spiritual, or whether you've been touched by the spirit of God, or whether you've had a spiritual experience. The truth to work with is that there are not good powers and bad powers, either of a material nature or mental nature. There is only one power, and that power is the power of Spirit. And it's not an overcoming power. The power of God doesn't overcome evil; the power of God doesn't overcome sin or disease; the power of God isn't an overcoming power. It is a creative, maintaining, and sustaining power on its own level. The moment the experience of God takes place within, the moment God is realized, that with which we have been faced in the form of material power or force, or mental power or force, dissolves.

The moment you know this, you stop the struggle against evil. You begin to come into the Christian dispensation in which you have been taught: "Put up thy sword . . . Resist not evil." Then you learn why: Evil in and of itself is not power. It is power only to the mentality that still accepts two powers, a good power and an evil power. When you no longer accept good or evil powers and accept a God of infinite nature—omniscience, omnipresence, omnipotence—right where you are, you will have found your demonstration. God is not to be attained, not to be gained, not to be sought after, not to go 'round the world looking for the Holy Grail, "for the kingdom of God is neither lo here nor lo there," it is where you are! "The place whereon thou standest is holy ground . . . the kingdom of God is within you." You don't have to go looking for it, not even in books. The only purpose of books is to reveal this to you, but even after it's revealed it will do nothing for you unless you put it into action. You might just as well read about how to play the piano and then try to put on a recital. You can read about it, but after reading about it, put into practice what you read.

It is the same with the Bible. The Bible is proba-bly—not probably—*is* the greatest book that has ever appeared in print anywhere in any time. But of what avail is it if you do not take the laws that are revealed in the Bible and consciously put them into action? What good is it to read that God is all power and then begin to fear the very next thing that pops up?

The first and greatest truth that a metaphysician must learn is that God is, and because God is, nothing else is truth except God, and that which God created, that which God gave forth, all that God made, is good. Anything that God did not make, was not made. Well, if disease isn't good, then be assured God didn't make it. If God didn't make it, it has no existence. Oh, yes, we're suffering from it. Of course we are, because we were born into this double-mindedness of two powers; consciously and unconsciously we accept two powers and thereby we come under the law of two powers. Do you think that it's easy to overcome that which we have been accepting for centuries? You may say, "Oh, but my child has only been here ten years. She isn't too much under the law." Nonsense! Your child has been born and reborn, and born and reborn, under the law for centuries. There isn't a single one of us that had our beginning on what we call our birthday. That, too, would make mockery of God. We have existed from time immemorial; we have coexisted with God, and we will live unto eternity. But in our human identity, we have been thrust into this world time after time, and always under the same laws of good and evil, matter and mind.

It isn't easy to come to a place where you acknowledge, in spite of all appearances to the contrary, that laws of matter and laws of mind are not power, that God is the only lawgiver and God is spirit, therefore all law is spiritual. Don't think for a moment that because this is said from a platform as truth—and it is truth, the most important truth ever revealed—that demonstrates the principle for you. It may. Some degree of healing can take place right in this room because of the consciousness that is uttering this statement. But don't rely on it too long, because you have to bring yourself to that place in consciousness where you declare: "Judge not after appearances; judge righteous judgement." I know all the appearances of material law. I've seen bullets operate. I know all about how bombs operate and how disease operates, too. Heaven knows, I've had plenty of it! But spiritual truth reveals that material law isn't law and mental law isn't law, for God is the only lawgiver. God is spirit and therefore the only law is spiritual.

Maintain that in your consciousness actively and consciously, day by day by day, forgetting all the other writings, forgetting all the other statements of truth, just abiding in that one truth until it registers, until the inner click or realization comes, until it dawns in your consciousness. Knowing "that is the truth!" will give you dominion. I know as well as you do, there are too many Infinite Way books. There should be only one. One is enough. But in our humanhood we cannot stay with one book and take it sentence by sentence, principle by principle, until we've demonstrated it. So we have twenty-five books, and as you read the same thing over and over, the same idea in a different context helps you to assimilate it. But one book is enough, just as one Bible is enough. One book of *John* is enough to save the world, if everyone would take the book of *John* sentence by sentence, principle by principle.

We have the metaphysics of life and the mysticism of life. The mysticism can come to you by divine grace, or you can bring it to yourself by practicing the metaphysics of it; but in doing that it must be the correct letter of truth. In other words, you can't declare God's allness today and then tomorrow wonder what wrong thoughts may be doing some evil to you; or wonder why mortal mind is doing this to you; or wonder if you're being punished for some sin of omission or commission. There has to be a consistency, as well as persistence, in holding to the truth that there is but one power. If you have sinned, that isn't a power because God didn't create the sin or the penalty for it. Therefore, it has no existence in that one mind, or consciousness, which is God. God being the only law, is a law of eternal forgiveness. And if you need to prove it to yourself, read the New Testament and find that Jesus had no condemnation for the adulteress; Jesus had no condemnation for those taken in the act. Jesus had no condemnation for any form of sin. Always it was: "'Neither do I condemn thee.' Start all over again." You begin to find that, instead of holding yourself in condemnation to a power of punishment, you begin to abide in your realization that God is an eternal state of forgiveness. God is starting all over every second of every minute and every minute of every hour. Every second is a fresh one; the past is dead, and the future never comes.

The secret of healing is not in the mysticism, but in the metaphysics of the Infinite Way message; and the metaphysics of the message leads to the mysticism in which one finds complete spiritual freedom. Then there is no longer an overcoming through knowing the truth. There is no longer any process. There is only a state of divine being. The mystics, like Jesus, who knew this principle and could say to Pilate, "Thou couldest have no power over me unless it were given thee of God," who could say to the crippled man, "What did hinder you?" proved there was no power in disease. "Come on, get up!" To mystics of that nature, healings were inevitable, as well as complete freedom for themselves and for all those within range of their consciousness. So for us to attain proficiency—first in understanding, knowing, the correct letter of truth, then in its application to every phase of our human existence until one by one these principles come alive in us—unfolds the mystical experience. After that, we need not live by taking thought.

You no longer have to take thought for your life, for your health, for your supply. You'll find that what Paul taught was literally true: "I live yet not I, Christ liveth my life." There is a spiritual presence in you which goes before you to prepare the way, and it provides for you everything necessary to the complete fulfillment of your life's demonstration. "Where the spirit of the Lord is, there is liberty." But it says, *where* the spirit of the Lord is. There must first be present in you the spirit of the Lord, not a statement. The statement, the quotation, will do nothing for you. There has to be the understanding of the statement and the demonstration of the statement.

I have told previous classes about this experience: I was sitting in a Christian Science church one evening listening to a very uninteresting reader, unable to concentrate on the lesson. My mind kept wandering up to the wall, and eventually it focused on a statement of Mrs. Eddy's that is printed on the front wall of every Christian Science church: "Divine Love always has met and always will meet every human need." I looked at it and looked at it, and finally a thought came to me: "Mrs. Eddy, how could you say that? Here I am looking around this church. I know everybody in it and all their troubles, and divine love doesn't seem to be doing a thing about most of them." I kept looking, and wondering, "Why did she say it? Why did she write it? Why did she want it on the walls of every church?" And all of a sudden it flashed into my mind that statement was true, absolutely true! "Divine Love always has met and always will meet every human need." But divine love isn't out there doing it to me. Divine love is something I have to express, and when I express divine love, it meets my every human need.

There is no divine love sitting on a cloud; there is no divine love floating around here in the air. The only divine love in this room is the divine love which we permit to flow out from us. And divine love doesn't mean human love, or emotion, or sensuality. Divine love means spiritual love, which means forgiveness, patience, cooperation, gentleness, charitableness. All of these things are embraced in divine love, and as we express them they meet our every human need. If we do not express them, they are unexpressed and are not meeting our human need. That experience is an illustration of what I'm saying to you in this entire lesson: that the truth up there did nothing for us. It was first the understanding it, then the putting it into practice. Then it operates, not only for me, it operates for all those who will grasp it, understand it—then practice it.

So it is with every truth, every principle, in our writings. The principle itself can do nothing for you, any more than the principle of electricity can do anything for anyone except the fellow who hooks it up. All of the principles of electricity, radio, television, the automobile, the airplane, have been in existence since before Abraham was, but they didn't help the world. Oh, no. Not until somebody came along and discovered those principles in consciousness and then put them into operation. Every truth, every law, every power, exists now in your individual consciousness. Why in your individual consciousness? Because the infinite, divine consciousness is your individual consciousness, not this human mind that you think with, but behind that, deeper than that. As you learn to turn within to that infinite source, you can also draw out music, art, literature, mechanics, whatever it is that your particular nature needs for fulfillment. We don't all draw out the same thing. God is infinite, therefore our natures are infinite. Some of us could not be fulfilled except through music, or art, or literature, or truth, and others could not be fulfilled except through benevolences, or inventions, or science, or architecture. Each one of us has something that fulfills our own nature, and by the ability to turn to that kingdom within our own consciousness, we draw forth from it that which is our fulfillment.

Now we know ninety-nine percent of the world is working for a living, not at a job which is their fulfillment, but doing something they just tolerate. The reason is, they started out young, got into the wrong line of work, got married, had to support a family, and had no time then to find their fulfillment. So they had to stick with that with which they were stuck. With this understanding, it is never too late because we can all turn within, we can all be patient until we reach that infinite source within ourselves and begin to draw forth our fulfillment. Then with patience, we will find that we're moved one step at a time to that which is to be our life.

Unfortunately, most of those who come into metaphysics expect this to unfold easily, but it can't happen that way. When the result does not come immediately, many are afraid of the time it takes to get it. When they may seem to be a failure to the world, when they may not seem to be bringing forth fruitage and expect just to be led from where they are to their heavenly estate without the experiences that often do come, when they have to give up the ways they tried yesterday for the ways of tomorrow, they often face bleak intervals of time, waiting for the result.

With wisdom, we learn not to be afraid of failure. With wisdom, we learn not to be afraid of lack or limitation. With wisdom, we learn to be patient with our transitional experiences until we do come into the fulfillment. Be assured of this: Our life's experience is the out-picturing of our own state of consciousness. Whatever limitations we're experiencing are the limitations of our own state of consciousness, and they're going to continue until our consciousness develops and deepens and becomes enriched. Then the outer experiences follow that pattern. We have to be patient during the transitional experience.

Now, I give you this: There are two parts to the message of the Infinite Way. There is the mystical aspect of the message and there is the metaphysical aspect of the message. Sometimes reading the mystical aspect may open you spiritually and lift you into a spiritual experience. But do not let this mislead you. Don't let it deprive you of the opportunity to study and practice the correct letter of truth so that you never fall into the trap of believing you have a God that is destroying evil, or that is healing disease, or that is bringing you wealth. Don't do it! You must abide in the consciousness of God as Spirit, governing eternally, immortally, and harmoniously, and let the evil or the negative appearances fall away from your experience without battle, without strife. Remember, even some of the Hebrew mystics knew this: "They have only the arm of flesh; we have the Lord God Almighty . . . And they rested in his word." And Jesus: "Resist not evil . . . Put up thy sword . . . Thou couldest have no power over me unless it came from the Father in heaven." As you abide in that, the mystical experience will deepen and enrich your consciousness.

Never forget the basic truth: God is not an overcomer. "I have overcome the world," yes; but I have overcome the world by learning and practicing this principle until that day comes when Christ takes over and I hear: "I will never leave thee nor forsake thee." After that I have nothing ever to fear except those worldly temptations that would cause me to give in to two powers, or to succumb to negative powers. Never can we fail in our demonstration. Peter failed; Thomas failed; Judas failed. All these disciples failed because they were not alert and awake to that which they had been taught, and they succumbed: Thomas to his doubts; Peter to self-preservation, the first law of nature; Judas probably to ambition. Ah! You see, even after you have the light, the world wants to tempt you. Oh, yes. Jesus was already engaged in his ministry when he faced the three greatest temptations of his life: the temptation to turn stones into bread, the temptation to seek fame, the temptation to demonstrate power over matter. Oh, yes, even after he was in the ministry these temptations came to him. So many in the spiritual ministry have found that they had a temptation of temporary lack and then resorted to human means to meet it; or they succumbed to the temptation of abundance and began to use their abundance for material satisfactions and pleasures and delights.

So temptations come, not only to those who have not been illumined, but to those who have been illumined;

and to those who have been illumined, it takes a great deal of alertness to hold to that light and never succumb to the material sense of good. Yes, too many metaphysicians believe that when they begin to experience a material sense of good, it indicates they are being more spiritual and enjoying more of God, not knowing that sometimes that very material good is to be their destruction. No, the spiritual path calls for alertness, but there can be no alertness if we do not know the principles which bring about the experiences and upon which the spiritual life is based. We have taken only one tonight, and the reason we've taken only one is that it is the most important one. This one, if you will remember it, will prevent you from praying to God for something. This one will prevent your expecting something from God. This one will prevent you from turning to God to overcome some evil. This is the major principle. This one, if you follow it, can save you many, many pitfalls.

It was a great joy this week to receive the newsletter on prayer sent out by a bishop of the Episcopal Church, in which he asked those who received it whether they expect things from God or whether they can trust the goodness of God to supply their needs. In it he quotes from the Infinite Way teachings, that we are not those who get or receive, but are those through whom God pours forth his bounty unto this world. He was teaching them that very point without saying it outright: Don't go to God for your blessings; let blessings pour out through you. You don't receive, you give. You are the instrument through which God's grace flows. If Jesus was the way-shower, then one of the ways he showed us was how to feed five thousand and have twelve baskets-full left over, even without storehouses and barns, merely by acknowledging that we

THE FOUNDATION OF MYSTICISM

already have God's grace. Then all we have to do is begin with the one or two loaves and the one or two fishes, and start pouring them out. And they'll multiply themselves.

It was also a source of gratification a few years ago to hear Bishop Sheen[2] conclude his radio broadcast by telling his listeners, "Never pray to God for anything material because God knows only spiritual good, and when you pray, pray for spiritual good." Do you see what I mean? If you do not know these principles, you cannot even pray aright. The greatest of them all is, *God is*. Therefore, that which you have been fearing is not a power, and as you maintain that truth in your consciousness, it loses its power and disappears.

Thank you, thank you until tomorrow night. Between now and then, please remember this: Don't use truth for any purpose whatsoever. Just abide in the realization that God is, and let that truth do its own work. God is!

---

[2]Fulton John Sheen, 1895-1979, was nationally known as a spokesperson for Roman Catholicism in the United States. His fame came principally from his radio program "The Catholic Hour" (1930-1952) and a television series "Life is Worth Living" (1952-1965).

~ 11 ~

THREE PRINCIPLES AND THEIR PRACTICE

Good Evening.

We are working now with specific healing principles of the Infinite Way that we are to apply in meeting problems of our everyday living. I recognize, and you must recognize, that there is going to be some difficulty with this because most of you have other metaphysical backgrounds. The major principles of the Infinite Way are not only *not* the principles of your previous studies, but some of them may appear to be very contradictory. I know that many students do have difficulties when they try to mix the principles of their former teachings with these principles of the Infinite Way. They make no headway or have difficulties in their demonstration of harmony.

Last night I explained one of these principles, and I hope I made very clear what is probably the most important principle in the message of the Infinite Way. God, being infinite, is never used for any purpose. God is never used for overcoming sin, disease, or death. In the Infinite Way, truth isn't used at all. The very opposite of that is the truth in the Infinite Way. We seek to become the instruments of truth; we open ourselves that we may be used by truth, by God, that God may manifest itself as our individual being, that God may live its life as us, that God may lead, guide, direct, govern, sustain, maintain, support, supply. And we are the instruments through which, as which, that takes place.

You see, the wisdom of God is infinite—omniscient—therefore it is ridiculous to believe that we can tell God, ask God, or inform God of our needs. It is an impossibility for us to know more than God. It is only possible for us to know as much as God if we first know that we know nothing, and then let the wisdom of God manifest as our wisdom. In other words, as I indicated last night, you develop a receptive attitude for the inflow of inspiration as you would if you were a composer, an artist, or a writer, always keeping your attention within as a listening attitude, almost as a vacuum, waiting for the new melody, the new idea, the new vision, the new invention, the new discovery to come to you.

This is perhaps best illustrated in the Zen teachings. We have it given to us very clearly in a book on Zen archery, in which the archer is taught how to hold the bow and arrow, then to wait until something releases the arrow so that it flies into the heart of the target. In other words, man doesn't aim it; man hasn't the power to hit the center of the target. But by correctly holding the bow and arrow and waiting for that influence to release the fingers, the arrow darts right into the heart of the target. So it is, when you are receptive to the idea of being an instrument and recognize the truth that there is a God of infinite wisdom, infinite life, infinite love, in silence and stillness it can manifest itself as us and perform its functions through us.

We can't use God or truth, but by attaining an inner stillness, God, or truth can use us. It can manifest itself through us as healing if we have chosen the healing profession, as inventions if we are inventors, as music if we are composers. God is infinity, and all that is, is an emanation of God. Whether it is to appear as engineering principles, scientific principles, literary works, art works—whatever it may be—it must be an emanation of God, and we the instruments through which and as which it is to function on earth. So you see, our approach to life is not learning how to use truth, but how to be so receptive and responsive to the divine impulse that truth can use us, that Life can flow as our life, that Wisdom flow as our wisdom—and we know right well it isn't ours, it is God's.

The power of God is infinite. Therefore, the afflictions, discords, diseases, and inharmonies, not only of our families and friends, but of the world with which we are so aware, exist in the human scene because we are ignorant of the basic truth that God alone is power. It isn't your ignorance or mine, personally. It is a universal ignorance which takes over the moment we're conceived, and it directs our life the minute we're born. It isn't your ignorance or mine, any more than the wisdom or power we attain is yours or mine. No, we come into this world ignorant of spiritual truth; we come into this world accepting the powers of good and evil. Long before we understand the meaning of them, we accept them. We become deathly afraid of evil, afraid of falling down, afraid of meeting strangers, afraid of automobiles, afraid of almost everything on the face of the globe, until finally we're sent to church to learn how to become afraid of God.

The first lesson to learn as students of the Infinite Way is that the nature of God is infinite, therefore there is no power, no law, to sustain anything of a discordant nature, of a material nature, of a limited nature. In learning this, we learn to "resist not evil"; we learn to "put up thy sword"; we learn to stand before every form of Pilate and say, "Oh, you look terrible, and from what I hear about you, you're very frightening, but thou couldest have no power over me unless it were given thee of the Father." It isn't a simple matter to come to that state of consciousness because we are born and brought up in material consciousness, and that means in the consciousness of two powers, good and evil. We are making the transition from that state of consciousness to one who is able to say, "What did hinder you? Pick up your bed and walk"; or "Lazarus is not dead, but sleepeth. Come forth, Lazarus"; or to the blind man, "Open your eyes and see," because there is no power to prevent it. There is only one power operating in consciousness, and that power is God.

Even if we intellectually accept this as the truth, because of our human birth we cannot demonstrate it until it comes alive in us, until we have an inner conviction which comes with practice. Then of course we are only able to demonstrate it in a measure. But that is the basic principle, and it is the one that gives all students the most difficulty, especially those in metaphysics who have been taught that truth may be used to overcome the error. It is difficult to realize you can't use truth. Truth is infinite; truth is God itself. No one can use God, no one can influence God, no one can sway God, no one can get God to do his bidding. We have a chapter in our new book, "Is God a Servant?"[1] Just think if you haven't

---

[1] *The Art of Spiritual Healing,* © by Joel S. Goldsmith (Atlanta, GA: Acropolis Books, Inc., cloth, 1997 - Harper Collins, paperback edition, 1992).

tried to use God, unconsciously of course, as a servant, telling God your need and expecting God to fulfill it; telling God what you want, and expecting God to produce it; asking God for this favor or that favor; or even commanding God as if God were a servant. The Master acknowledged himself to be only a servant of God—not a master, but a servant.

Now we come to another principle, and all our healing work is based on this. Again, to those of you with metaphysical backgrounds I say: If you wish to really understand and demonstrate this principle, you'll have to work with it and work hard, until you break through your former beliefs and come into the understanding of this principle. Listen well. There is no such thing as personal evil; there is no such thing as evil for which you are responsible; there is no such thing as your being responsible for any of the sins or diseases or lacks or limitations that come into your experience. It is not your wrong thinking that produces error; it is not your envy or your jealousy or your malice that produces it; it is not your greed, your lust or your mad ambition that produces it; it is not any fault that is to be found in you that produces it. You have no responsibility for the evil which expresses itself in your experience. Ah, this sounds wonderful right now. It only becomes difficult when I tell you that neither is your wife nor your husband responsible for any of the evil in their lives. You see, the truth about you is that you are the child of God. God has manifested its own life as your individual being. God has expressed itself individually on earth as you. The life which is God is your life, therefore it is eternal and immortal. Your mind is actually that mind which was also in Christ Jesus: infinitely wise, infinitely pure.

Your soul is spotless, and there isn't anything you could ever do that would change that because God is your soul. God is your very being. And we'll go one step further to acknowledge that your body is the temple of the living God.

This is the truth about you and your life, your body, your mind, your soul, your being. Then, why all these discords? In ancient days, they created an entity called the devil or satan; and in later days Paul, who probably didn't like the term devil or satan, called it carnal mind. Then, when metaphysical language developed, it was called mortal mind. It makes no difference which of these names you would like to use, they're all correct. There is a devil, satan, and there is a carnal mind, or mortal mind, which is the source of all evil. Therefore, if you see a man stealing, do not call him a thief. He is just the instrument through which the carnal mind is operating. Regardless of what sin, disease, lack, or ignorance you witness in any individual, do not condemn him; he is but the instrument through which this carnal mind is operating. It is the carnal mind which is the anti-Christ, which is the anti-everything of God and which, if it is believed to be a power, will destroy you.

When it was discovered that man personally wasn't a sinner, that there was a tempter called devil or satan, a mistake was originally made claiming that this devil or satan was the opposite of God, the opponent of God, and it was God's function to try to get rid of it. All religions, down through the ages, have been dedicated to that one purpose: overcoming the devil. And the devil hasn't any power, the devil isn't anything except what we agree to make it. Metaphysical teachings have made the same mistake. They will tell you in another way that there is no devil or satan, just mortal mind. Then they will invent ways to protect you from mortal mind, using all kinds of quotations and affirmations to overcome this mortal mind, and thereby taking a licking from it. It must be recognized that all evil is impersonal, comes from an impersonal source, and that source is the belief in good and evil. That is all there is to what is called mortal mind. There is no such thing as mortal mind as an entity; there is no such thing as carnal mind as an entity; there is no such thing as devil or satan as an entity.

There is a universal belief in two powers, and that belief itself causes every bit of discord and inharmony that ever existed on the face of the earth. To the degree that you recognize this, you come back to the example of the Hebrew, Hezekiah, who, when confronted with an enemy twice as strong as his own army, could say to his people, "Fear not, fear not, they have only the arm of flesh." Because they rested in his word and did not take up the sword and go out to fight the enemy, the enemy fought amongst themselves, destroyed themselves, and left all the loot on the battlefield for the Hebrews.

In the same way, the Master said, "Resist not evil . . . What did hinder you?. . . Pilate, thou couldest have no power over me unless it were given thee from heaven . . . Peter, put up thy sword. Those who live by the sword will die by the sword." In the degree that you battle this so-called mortal mind or any of its individual forms and expressions, in that degree will you lose in the end because you have created an enemy greater than yourself. It is an enemy that God can't help you with because God has no knowledge of it. God is too pure to behold iniquity. Jesus never prayed to God, "Please destroy my enemies. Please go before me and slay these horrible people." Those were ancient Hebrew prayers, not Christian prayers, but we indulge them and we expect, even in metaphysics, that God will overcome mortal mind, or sin, or disease. Don't ever believe it.

The overcoming has to take place within you. It is your recognition of the truth: "I will never leave you nor forsake you. . .If you go through the waters, you will not drown. If you go through fire, the flames will not kindle upon you." Why? They haven't any power. As you realize this, and as you realize the mission and message of Christ Jesus, you'll understand why he could be so big-hearted as to forgive the woman taken in adultery, the thief on the cross, or the Judas who betrayed him. Because he knew; he knew by divine revelation that these are not power. "Crucify me if you want. Destroy this body. In three days I'll raise it up again."

Certainly, depressions may come to deprive us of our savings, our wealth, or our investments, but they are only the body of supply. They are not supply itself. God is our supply, therefore, if we lose the body of supply, we start right over tomorrow to build it again. There's no such thing as a limit; there's no such thing as having only one chance or two or three—none of these things! The question is, what spiritual principles do we accept and practice until they become living forces within our own being? Don't think that I don't realize how difficult it is to see the sins and diseases and horrors of the world and believe there is no power in them. It is only after we feel a certain rightness about these principles within and then are willing to put them into practice, until such time as we witness the first healings with them, that the belief in two powers will gradually cease demonstrating in our lives.

The first time you heal anybody, the first time you've been instrumental in bringing about a healing and are able to rest in that word and see the enemy or the appearance destroy itself, you say, "Ah, I have witnessed the truth of this principle. I have seen it demonstrated." Then you have the courage to go on and on and on until you are able to do some of the greater works.

Humanly, we have been taught to judge, criticize, and condemn–anybody, any time, anywhere, for anything–if it doesn't fit with our sense of what's right or wrong. But in this work, we have to change our entire attitude so that we are never guilty of judging, criticizing, or condemning a person, but are always recognizing that the source of whatever is wrong is the carnal mind, and it hasn't power. If someone of questionable character comes to us seeking help through spiritual means, they will receive it. But even if they don't seek help, we still have to take the approach that all whom we meet in life, even political candidates, are children of God. That doesn't take from us the ability to determine which man or woman is the better candidate for that particular office, but it does prevent us from sitting in judgement over them and holding them responsible for the evils of which some of them are guilty. It does help us when we remove from them the burden of guilt, and sometimes it even frees them.

There are three principles in the Infinite Way healing work. The first principle is one which we embody at all times: the realization of one power, of not fighting or trying to overcome negative powers or beliefs or the claims that come before us. The second principle is impersonalization. The moment John Brown asks for help, be sure you put John Brown out of your mind.

Don't dwell for one single second on John Brown, and above all, even if you see it, don't believe anything evil about John Brown. Dismiss it instantly. Get it out of your thought as quickly as possible. Get John Brown out of your thought, because your first function in healing work is impersonalization. Remember that word, *impersonalization.* This claim is not a person, not a condition, not a thing. It belongs to nobody. It is an impersonal activity or substance or imposition. We could call it the carnal mind or mortal mind. Use devil or satan—whatever term you like—but impersonalize it. Take it out of the person. Realize that it isn't a person, it hasn't a person in whom to work. It is an impersonal claim of the universal mortal mind, the universal carnal mind.

When you are sure that you have impersonalized it so that you have absolutely no thought of the individual in your mind, then take the third step, which is nothingizing. That means you have to go back to *Genesis*: "God made all that was made, and all that God made was good. What God did not make was not made." Therefore, anything God did not make does not exist. And all that God made was good. If God made all that was made and all that God made was good, then God didn't make a carnal mind, or mortal mind, or devil, or satan. They have no existence except as mental concepts in the human mind.

If you want to know how powerless a human concept is, close your eyes and build the biggest bomb you could possibly build. Build an atomic bomb and combine it with hydrogen and all the forms of nuclear fission you've ever heard of, and multiply that by a thousand. Now throw it up here at me to see what it can do. Do you understand that? That's a mental concept. It has no substance; it has no law; it has no entity; it has no being. It only has form as thought. That's why you can see it in your mind, but you can only see it in your mind as a mental image.

Once you begin to understand that all there is to the devil is an entity made in the mind of man (not in the mind of God), and that it has no law of God, no substance of God, no activity of God, no source of God, no avenue, no channel through which to work, you nullify it. You've recognized it for what it is: temporal power, the arm of flesh, nothingness. That's where your healing work begins. Actually, regardless of the name or nature of the problem which confronts you, you can be assured of this: it is nothing but a temptation of the devil, or carnal mind, coming to you for acceptance or rejection, and this devil is neither more nor less than a belief of good and evil in the human mind. Once you have no belief of good and evil, the human mind, the mortal mind, dissolves. Then you operate in and through and with the infinite mind of God. Only as you believe in good and evil do you experience limitation, finiteness, negativity.

Often, when we are working with our friends, our parents, or our relatives, we revert to that human sense of criticism and judgement, or the metaphysical sense of saying to them, "Well, it's your wrong thinking. There's something in your mind that has to be corrected." Of course there is, but it is the belief in two powers. The only belief that has to be corrected in all of us is that God isn't omnipotence, God isn't omniscience, God isn't omnipresence. The whole theory of resentment causing rheumatism, jealousy causing cancer, or sensuality causing tuberculosis is a lot of nonsense. Not only have metaphysical practitioners failed to prove it, but psycho-somatic medicine has failed to prove it. They claim, "When you get rid of your resentment, you'll be healed," but that's because they don't know how to get rid of resentment. They don't know how to get rid of the negative qualities of human thought that all of us are heir to.

You do know how: by understanding they are not personal, they are impersonal, and they are not power—they have no law to sustain them. Because it has never been revealed in our human life that every discord coming to us is mesmeric influence, we do not know how to protect ourselves from the human belief in two powers. In other words, when you are in the midst of an epidemic, you are not necessarily suffering from the disease but from mesmerism, and the mesmerism is enhanced by publicity about the disease. Probably just as many people die from the mesmeric influence of the publicity as from the mesmeric influence of the disease. In the same way, there have been fires in large buildings in which the flames probably took a few lives, but more people were killed by the mesmeric sense of panic, fear, and lust for life.

This universal belief of good and evil operates hypnotically in the life of any and every individual in this world. When you leave your home in the morning, you have no assurance you're going to get back at night. Between coconuts falling from coconut trees and automobiles hitting each other and lightning striking, and this and that and the other thing, you may become a statistic. On any morning of the week, they can tell you downtown how many deaths there will be by six o'clock. They can't tell you who will die, but it might just as well be you, or me, or anyone else. We are statistics, and every night at six o'clock there must be so many deaths for this reason and that reason, and so it goes day after day.

The question then arises, "Is there a way to avoid all this?" Yes, indeed there is. If those who are taught the principles could break through their mental inertia in the morning to consciously realize, "There is but one power operating in this universe—not a power of accidents, or death, or disease, or sin—only one power. This same power causes the sun to rise and set; this same power causes the tides to come in and go out; this same power creates fish in the sea and birds in the air. That's the power that is operating in this universe, that's the power operating in my consciousness, and that is the law unto my experience." Then there is no power in this mesmeric suggestion of statistics; there is no power in the belief of infection and contagion; there is no power in mortal mind, carnal mind, or any of its forms or beliefs, individually or collectively.

And watch, watch to what degree the ordinary everyday mishaps do not come into your experience. "A thousand shall fall at thy left hand, ten thousand at thy right hand; and it shall not come nigh thy dwelling place." Where is thy dwelling place? In the individual who "dwells in the secret place of the most high." Not who dwells in a house, not who rides in an automobile, not who flies in an airplane, but who dwells in the secret place of the most high. And how can you do that? It has to be done consciously. Everything in your life is either an activity of your consciousness expressing itself, or it is your unwillingness to let your consciousness express itself. Then you become a blotter for the beliefs of good and evil that permeate the world. You either become a blotter taking it all in, responding to it, showing it forth, or else you become master of your fate and captain of your soul. But only by an act of consciousness, not by saying, "Oh, well, God will take care of it." There is no such God. There must be an activity of truth in your consciousness, and that activity of truth has to be built. No matter what form of treatment you give, it has to be built around the principle that there is only one power, that nothing but God is power, and that any sense of evil is impersonal and is nothing but the activity of the fleshly mind, the arm of flesh—nothingness.

Every treatment has to be built around these principles. It makes no difference whether you're going up in an airplane or down in a submarine; it makes no difference if you're going to war and you're going to be at the front, or whether there will be bombers overhead. It makes no difference what the nature of the human claim is, it has to be consciously dealt with. Every treatment or realization must embody these principles: realization of one power; not a protection from evil power, but the realized truth that God itself is infinite and only God is power; and that every appearance is mesmeric influence, the temptation of the devil coming to our consciousness to be accepted or rejected—and it has to be consciously rejected. That's why I said last night that the one thing the world is suffering from is mental inertia. It won't wake up and think; it doesn't want to think conscious thoughts. It wants to look at pictures. It doesn't want to give voice to concrete truth; it doesn't want to sit back and live with truth. It wants to depend on an unknown god, and not only that, but a god that's failed mankind for thousands of years. It's so easy to sit back and say, "God will do it." God won't do anything God is not already doing. Don't ever believe for a moment that God is going to do anything a minute from now that God isn't doing now. Don't think for a minute that you're ever going to know enough truth to influence God to do something for you or for anyone else. Don't ever think you're going to be so spiritual that God is going to be your servant, is going to fulfill your wishes, your hopes or your desires. There is no such God. God is. And God is "ising" this very second. God is being this very second, and God is being all that God can be. There is no way for God to change. God is the same yesterday, today, and forevermore. God is from everlasting to everlasting. Don't try to get God to be anything or do anything. God is.

The responsibility is on your shoulders: "Awake thou that sleepest! and Christ will give thee light." But wake up to the fact that your experience is going to be your own state of consciousness, objectified. If you want to lie around all day reading books, that's probably what you'll exemplify and that's what your life will bear witness to. If you insist on going around all day without living consciously in the realization of God-omnipresent, God-omnipotent, God-omniscient, God here and now, the all and only power, and then impersonalizing all phases of evil, realizing that they exist only as the arm of flesh or nothingness, you won't bring harmony into your experience. Paul called it "praying without ceasing," and to the degree you do this, you will succeed.

The strange part of it is that for about a year it's hard work, because we forget more than we remember. It's usually ten or eleven o'clock in the morning before we remember how much we've forgotten that we should have been consciously knowing since seven o'clock. Then we have to start in at noon to make up for lost time, and by the time we get into bed at night we've really got ourselves in a jam because then we have to undo all the forgetting we did throughout the day. It's a discipline for a year. As an experiment—make an agreement with yourself that you will try not to eat a bite of food or drink a drop of water without consciously recognizing that God is the source. Then count how many times you forget that when the end of the day comes around. You will see how difficult this is. But watch the magical effects in your life when you persist. See if you do not reach a place where you don't forget, where you consciously recognize with every bite of food and with every drink of water you take that but for God it would not be here; but for God's grace you wouldn't have it; but for God's grace it wouldn't be on earth; but for God's grace you wouldn't be digesting it.

Come to the realization that the trifling acts of your day, waking up in the morning, sleeping at night, cannot be performed without an activity of God, an activity of this invisible Spirit, and find out what happens when you begin to "acknowledge him in all thy ways." See what happens as you consciously remember when you get into your car that God drives, not only your car, but since there is only one being, one selfhood, God drives all cars. It is your conscious recognition of this that sets you free from the statistical beliefs.

For a year this is difficult work. Sometimes it takes a little longer than a year, but eventually something beautiful begins to happen. You don't have to consciously think these things, they automatically arise within you. Then it isn't long before you really understand what Paul meant,

"I live; yet not I, Christ liveth my life." After that, there is no, or very little, conscious effort. Now it all flows from within. Now it all comes to you; you don't have to go after it. The idea is, of course, that early in our experience we are searching for God. No one should have ever coined that term because it's incorrect. It's God that has been searching for us, and we have to learn to let God catch up. And that's what eventually happens to us: We find that we've been using a lot of energy we don't have to use. If only we realize that God is chasing us, then we can be quiet and let him catch up.

Now let's have a rest. Then we'll continue with this lesson.

~ 12 ~

REALIZING THE PRINCIPLES

Please remember, it is only in the first months or year that living the Infinite Way may seem a bit burdensome and difficult. Be willing, for the sake of its fruitage, to undertake some of the labor that goes with this work in the beginning. In living the Infinite Way you are doing two things all day long: You are doing protective work and you are doing treatment, or healing, work. You are engaged in those two activities throughout the day whether or not anybody asks you for help, and you are always using these three principles—the realization of one power, impersonalization, and nothingizing—as the major part of your work.

From the moment you awaken in the morning, you are to do protective work. Now, don't think of protective work as protecting yourself from evil or protecting anybody else from evil. Remember, protective work is the realization that there is no power from which to protect one's self. Protective work is living in the realization that since there is only one power, there are no other powers to do anything or be anything. Any other suggestion is mesmeric influence, mortal mind, the arm of flesh, nothingness.

Without protective work, even though you're not consciously thinking of accidents or discords or diseases or sins or temptations, you are permitting yourself to accept unconsciously, or subconsciously, the world's mesmerism, the world's hypnotic suggestions. In other words, this evil touches your life in very much the same way as subliminal perception operates. Something enters your consciousness which you do not see, hear, taste, touch, or smell; it enters in the form of suggestion, or mental imposition.

You don't have to see a headline to know there is trouble in the world. You inwardly feel it. But even if you can't sense the trouble, you can tell it if you've awakened with a headache, or you've awakened with a dullness, or you've awakened with a sense of fear. None of this originates in you; none of this is part of you. You may not even have read that there's a flu epidemic going around, but the first thing you know you have the flu. You weren't exposed to it, you didn't consciously entertain it, but the suggestion entered your thought, your consciousness. When there is no protection in your consciousness, that is, no understanding that this is hypnotic or mesmeric influence (a mental malpractice is what it really is), unless you realize that this hypnotic influence isn't power, that it is not an emanation of God, it can take root in you and appear in any form, or every form. And it does appear. That is why you have these human experiences.

In the beginning stages of consciously living the principles, you must be alert throughout the day to suggestions of accidents, sickness, sin, wars, depression, lack, or unemployment. As soon as these touch your consciousness, it is necessary to know that these are the tempters: "This is a temptation, this is a universal mesmeric power and presence apart from God. I reject this in the realization that it is nothing but the fleshly mind, the arm of flesh, nothingness. This is not a power that is God-ordained, it has no law of God behind it." And then you're through with it. It takes a minute, but in that minute you have established within your consciousness the power of truth, and truth being infinite, nothing else can enter "that defileth or maketh a lie."

In the same way, you are always engaged in treatment or healing work. On every side you witness sin, disease, death, lack, limitation, unemployment, disfigurement, alcoholism, drug addiction, poverty. All of these confront you on the streets, in the press, on the radio, and you can't afford to be like blotting paper; you can't afford to simply let those things go into your consciousness and take root. You are consciously alert to realize, "Yes, these are pictures of sense; yes, these are suggestions. But in our understanding of one God, one power, one law, these are nothing." Then you'll find you are abiding in "the secret place of the most high, and none of these things will come nigh thy dwelling place" (and if not literally "none of these things," few) and when they do come, you have the principles with which to free yourself.

As far as I know, it is absolutely true that no one on earth completely avoids discords and inharmonies, not even if they lock themselves away in monasteries or convents, because that same human mind follows us wherever we go; it accepts subliminal suggestions even when we're not aware of them. So there's no place you can go to hide from the world's troubles because your mind is a receiving station, and you don't have to see, hear, taste, touch, or smell mesmeric suggestion to become aware of it. You can get it right from the atmosphere.

Train yourself to realize that all these inharmonies are appearances. That's what Jesus called them: "Judge not after appearances; judge righteous judgement." Everything that came to his awareness was an appearance and he didn't judge by that. He let it pass by in the realization that it was only an appearance. "Thou couldest have no power over me . . . What did hinder you?" In other words, it isn't a power. Then it can go by. As you engage in this practice, you will find two things: First of all, you will save yourself from so many of this world's woes, from so many of this world's negative experiences. But what is even more important is that once you prove this in your own experience, you will see how quickly your awareness of these principles begins to set others free. They don't have to know you are realizing the truth for them or about them, and yet you'll be surprised at how many will receive healing without knowing from which direction it comes. And of course, since we're not out for personal glory but to realize principles in operation, we are not concerned about getting credit.

To us, the joy and satisfaction is that we have discovered principles of life we can live by and which will benefit those who are receptive and responsive to them. Getting credit is nonsense because it makes no difference how many medals are pinned on you while you are here, you can't take them with you. It makes no difference how many honors or titles you receive in this life, you don't take them with you. So, really, we don't require any personal recognition. Do you know what we take with us as we leave this plane? We take our spiritual enlightenment, our knowledge of good. This is stored up where neither moth nor rust can corrupt, and we take it with us. That becomes the foundation of our next experience.

Try to remember we are storing up spiritual treasure. The good we bring into our experience is what we take with us. Temporalities, such as money and stocks and bonds, we check at the probate court as we go out. As for the medals, they go to the Smithsonian—and our family takes our certificates of titles and honors off the wall, sends them to the basement for a few years and then burns them. They are of no avail to us, not one bit. Even the good that is sometimes spoken of us is relatively unimportant. Probably just as many are saying the opposite. But every principle of life that you embody in your consciousness becomes your state of consciousness throughout all time, just as every skill you attain here is yours throughout your life on earth. You don't lose your skills, you don't lose your abilities, you don't lose your wisdom. You carry these with you. We are not trying to build rewards for the next life. We are establishing an understanding that the spiritual principles which we learn—the principles of spirit—are our protection, our health, our safety, our security, and our peace. And these principles will bring freedom to every individual on the face of the globe as the world awakens to them.

You may think you live your life privately, that nobody else is affected by it. You may think you are unimportant, or that you have no influence. I want to tell you, that is the most disastrous state of thought in which you could possibly indulge yourself. There wasn't anybody more unimportant than Thomas Edison when he was selling newspapers on a train. There wasn't anyone with less influence, money, or standing in the world than Mrs. Eddy. There wasn't anybody further removed from the possibility of doing anything for anybody in the world than I was when I was buying and selling merchandise. And yet (the experience of thousands and tens of thousands bear this out), if I live my life unto myself and if I concern myself only with attaining some of this wisdom for myself, I cannot keep it bottled up. It has to spread. Somebody witnesses the fruitage of it, wants some of it, and that's how it begins. There isn't one of us who knows how unimportant Jesus Christ was as a Hebrew rabbi, but certainly every one of us knows how true his words became: "My words shall not pass away," for they still live in our consciousness awaiting our demonstration this very day.

There is no one who is unimportant. Nor is there anyone living solely and exclusively unto themselves, even if they seem to be. As Emerson[1] told us: "What you are shrieks so loudly I cannot hear what you say." In other words, what is taking place in your consciousness is an influence, and if you are studying these principles for no other reason than to learn them and to find out what the secret of life is, eventually these principles will do something to your life, and then through you to someone else's life—and you have no way of knowing how widespread that becomes in time.

There are unimportant people in this world, but they are people who believe they are unimportant and that's what keeps them so. We are important to each other, we are important to the entire world; we cannot live unto ourselves without benefitting others. If our attention is on searching for the secrets of life, they will not be hidden. Do you know that Albert Einstein expected to go to his grave keeping secret all that he knew about the atom? He pledged to himself that he would never reveal his knowledge to anyone, not because he didn't understand the

---

[1]Ralph Waldo Emerson, 1803-1882. American lecturer, poet, and essayist, the leading exponent of New England Transcendentalism.

great good that would come to the world through right use of the atom, but because he knew that in the wrong hands it would become destructive and produce evil results. He didn't feel the good it could do was worth the evil if this information got into circulation. He only gave up his knowledge on the promise that it would never be used for destructive purposes. Well, of course, that promise wasn't kept. But the point is this: Eventually the day will come when the knowledge he gave to the world will be of tremendous benefit. When we're long past the thought of its destructive power, we'll find the greatness of its constructive power, and then the whole world will be rebuilt. So, even if you want to, you can't keep these secrets, these principles, these laws, bottled up within you.

Please understand that these spiritual laws and principles do not manifest themselves only as spiritual healing or spiritual living. Ah, no. It isn't meant that everyone on earth should be a mystic or spiritual healer. These spiritual principles manifest themselves as new forms of music, new forms of art, new forms of literature, new scientific discoveries. Never forget that. It must have been five years ago that I said to classes that probably within twenty-five years there would not be a need for spiritual healers because there would not be any more diseases. Medical science has wiped out much of the disease on earth, and I have a very firm conviction that within twenty-five years it will have healed the rest, more especially the major ones. That would put us out of business! Of course, some doctors are already afraid we're going to put them out of business. We never will. And if we expect to be healers all of the time, take my word for it, they will put us out of business. But that is not our function. Healing is only one of the temporary landmarks along the way; it is only one of the temporary signs following the spiritual principles. I know that it will not be too long before medical science wipes out the major diseases. Then our function will be greater than ever, because without having our own or anybody else's health to concern ourselves with, we can give our entire attention to living with these spiritual principles, letting them come forth as new forms of peace on earth, new inventions, new expressions of life.

You probably know that for several years I have been trying to ensure that the University of Hawaii becomes an international institution. To that end, I have worked with their publication. Spirit operates on that plane of consciousness to unite East and West, to unite through culture, through language, through literature and art of the world. Don't think for a moment that this grand work we are doing is limited only to healing the body or mind. That is its minor function. Our major activity is to live by spiritual principles and through the development of our spiritual awareness, or soul faculties, to bring forth greater beauty, greater harmony than this world has ever known, and to bring it through from every direction. I should hate to believe that we are dedicating our lives merely to making a few of us a little more comfortable in our bodies. No, every healing is to be a witness to the principles of life and, when understood and practiced, will bring forth harmony—harmony of body, yes; harmony of mind, yes; harmony of purse, yes—ah, but now go on from there: new forms, infinite forms, of harmony and beauty and goodwill and peace.

Travel is a wonderful activity for many different reasons, but in my lifetime of travel its main function has been meeting people. My interest is people. I've seen all

the scenery, sometimes once, sometimes twice, and
that's enough for me. I've visited art galleries too; but I
like people and I don't go back around the world over
and over and over again to see more scenery, or even to
see more art. I travel to meet people, because in our
relationship with each other lies the secret of life. Life is
for living, and life cannot be lived except as it is lived
with each other. No one can live a life unto himself and
be fulfilled. No one. And no nation, no race, can live
unto itself and become anything but ingrown. Now we
can travel to places faster and cheaper than at any time
in the history of the world. We are all travel-conscious,
and although many do not realize that the purpose of
travel is more than seeing scenery, nevertheless you'll
find that the more traveling takes place, the more
meeting of minds there are, the greater will be our
understanding of each other.

Ah, but that's on the human level. Think, now, how
each one of us is aware that we are the temple of the
living God and are no longer ascribing evil to each
other, no longer believing that evil is a component part
of this race or that race, or this nation or that nation.
Think. As we embody these spiritual principles we
discover that this spiritual illumination is a bond, an
invisible bond, between all of us. Then you'll begin to
understand the greater functions of a message like the
Infinite Way, and you'll understand why you cannot
fulfill that function until, first of all, you have a God. In
having a God, you lose all fear: fear of person, fear of
thing, fear of condition, because you cannot have a God
and have fear, too. Only an atheist fears, and anyone
who fears is an atheist, so, regardless of how many
churches he belongs to, he hasn't yet come nigh to any

faith or belief or understanding of God. "Where the spirit of the Lord is, there is liberty," and wherever there's an understanding of the nature of God, one cannot fear. One cannot fear life and one cannot fear death. "If I walk through the valley of the shadow of death, I will fear no evil for thou art with me." The very moment we have a God, fear goes out the window because in having God, we have the only presence, the only power, the allness; and that we share with each other.

So we practice this one power, and we practice our two other healing principles: impersonalizing and nothingizing. As we do this, we are lifted into a higher spiritual atmosphere in which we have contact with each other on a spiritual plane, in which we have contact with the wisdom of the world. Do you know that every person on earth would have supreme wisdom if there weren't this mesmeric activity keeping it from them? In other words, this belief in two powers? Without that, there is only one infinite consciousness, manifesting itself as individual consciousness. Remember this: God-consciousness is your individual consciousness, and all that God is I am; all that God has is mine: "Son, thou art ever with me, and all that I have is thine." That doesn't refer to money; it refers to life, wisdom, love, peace, joy, dominion. "All that I have is thine." What prevents us, then, from being infinitely wise and infinitely loving? Nothing more nor less than this human mesmeric influence that was built around us when we were conceived. It begins to dissolve the moment we recognize this and realize, "Ah, but this isn't a power. It has acted as a power in my experience because I accepted the world belief of two powers, and now I know there is but one power."

Then you find that as this world belief becomes nothing, your consciousness becomes the inlet and the outlet for all the wisdom of God, all the art, all the literature, all the music, all the science—anything and everything which is your birthright. Actually, because of our differing natures, it isn't very likely that we will develop infinitely in more than one direction, but there have been those who have developed in four, five, and six directions. There have been many such people in the history of the world. We call them cosmic minds because there was no hypnotism, there was no mesmeric influence, keeping out God-wisdom, God-knowledge, God-power. They were a transparency through which art, science, literature, and many other talents, could manifest.

Now watch the transformation that takes place in your own experience, watch the limitations that are removed, the moment you realize there is nothing keeping you from being a transparency for the infinite nature of God: the infinite wisdom, the infinite life, the infinite truth, and infinite love of God. Nothing is operating but this universal belief—and it isn't a power. It has operated only because—unknowingly and unconsciously—you have accepted the world's estimate of two powers, and because of that belief, it has functioned in your consciousness. As you nullify it, it begins to lose its power in your life and you become a greater transparency for divine wisdom, divine love, divine life, divine power.

I told you last night that when this work and message were given to me, I was told, "My consciousness will be your consciousness. I will do these things as you, through your consciousness, which will really be My consciousness." That infinite divine consciousness has operated in me and through me and has gone before me to do this work of the Infinite Way. This same voice said: "My consciousness will be the Infinite Way consciousness throughout the world. My consciousness will function as the consciousness of the Infinite Way, of its students, of its work." That was given to me on April eighth, and I know it is functioning now because I see from students' letters how many are receiving light and illumination and spiritual experiences that they never had before that date. So I know this consciousness is operating as their experience, and it will go on to greater unfoldment.

Actually the truth is: This consciousness is the consciousness of every man and woman in the world, but it cannot function through selfishness, it cannot function through the minds of those who are on the make, who are seeking only to get and achieve, for me and mine. It can't function that way because the nature of that mind is an expressing mind, a giving, a bestowing, mind. It is a benediction; the mind of God is a benediction to this world. It is a full-flowing mind of blessings, and we have hindered its operation. Not consciously. Oh no, no. Let's not go back to blaming anybody. In our ignorance we have accepted self-preservation as the first law of nature; we have accepted two powers; we have accepted the human mind, and then started to count how little or how much education we had and judged by that. We limited ourselves instead of realizing that God-consciousness has no limitations; it embodies infinite wisdom, and it imparts it to all who are a transparency for it. To be a transparency for infinite intelligence and divine love means to recognize that this thing called devil, mortal mind, carnal mind, this mesmeric influence of two powers, is not power, is not functioning in your experience, has no law of God to maintain it or sustain it. Then gradually you find how freeing it is and how free you become inside.

You must remember what I have said to many students who told me or wrote to me that they're discouraged because they don't feel spiritual. My answer has always been: "And you never will." If you meet people who say they feel spiritual, don't believe them; they're lying to you. There is no such thing as feeling spiritual, any more than there is such a thing as feeling moral. Have you ever felt moral? You can be moral, but you can't feel that you're moral. You can be honest, but you can't feel that you're honest. Why, you'd go around praising yourself all day long if you could feel that you were honest, or feel that you were moral. You don't. It is what you are, and that is your natural being. The very minute this mesmeric sense is broken to the extent that you can grasp even a little bit of the truth that there is only one power, you are spiritual. The very minute you are not depending on bread alone for your life, you are spiritual. The very minute you know that money isn't supply, that money is only one of the forms that supply takes for our temporary use—the minute you know that—you're spiritual. The minute you know that God is infinite, the only power, you're spiritual. But you can't feel it. You can be it. You can experience it, but not feel it. I don't think musicians feel musical. There is no such thing. So don't try to make an emotional experience of this and try to feel spiritual. Don't try to feel mystical. Don't try to feel anything. Be it. Don't feel it.

The realization of these principles begins instantly to operate as a freeing influence in your consciousness. It doesn't heal you of anything, it doesn't enrich you, it doesn't improve your morals. It breaks the mesmeric sense and leaves you as a spiritual being, a harmonious being, which you are naturally. I don't know how to describe that, except that there are times when we have a limiting sense of ourselves and then there are other times when, for one reason or another, that limiting sense disappears and we are our natural selves. Or, there may be times when we have a fearful sense and for hours we may walk around in fear or dread, and then all of a sudden it dissipates, it's gone, and we are our natural selves.

Well, that's what I mean by this: Every sense of limitation, every sense of discord, every negative trait of character is nothing more than an erroneous sense that's gripping us. The very moment we realize one power and the non-power of this mesmeric sense, a sense of freedom takes its place, and you're the same person you were, only now you're free. "Whereas before I was blind, now I see." Whereas before I was in a sense of limitation, now I feel free. Whereas before I may have even felt inadequate, now I feel adequate to whatever situation is brought into my experience. The whole thing really is de-hypnotization.

Many, many years ago, when I was spending all of my time in the healing practice, as patients came to me, I recognized, just watching them, how they were functioning from a sense of limitation, from a sense of fear, and from many other things that aren't normal or natural to man. And I heard friends in the practice say, "Oh, if so-and-so would only do this, or if so-and-so would only be this way, or if so-and-so would only overcome this," and through this I saw that these inequities, these injustices, these bindings to limitations, were nothing more than mesmeric sense.

Then the question would come to me: "How do you break this hypnotism? How do you break this hypnotism that's binding this person to greed, and this person to miserliness, and this person to lust, and this person to fear? How do you break this mesmeric sense?" And don't think it wasn't years of meditation, and years of almost breaking my heart trying to get at the secret, before it was revealed to me that the way to break the hypnotism was to know that hypnotism isn't a power. That is the only way. And that has been the practice and function of my work from that day to this: not trying to break hypnotism, not trying to free anyone from being hypnotized, but knowing that hypnotism itself is an activity of the carnal mind. Therefore it has no power, it has no law.

That is how we worked when subliminal advertising was offered to the world and was succeeding. From the day we went to work, it hasn't succeeded. They had to scrap all the machinery they had built, they had to stop all the experiments, because from that day there wasn't one percent of success in any of their experiments. Up to that time they had been having an average success of fifty-seven percent, but it dropped from fifty-seven percent to zero, and it's been zero ever since. Why? Because the activity of subliminal perception is a hypnotic influence that comes out of the mind of man, or carnal mind, and therefore it isn't a power. It has no law to sustain it and so it becomes inoperative.

One with God is a majority. Watch it with the weather, watch it with tidal waves, watch it with storms, and see how quickly you dissipate them. The very moment you know these are not conditions of matter,

THE FOUNDATION OF MYSTICISM

they are activities of the mesmeric mind, watch and see how they stop instantaneously. They can't last long in the realization that God is the only power.

In his talk the other night, Dr. Suzuki[2] asked, "If you see a flag waving, is the flag waving or is it the wind?" And he said, "Neither. It's the mind." His audience laughed and ridiculed him, but they didn't realize how true that is! Nothing happens outside the activity of the mind. Not a thing. Therefore, if it's the mind of God you can't change it, you can't alter it, you can't improve it. And don't try! Don't try to fool with two times two is four; don't try to fool with the movement of the stars or the sun or the moon or the tides. Don't do it. These are activities of the divine mind, the divine consciousness, the infinite, immortal, eternal That, which existed before there was a human being to know it. But you can nullify anything that exists as an activity of the carnal mind to the degree of your awareness of these principles. You may start with only small things, minor things, but you'll work up to the greater ones because it's all proportionate to the degree of your realization, just as Jesus could probably heal better than the disciples, and the disciples better than the apostles. So it is all a matter of degree, the degree of our awareness. It has nothing to do with God so far as God is concerned. God is infinite and has nothing to do with error so far as error is concerned. It is nothingness; it is the "arm of flesh."

What does matter is the degree of your awareness of these principles. Any moment you know that anything

---

[2]D.T. Suzuki, 1870-1966: Daisetsu Teitaro Suzuki, Japanese Buddhist scholar, considered the chief interpreter of Zen Buddhism to the West.

that is the emanation of the carnal mind, of the devil, of satan, of mortal mind, is without law, without God-being, God-presence, or God-power, you have started to annul it. And in your present state of consciousness, if it doesn't yield the first time you know it, keep at it a hundred times. Sometimes it takes a hundred times of knowing to break it. If you had found the Master at his spiritual height, he would have broken it the first time. But you and I aren't at that level. Let's go back at it the second time, the third time, the fourth time. Those of you who have ever asked me for help know that I have never been impatient if the problem didn't yield at once. I'm perfectly willing to go back the next time and the next time, until it does yield, because I know it's only the degree of our awareness, the depth of our awareness, that really meets the situation. And if we haven't got it today, let's go back at it tomorrow, and keep at it until we accomplish it.

Above all things, remember this: Every word I have said to you tonight is absolute truth. And also remember that this truth will not do a thing for you except to the degree that you embody it in your consciousness. Consciously utilize these principles in what you would call prayer, treatment, contemplative meditation, making these principles active in your consciousness. The time will come when you find that there will be very little human effort involved, very little mental effort, but that will only come as these principles are embodied within you and become real to you.

Thank you. Thank you.

~ 13 ~

QUESTIONS AND ANSWERS
REVELATION OF SCRIPTURE:
THE TRUTH ABOUT PRAYER

Happy to have a few questions on the table. We'll answer these first.

Question: *You don't mention the Lord's Prayer. How does it fit in?*

Answer: Please let me explain to those who do not know this: There is no part of the Infinite Way message which is mine, that I have ever thought up, or conceived in any way. Every principle that is in our writings and in our work has been given to me from an infinite source, and it does not represent my opinion, my belief, or my concept, separate and apart from the fact that it is mine because it was given to me. In the same way, every passage of scripture that has been spiritually interpreted in our writings has been given to me. Those for which I have not received spiritual interpretation, I have never included in my writings and never will until the interpretation is given to me.

The Lord's Prayer is a passage about which I have never had any spiritual unfoldment or revelation. However, there is one part of it that is very much a part of our work because it is a confirmation of other scriptural passages which have been given to me, and which are included in the writings, and that is: "Forgive us our debts as we forgive our debtors." That I understand full well. Only that which I release can be released within me. Anything that I hold is held against me, but not by any God. It is a reflex action of my own state of consciousness. Therefore, any time that I am holding an individual in absolute, complete unforgiveness, I may rest assured that somewhere, somehow, sometime, I too will be held in unforgiveness, not necessarily by a person, but by my own erroneous clinging to the false sense of man.

So I do know this: Whatever you release, you are released from. What you cling to is that which binds you. You are your own liberator. If you cannot accept spiritual principles as they have been revealed by the mystics, you cannot come into the fullness of mystical life, which is a life of freedom: "Where the spirit of the Lord is, there is freedom." And this means mental, moral, physical, financial, freedom, and freedom in human relationships; but you can't enjoy this any more than you can give of that enjoyment.

Since we are in the Western world and the Christian world, we accept, not only the revelations of all mystics, but more especially the teachings and revelation of Jesus Christ. Therefore, if we are told, "Pray for your enemies that you may be the children of God," we do this because the revelation was given to Jesus and proved in his experience. We who have followed in his footsteps have since proven it to be true, that as we pray for our enemies, we ourselves are prayed for. In other words, to pray for one's enemies means not to hold them in bondage, not to want them to be punished even for their sins. To pray for them doesn't mean we ask God to prosper them in their iniquities, but rather to release the sin and discord from their consciousness.

The principle of praying for your enemy is not merely a beautiful teaching of scripture, it is a spiritual principle, and you either live by it or suffer from the violation of it. You have no choice in the matter; it's going to be one way or the other. All your prayers to God to release you from your offenses have no power unless you have already released everyone in this world, not only those who have offended you, but those who have offended mankind, those who have offended freedom, liberty, justice; those who have offended nations, races, or religions. Unless you can come to the full agreement of not holding them in bondage to their ignorance—"Father forgive them, they know not what they do"—unless you can readily see that, you yourself will be held by yourself in some form of bondage. Do you not see that? That these revelations of the mystics are not beautiful statements, they are laws? Violating these laws does not bring the wrath of God upon you, it brings the wrath of your sin upon you. You are never punished for your sins, never. And you never will be. You are punished by your sins, and you can't avoid it.

"As ye sow, so shall ye reap." That is not a beautiful passage in scripture, it is an absolute spiritual law. What goes out from you is what comes back to you. "Cast your bread upon the waters." Why? So that your bread can come back to you with butter and jam. But remember: If you do not cast your bread upon the waters, there is no bread on the waters to come back to you. You can't have the bread that belongs to somebody else. That bread is on its way back to the one who cast it upon the waters. You can't even get away with stealing it. That is why it has been clearly revealed in this message of the Infinite Way that there is no such thing as competition; there is no such thing as anyone taking from you that which is yours, except in the human picture. If you are living in obedience to the spiritual principles which constitute this message, it would be an utter impossibility for anyone to take away from you that which is yours.

We had one of the most wonderful experiences of this in California. For some months, when offices weren't available because of war conditions, one of the foremost and best known practitioners in California allowed me to use his office when he wasn't there. And so I had my Hollywood office hours from Friday noon until Monday noon, and he had the office the rest of the week while I conducted my work at home. When he had an injury and I was able to help him, he said, "Now I know you can take care of my practice. For years I've been wanting to go to England to buy cattle for my ranch, but I haven't been able to get away from the office. Now I'm leaving for England, and you're taking over my office and my practice." And I did. For nine months I was in that office every day and took care of his work.

When he came back, he came in one day and said, "You've done a mighty fine job. My people just love you, so I've decided you're going to stay here and keep my practice because you've earned it. I'm going to move away and start over again, fresh." And I had to say to him, "I'm surprised at you–very surprised. Surely you must know that your practice is your demonstration. No one could take that from you, and you can't give it away. Certainly I could care for it in your absence with your consent. But that is only caring for it, that is not possessing it. It's yours. You've demonstrated that it is an activity of your consciousness, and I might just as well try to separate you from your right arm as to separate you from an activity of your own consciousness." So we put up a glass partition to divide the room, and we shared the office. For a whole year those who came in could walk into whichever office was vacant at the time and leave their money with whomever wasn't too busy to give the treatment. That went on for a year and then, finally, I was called to write *The Infinite Way*.[1]

I tell you this to illustrate the point that anything that represents an activity of your consciousness is yours. If anyone were to try to take it from you, I can assure you their fingers would be burnt right up to the elbow. Never hesitate to be very liberal and loose with your possessions, because no one can take them from you if they are the result of your own demonstration and of your own consciousness. That is spiritual law. Nobody can break asunder any tie that God has made. Nobody can deprive you of anything that is the product of your consciousness, and if for any reason there should be a temporary loss through some human circumstance, be assured of this: it will be re-established, pressed down, and running over.

Now, back to the question. I cannot answer about the Lord's Prayer, except that one passage, for I have had no light on it. Many of you know that for years at every class, the question was always put on my desk, "What about the Sermon on the Mount?" And every time, I

---

[1] *The Infinite Way*, Joel S. Goldsmith, Op. Cit., see chapter 9, "Supply".

gave the same answer that I am giving you on this question: I can't answer you because I have no spiritual light on the subject. Then one Wednesday night in Chicago, we had a beautiful meditation in our class and the voice said to me: "Open the Bible to the Sermon on the Mount." I turned around and said, "It's no use. I don't know anything about it." It came back a second time and said: "Open to chapter five, *Matthew*, The Sermon on the Mount." I said, "It wouldn't do any good. I don't understand it." Again, the third time it came back, so then I said, "Well, maybe I'm going to be taught." I opened the Bible to chapter five in *Matthew*, and the revelation of the Sermon on the Mount was given to us, and if we can ever get through with our editing work, it will be in a book.[2] We have a very beautiful spiritual interpretation of The Sermon on the Mount, but it was given to us; it was given to me at the same time it was given to those who were in the class. The spiritual interpretation of many other passages has been revealed in that same way. So, when you read the interpretation of a Bible passage in any of the Infinite Way writings, you are reading what has been spiritually interpreted or explained to me. Please remember that you are not getting my opinion; you are getting a spiritual interpretation that was specifically revealed to me and merely passed on from me.

---

[2]Contained in "Part Three" of *The Thunder of Silence,* © 1961 by Joel S. Goldsmith (Harper, San Francisco). Ed. Note: Tape recordings of Mr. Goldsmith's classes, 1956 Seattle Closed Class, Tape 2, Side 2: Sermon on the Mount, First and Second Genesis; 1956 Portland Closed Class, Tape 4, Side 1: From Law to Grace through the Sermon on the Mount; The Infinite Way, Peoria, AZ.

Question: *In most cases where we are faced with the task of impersonalizing evil, I would think that it is almost impossible to achieve it unless we are first able to have deep spiritual contact with God. Please speak about this.*

Answer: In a sense, that is absolutely right. Impersonalizing evil must come as the result of some measure of spiritual realization. If I were to go out to a street corner and preach there are no thieves, there are no immoral people, there are no bad people, can't you imagine what would happen to me, because all those people would be listening with a mind that has no spiritual discernment at all? Whereas, when I say to you there never has been an evil person in the world, and there never will be, you understand that through spiritual discernment. Certainly there are times when we are the instruments through which evil manifests, and if we aren't, somebody else is. But that doesn't make us evil. That just makes us ignorant of how to protect ourselves from that mesmeric influence. By the time you have arrived at the state of consciousness where you are in this room, it must be clear to you that evil is impersonal, and you must have a degree of developed spiritual consciousness or I doubt very much if you could have worked your way into this room. Being in this room is a matter of demonstration, not that anybody was here to hold you out. But neither was there anybody to pull you in. If you are here, you came as a result of the activity of your own consciousness. And if you hadn't been prepared for it, you would have been led in some other direction and you wouldn't be here. Therefore, anyone in this room is sufficiently developed spiritually to be able to accept the fact that evil is impersonal, that as we face our daily existence, regardless of what we witness any person doing, it is possible for us to realize: "I know that it isn't you; it is the carnal mind. Wake up. Do not permit yourself to be an instrument of evil. You have the capacity to refuse it."

Surely every spiritual principle that is ever voiced is utter nonsense to the human mind. It takes some degree of spiritual illumination to accept these principles: resist not evil, put up thy sword, pray for your enemies. You know it is taught that this is impractical in this age, but you also know there are millions of people in this world living by just such principles, and it isn't that impractical. It was said to me one time in California: "Joel, you're a fine fellow, but so impractical." If so, it has been a very practical impracticality! I had to turn down a man today who wrote me from New York that he's just had a brilliant idea for promoting the Infinite Way on a worldwide scale. I'm too practical for that.

Question: *Why is it all right to pray for light, wisdom, understanding, and other spiritual qualities?*

Answer: Why is it? In the first place, it is an acknowledgment that at this moment we haven't all of the light, the wisdom, and the spiritual understanding to which we are entitled as children of God. In acknowledging that and turning to the spiritual center of our own being for that light, we are praying for it. If you mean, "Why is it all right to ask, or plead, or beg?" I answer you, that isn't prayer. That is something that has been taught for a long time in orthodoxy under the name of prayer. It is as far removed from prayer as any form of paganism that ever existed in the days of Rome or Greece, because that was their mode of prayer. They prayed to all kinds of gods for all kinds of things. That same type of prayer was merely taken over by the churches and continued until now, but that is being changed by many ministers, many bishops, many priests, who are waking up today to the right sense of prayer, which is conducted without words and without thoughts.

But there have to be steps leading up to that state of consciousness, and one of the steps is, that since we are in the habit of asking in prayer, let us at least ask for spiritual things, spiritual unfoldment, spiritual understanding, spiritual good. Do not believe for a minute that you are really asking God, and that God is going to answer. You are turning to that center within you from which the answers must come. I realize there are some teachings that claim we are completely perfect and spiritual now, and therefore all of this would be unnecessary. In our spiritual identity that's true; but it certainly isn't true of our humanhood. And it is our humanhood, or to our humanhood, that we are trying to bring light so that we may outgrow this humanhood. But denying that you are a human being, and stating that you are already perfect and already spiritual and already have the mind of God, is merely a form of affirmation. You are claiming something for yourself that you haven't demonstrated.

Never forget this: It is true that "I and the Father are one." It is true that "all that the Father hath is mine." It is true that "the place whereon I stand is holy ground." This is the truth, but it is the truth that I am now trying to prove in fuller measure. We have only proven it to a degree, so if you think for a moment that any individual can come to this platform believing they know it all and don't have to pray for light or guidance, you haven't seen me before class work or lecture work. There is nothing more definite than this, that "I of my own self can do nothing"; that I of my own self am nothing; that I of my own self have nothing. "The earth is the Lord's and the fullness thereof." That only becomes mine to the degree of my ability to be humble enough to know that I know nothing, to know that I have nothing, and to be willing to sit here and wait for it to come from that infinite source, which is closer to me than breathing, nearer than hands and feet. And it is nearer to you than breathing, nearer than hands and feet; it "is neither lo here nor lo there," it is within you.

You have to turn to that within-ness in the deepest kind of humility, not with any belief at all that you are the child of God. Of course you are in your essence, but so was the prodigal son when he was eating with the swine. He was still the son of the king, heir to every-thing, and that didn't do him much good. Neither does our heirship in Christ do us much good until by contact with this center within our own being we re-establish that oneness. Then the infinite good of God flows through. Regardless of how high you ever go—and I'm granting that you may even go as high as Jesus Christ—you will still be at the place where you will have to pray for light, wisdom, understanding. If you don't believe that, go back to the Bible and read the incident of Gethsemane and see if Jesus didn't pray, and if he didn't ask the disciples to stay awake and pray with him. Pray for what? The realization of God's presence, God's grace. Wasn't it there with him? It was, but it doesn't do any good until, through prayer, it becomes alive in you.

This is a mistake too many students make: stating these absolute truths as if they were already an accomplished fact. They aren't; they aren't. Why do you think Jesus said that he came to earth to heal the sick, open the eyes of the blind, open the ears of the deaf, forgive sinners? Did he at any time say, "Oh, you are already spiritual; you are already perfect?" Did he at any time say, "You don't need healing, you are already in the kingdom of God?" Oh, no, he didn't. No, he acknowledged his responsibility to serve humanity by revealing the kingdom of God, thereby establishing the health of those around him by feeding them food when they didn't have it, by forgiving their sins. He didn't tell them they weren't sinners. He didn't say, "You are too spiritual." He said, "I forgive you your sins." He did more than that: He warned them about sinning again, acknowledging that we are here seemingly in the flesh, and even if we have been healed of sin, we can sin again. That is why we have to be alert; that is why we can never stop praying. And heaven help anyone who falls into the trap of believing they have gotten past the stage where it is necessary to pray without ceasing.

Always remember this: If the day ever comes when the fullness of Christhood envelopes you, you will be invisible to the world. That will be the day of your ascension. So as long as you are still visible to us, please accept the fact that you are at that stage where the Master was, even in the Garden of Gethsemane. Pray, pray, pray. Pray that this cup be taken from you unless it is the will of God, and then let it come. Don't pray to God for automobiles, don't pray to God for good weather. It won't do you any good. God doesn't answer those prayers, because God knows nothing about weather or automobiles or food. Pray to God for light and wisdom.

Now, don't think for a moment that you haven't got control over the weather, for you have—not by going to God for it but by knowing the truth. When you definitely and specifically know the truth about the weather, you have control over it. Whether it is a tidal wave, a hurricane, or any form of abnormal weather, you can control it. I don't say this to you as theory. This has been part of our practice, and it has been beautifully demonstrated over and over again. The weather responds more quickly than our human patients do. But it is by knowing specific truth. Please believe me, prayer is your contact, your agreement, with God. Prayer is the means whereby the relationship of God the Father and God the Son is established as demonstration—the word made flesh. Prayer, when it is understood, is the means whereby you overcome all material sense, material living, and bring yourself to that place where your life is spiritually governed, spiritually protected, spiritually guided, spiritually experienced. And what I mean by that is this: that while you may eat a very good and enjoyable meal, and you may outwardly express the fact that it is good and enjoyable, inwardly you won't believe it yourself. It will be a concession to this world, because it is of such relative unimportance whether or not it is good that actually it doesn't leave you with a sensation of being good.

When that contact is made there are spiritual joys, there are spiritual experiences of harmony, of peace. Actually, even the most beautiful scenery is just scenery, and even though we do say, "Oh, yes, it was a beautiful day in Switzerland and the mountains were gorgeous," or "Yes, here in Hawaii we probably have the most beautiful scenery in the world," nevertheless, that is merely a statement of human fact that is of little moment beyond the comment given, because of the company you're in. Once prayer has been achieved, there are spiritual experiences that take place within you which are your real joys and which you value the most. It isn't money that you count any longer as your wealth. No, it is the love you continuously experience which prompts someone to be kind to you, whether they offer you money or whether they offer you a little remembrance, or an automobile ride, or a meal, or some courtesy on the trip. It isn't the material object at all that pleases you or thrills you. It is the love which prompted the kindness; and that you glory in, that you love, that you feel, because of your oneness with the individual who brought that out.

Prayer establishes us in a spiritual universe. It reveals spiritual beings. It reveals you as you really are. That is why it is very often easy to fool mystics. I guess mystics can be fooled by people and probably taken in, because they are never seeing the human condition and they are never really valuing the human thing, the property. They're living in the conscious awareness of you as you actually know yourself to be. I know for a fact that there isn't anyone in all the world who doesn't know inwardly they are a far greater person than they appear to be on the outside. I know that there isn't an individual on the face of the globe who doesn't know that their own inner standard, their own inner being, is far higher than anything they're exemplifying outwardly. I know that. I have seen it thousands of times, not only that which you are, but that which to some extent you know you

are, but you don't really know all of it. And you do
know in spite of many faults, in spite of many sins, this
is not you. You know who you are and what you are,
and that is why you can forgive yourself; that is why I
can forgive myself.

Understand, as I told you the first evening of our
classes: The metaphysics of this message is what makes
it possible to do the healing works. The mysticism of this
message enables you to live in God, live in spiritual
consciousness, live and move and have your being in
the fourth dimension of life. Then your experiences in
the outer plane become sort of a "suffer it to be so for
now," and yet it's very enjoyable, especially when you
meet people seriously trying to live a spiritual life. That
is what has constituted so much joy, not only for me, but
for many of our students who have been in class work in
many cities and foreign countries. They found the same
aloha spirit that we have here, which really exists as the
Infinite Way spirit. Those students who have experienced this in other cities and in other countries know
exactly what I mean, that there is a relationship between
us which is described on every front page of the Infinite
Way writings.

Spiritual illumination is the bond between us, and it
is a bond of love. It sets us apart from any other form of
relationship that exists between humans. I know this as
I travel around the world and come into the companionship of Infinite Way students. I have never yet met a
student who has been with us in other cities and in other
countries who has not found exactly what all of us are
finding here this week, what we found in 1957, what we
even found in our very first Honolulu class, which was
really a tremendous experience and revealed this same

oneness, this same spiritual being. From that day to this, every one of us here in the Islands has had the experience of being one: of never demanding anything of each other, never wanting anything of each other, never intruding into the lives of each other, and yet able to have the most glorious relationships with each other on about as high a plane as can be imagined. It is beautiful; it has been beautiful. I have had this same experience in every city and in every country, and not only have I had it, but so have all the students. I know there are many of you here who have been with us in California, Chicago, Seattle, Portland, New York, Melbourne, and London, who experience this oneness. You know that this is the same experience we find everywhere, and that it isn't a human relationship. This is a relationship which has evolved because of our prayer work and because we have always had as our goal, conscious union with God.

Remember the theme of the book, *Metaphysical Notes*[3]: "My conscious oneness with God constitutes my oneness with all spiritual being and idea." From the very minute those words came through my lips in San Francisco, it has been demonstrated that this is the truth. Since I am consciously one with God, I am consciously one with all that God is God to, whether appearing as person, place, or thing. Anything and everything necessary to my unfoldment appears as it is necessary. Why? My conscious oneness with God constitutes my conscious oneness with you. My conscious oneness with God constitutes my oneness with anybody, any place where I may travel. And always a group is waiting for the message. Why? It was established in the beginning

---

[3] Op. Cit., p. 161.

as conscious oneness with God. There again is another of our tremendous principles in this message of the Infinite Way.

Years ago it was revealed to me that it is nonsense to pray for anything at all, because it isn't possible to get anything through prayer. The principle behind that is this: God is the substance of all form. Therefore, if you haven't God, you haven't the form; but if you have God, you have all the forms that God constitutes. Always remember, you must be consciously aware of God. You must have a conscious experience. It's an experience that has to take place consciously in your consciousness. When you sit down in the morning to pray, to meditate, be sure that above all things, you do not have your mind on any thing or on any one, that you have no desire for person, place, or thing. If you cannot purify yourself before going into prayer, don't waste your time. You have to be completely free of desire for person, place, thing, circumstance, or condition, so that you are able to say as you go into prayer, "My only need is God-realization."

To know thee aright is life eternal. To be in conscious union with God is to realize:

Thou and I are one. God and I are one– not two– just one. Here and now where I am, God is. All that God is, I am: God the Father, God the Son. Having God, I have infinity in any form and every form necessary to my unfoldment, and I need not outline what that is. I need not tell God, I need not instruct God, I need not ask God. I must realize God's presence. Where the spirit of the Lord is, there is liberty. In thy presence is fullness of life. Where is thy presence? Thou art infinite, therefore, thou fillest all space. Therefore this place whereon I stand is holy ground, for thou art here, here where I am. In thy presence is fullness of life. Thy grace is my sufficiency in all things. Having thee, I have no other need.

Isn't it true? Can you imagine being in the actual presence of God and still wanting something or somebody? Wouldn't God itself be the fulfillment of anybody and everybody and anything and everything? What can one want beside God? So it is, when you realize that "in thy presence is fullness of life. Thy grace is my sufficiency," you consciously establish within yourself the realization of God's presence. You are bringing to conscious remembrance the fact that God already is in the midst of you and God is mighty. God's hand is not shortened and God's grace is not limited. "Thy grace is my sufficiency in all things."

Do you not see, as we have been bringing out here for two nights, that first of all you must know the principles? Then, knowing them, they must be put into practice until they become such a developed state of consciousness that it is no longer necessary to take conscious thought about them. But how can you bring yourself into conscious union with God if you do not understand the nature of the experience, or the meaning of the experience? And please don't ever believe that the function of God is to increase your material good. Too many metaphysicians have spent too many years trying to make a spiritual God increase their human sense of good instead of being willing to abandon the human sense of good for the spiritual reality.

Once you understand the nature of spiritual good, human good will be of very little moment in your experience. You'll still have it, and to a certain extent enjoy it. But I can assure you that it will be in a minor way. There is a heavenly kingdom; there is a spiritual kingdom; there is a spiritual sense of life; there is a spiritual sense of body, a spiritual sense of being, a spiritual sense of supply. Money isn't supply. Too many of you know that money takes wings and it isn't there anymore. Money isn't supply. Money is a form of supply in our experience, but it isn't supply. To get money humanly is to find that often it doesn't bring the satisfaction that is promised. I've told students in previous classes what my life's ambition was as a youngster. It was the same for years and years and years. All I wanted was a hundred thousand dollars, and with it I was going to buy a four-hundred-dollar-a-month annuity, and then I was going to move to California and read all the books in the library.

I don't mind telling you that three times in my business experience, I came close to having that hundred thousand dollars, and each time it took wings. When I started over, I started over again with two hundred fifty dollars, and surprisingly enough, I think I have read all the books in the library without that hundred thousand dollars and without that four-hundred-dollars-a-month guarantee. You see, even after you get it, it isn't what it promises to be. It doesn't always do what it promises to do. Certainly it doesn't give the satisfactions it promises. But for us on the spiritual path, we realize what we are really seeking is the consciousness of God's presence, and then the conscious realization of this presence brings us everything we formerly believed money would bring us—and somehow or other it always seems to bring some money along with it too, at least enough.

But that isn't the important thing. There are spiritual values and you can enjoy those values with little or no money, without even an awareness of money. If you are threatened by a tidal wave or a hurricane, and you wish to avoid the experience, you can, and you won't need God's help. All you'll need is to know this truth, that this threatening storm isn't a thing at all. It is an activity of the carnal mind, but the carnal mind hasn't any law, being, substance, or cause. Therefore, it is nothing but an image in thought like the bomb we built here last night. It is nothing but an image in thought, and it has no power. Your realization of all this will dissolve the storm—and it has dissolved the storm. We had one specific experience in a city where it rained every day for eighteen months without stopping, and three quarters of the businessmen in the community had gone bankrupt. Then, finally, a telephone call came to us out here in Hawaii asking for help. The next morning there was no more rain. The weather bureau reported, "Don't be fooled. The rain will be back with us because the condition that kept the rain here all this time is still present. So we don't understand why it isn't raining, but it will rain again." It didn't, and three days later the condition that was causing the rain disappeared.

God doesn't stop the rain. God knows nothing about the rain. If you know the truth, the truth will make you free. Once you begin to realize that these errors, these evils in any form, are merely the product of this universal mesmeric mind and then nothingize it in the realization that it's not of God, it will make no difference to you if it's the weather, false appetite, sin, disease, lack, limitation, unemployment. They'll all disappear. They'll all disappear, or begin to disappear, the moment you recognize that they only exist as an activity of this universal mesmeric mind, that which has been called carnal mind, mortal mind, devil, satan. But it isn't God ordained and has no God law. One with God is a majority.

~ 14 ~

Overcoming Mesmeric Sense

Now I'm going to explain a mystery, and if it shocks some of you don't hesitate to pray about the subject within yourself. Don't go to anyone and ask them to explain it. Certainly don't complain to anybody because I said it; but take it into your own inner sanctuary and ask God for light on this subject.

You know there are pilgrimages to Lourdes, and that out of every hundred-thousand people who go there only fifteen are certified as being healed. You know there isn't a day, an hour, that churches, synagogues, and temples aren't open where prayers are uttered for the sick. And you know what would be happening if *materia medica* weren't right on the job! Haven't you wondered why all of these prayers to God have not healed the sick? Haven't many of you prayed to God for your children or your parents or your wives or husbands, and wondered why you didn't get an answer? Then let it be clear to you now that God knows nothing of disease and therefore has no possible way of healing it.

God would first have to know you were sick before God could heal you, and if God knew you were sick and did nothing about it until you prayed, what kind of a God would you have? In other words, humanity experiences a complete separation between God and man "whose breath is in his nostrils." If there weren't such a complete sense of separation between God and humanity, humanity wouldn't be sick, sinning, dying, aging, or decrepit. You can't believe for a moment that if God were on the field such things would be happening in the lives of millions. Do you, any one of you, actually believe that God knew there were seven million Jews being burnt up in ovens? Do you really believe that God knew that? Is there one of you who does not know how sincerely the Hebrew people prayed to their God, how earnest they were in their devotions? But they were burnt up! Do you know that seven hundred thousand Hebrews lived in the city of Amsterdam before the last war and only ten thousand of them survived? Do you believe God knew that? Do you believe that they prayed, as you know they must have prayed, and God ignored that?

There is such a complete sense of separation between God and the man of earth that the two never come together. That is why, in order to live under God's grace, what Paul said must necessarily follow: "The spirit of God must dwell in you, otherwise you are not under the law of God, neither indeed can be." Only when the spirit of God dwells in you. There is other scriptural confirmation about this: The Ninety-first Psalm says, "A thousand shall fall at thy left side, ten thousand at thy right side, and it shall not come nigh thee." Who is this "thee"? "They who dwelleth in the secret place of the most high." They are the only ones who can be certain that these evils will not come nigh their dwelling place. And this is the teaching of Jesus Christ: "If you abide in this word, and let this word abide in you (let me abide in you—God, the spirit of God), you will bear fruit richly; but if you do not abide in this word (that means not consciously living in this word, not acknowledging that I is God in the midst of you), you will be as a branch of the tree that is cut off and withereth." What's the use of quibbling? That's the way it is. That's the way it is stated in scripture. Heaven knows we have witnessed man's inhumanity to man for countless centuries, with no lessening of it, and thereby we know God isn't in this scene. That's why there is no use asking God to heal disease, to stop tidal waves, or to end the depression.

But Jesus also taught: "Ye shall know the truth, and the truth shall make you free." Understand why this is. God is. And God is infinite, omnipotent, omnipresent, omniscient, and because of this there is no evil. If you have an infinite, eternal, immortal God, and in the entire kingdom of God there is no evil, then, as scripture says, "God is too pure to behold iniquity." Certainly God wouldn't tolerate it today and then heal you of it tomorrow. That would make of God a human being, and not even a very nice one. Oh, no! The reason healing is possible is this: God is, and God constitutes this universe, and God constitutes your being which is perfect. But because of this sense of separation, you are going to be bombarded with mental miasma, which is malpractice, a constant hypnosis coming out of this carnal mind belief of two powers. Without your consciously knowing it, it is getting into your system (the same way that subliminal advertising is thrown into the unconscious or subconscious mind) and then you respond to it. That is the wherefore of error. Error is nothing more than a universal hypnotism which comes out of an impersonal entity called devil, mortal mind, or carnal mind.

Now, you know this truth and can look right out at any phase of error whether it is appearing as a man, woman, child, or condition, disease, or weather, and realize:

I know thee who thou art: you're not a person, you're not a condition, you're nothing but that mental malpractice; you're nothing but that carnal mind in action—an image, a nothingness—the arm of flesh, the fleshly mind, that which has no law of God, no life of God, a nothingness. I don't have to fight you. I have to recognize you for what you are: a mental image in thought without substance, cause, reality, or law.

What happens then? The hypnotism is dissipated and you are living a spiritual life, a God life. God was doing its job all the time. God was always manifesting its spiritual perfection as you, but only by seeing through a glass darkly did you see yourself in sin, disease, death, lack, and limitation.

Some of you have undoubtedly watched hypnotists at work, especially in the entertainment field. You know it is possible for them to make you see things that aren't there and feel things that aren't taking place. Suppose a hypnotist makes you see pink elephants? Is the remedy to remove pink elephants? It can't be done. The remedy is waking you out of that hypnotic sleep. If you are crossing the desert and you see the road flooded with water, is the remedy draining the water off or waking to the fact that you're beholding a mirage, and then going forward?

There is a God maintaining and sustaining the integrity of this universe, and it is perfect except when you see it through a glass darkly, or when you see it through a sense that has been to some extent mesmerized by the belief in good and evil. The healing agency is your realization that God's universe is intact and therefore I am intact, for all that God is I am, and all that the Father hath is mine. So that which is appearing is just the product of mesmeric sense, but since it isn't God-created, God-ordained, God-maintained, God-sustained, it is nothingness. "They have but the arm of flesh; we have the Lord God almighty." As you abide in this truth about the unreal nature of evil, the evil begins to dissipate right before your eyes because it doesn't exist as a God-created condition. It doesn't. It exists as a mesmeric influence, which you have accepted as real because of that mesmeric sense.

I knew a man from Germany who was my friend for forty-nine years until he passed on. At one time he was one of Hitler's right-hand men and destined to be the Secretary, or Minister, of Commerce when Hitler came to power. But it so happened that at one of their meetings, Hitler made the remark, "To accomplish my goal I don't care if two hundred thousand German youth are killed." Well, my friend had been through the First World War and had been heavily decorated in action, and he said to Hitler, "Not with my help. I wasn't born to help kill two hundred thousand German youth. You'll have to do it without me."

With that remark, my friend had issued his own death warrant, but Mr. Hitler thought he would win him over. Soon after, somebody reported to Mr. Hitler that my friend was a Jew-lover and that his best friends were Jews. Mr. Hitler sent for him and said, "You know we can't have this, so I think you'd better move to Switzerland. You can have twenty-five thousand dollars a year income for the rest of your life, just leave Germany." Hitler didn't kill him; he didn't turn on him for the rest of the war. My friend lived in Switzerland and Italy as long as money was sent to him. Then later, he formed the underground against Hitler and became his enemy openly, and of course the income was stopped.

The point I'm trying to make is this: People aren't evil, even if you call them Hitler. They'll be evil to you if you see them as evil. They can't be evil to you if you see them as they are spiritually and realize that the evil you're beholding in a person isn't an evil person, but a mesmeric influence which is being accepted as reality. If you don't accept it as reality, it cannot function against you. That's the secret. "As ye sow, so shall ye reap." If you believe there is a sinful person, then sin can be committed against you. If you believe there is a poverty-stricken person, poverty can knock at your door. If you believe there is disease and death, you can experience it.

Classes have heard me say over and over again, right from the mount of spiritual intuition, that in all the history of the world not a single man, woman, or child, has ever died. There has never been a death in the entire history of the world—never! Passing from our sight is part of this mesmeric influence. Those who are born must die. Those who believe in death, those who have not been able to see that this human picture is really and truly the immortal, eternal, spiritual reality, are looking at life through hypnotized eyes. If you were hypnotized into seeing pink elephants and then were awakened out of that hypnotism, you'd be your own natural self—and without pink elephants!

And so it is, to the degree we become dehypnotized, we do not experience birth or death, but an ongoing evolutionary experience which will eventually take us out of what we call this human scene to bring us into higher unfoldment. It isn't in the cards for the world to stand still. It isn't in the cards for infants to remain infants, children to remain children, youth to remain youth. It is inevitable that we mature, not only in years, but in spiritual understanding and demonstration. The beginning is to know that God is, and that God is the substance of all that is—the life, the activity, and the law of all that is—and therefore this is an immortal and an eternal universe, and we are eternal and immortal beings.

That which we behold as a limited, finite world, that which we behold as evil in any form—sin, disease, lack, limitation, war, depression, storms—must be seen and understood as the product of this universal mesmeric sense. This was originally called devil, but is now called carnal mind or mortal mind. Because it never was of God, but was formed in this mind of man after the fall of man, and exists only as a mental picture without power, without continuity, it begins to fade and fade and fade. The basis of our healing work is accomplished not by praying to God for help, for employment, or supply, or activity, or for a profession, an art, or a gift, but by realizing that the mind of God is actually our very mind. The fullness of that God-mind is our capacity, our art, our good. We realize that the picture that confronts us is this mesmeric picture that is forever without law. Then watch it begin to recede. Watch the healings that take place, and not because God has done you a favor or because you have found some person who is closer to God than you are. That is all nonsense. There isn't anybody closer to God than you are. There are only those who have learned about the origin of sin and disease, and thereby know how to nullify it.

If disease or sin or any of these earthly conditions were really and truly a fact–a being–God would have to be responsible for them, and their nature would be good instead of evil. It isn't possible for God to be divided against itself. It isn't possible for an infinite intelligence to act destructively against itself or its own creation. Therefore, you can accept the fact that God is perfection itself, and all that God has done is good. All that God has made is good, and anything that God did not make was not made. Therefore neither sin, disease, death, accident, nor anything else like that was ever made. It appears to us only out of this mesmeric sense. Our realization of this is the healing influence. Our realization of the nothingness of that which is frightening us, confronting us as evil, is the very presence and power that nullifies it. Nothing else will do it, be assured of this.

"Ye shall know the truth and the truth will make you free." This is the way the Master did his healing work. He never healed a crippled man. He merely asked, "What did hinder you?" He never healed a blind man. He just put some spittle on clay, laid it on the man's eyes, and told him to open his eyes. That was his way of healing: never acknowledging any power in disease. Jesus never asked God to heal any of his patients. Jesus never told any of his patients that God made them sick, or even that God made them well. Jesus never told any dying people that God was calling them home. In fact, he never declared anyone was dead. On the contrary, "Lazarus sleepeth." And to the boy who was being carried to his funeral, "Come on, get down from there."

If Jesus had recognized these conditions as conditions, can't you understand that he would have prayed to God to do something about them? But he didn't. He prayed constantly, but that prayer was communing with the Father within by going into his inner sanctuary. That was his prayer. That is our prayer. But we desire no benefit from God; we desire no favors from God. That, to me, would be the height of ridiculous living: to go to God and ask for anything. It would be ridiculous. Oh, to ask for understanding or light is different, because you're acknowledging your own emptiness at the moment and asking that inner self to reveal itself as truth. To actually ask God for something, you first have to assume that God is withholding it. If you asked for health for anybody, aren't you saying, "God, you've got this health, but you won't give it. But I'm asking you, let go! Give! Give!" To God, that's sacrilege. God isn't withholding anybody's supply; God isn't withholding anybody's employment; God isn't withholding recognition from anybody, or reward, or talent—impossible! God is the very talent, the very supply, the very wisdom, the very substance of our being. God is all of these things. God isn't withholding them. So let us not ask God, but let us recognize that God already is everything. God constitutes our very being. God constitutes the very mind and life and soul of us. Even our body is the temple of the living God. Then when we're faced with discords, inharmony, unhappiness, lack, and limitation, let's not go to God. Let's turn away and look right out into the world and see: "Aha, this is part of that universal mesmerism trying to convince me that God is not on the field, that God is not my life and being, trying to convince me there are two powers on earth. But I know better. There can't be an infinite God and an evil power." By abiding in that word and letting that word abide in you, you break the mesmerism. "Not by might nor by power," but by understanding.

You can't take heaven by storm. You can't gain heaven by might or by power, but only by an inner silent, sacred, communion—not for any purpose, except the joy of communion. When there is something interfering with your well-being, or anyone who is looking to you for that help, God is on the field. God is always there. You don't have to concern yourself with God, or stir him up on anyone's behalf. All you have to do is face the impersonal source of all worldly evil and recognize its nothingness, its lawlessness. Then be still, be quiet, be calm, and watch—watch the hypnotism and its pictures pass away from you. That's how it's done.

Question: *Please discuss contemplative meditation.*

Answer: And that's what I've just been doing. That is contemplative meditation. When I sit with some facet of truth in my mind, I do just what I have done, only I do it silently, reassuring myself:

God is. Life is eternal. I and my Father are one. There is no discord in God's creation, God is the substance of all form; God's world is perfect, and if there is a "this world," then this world is perfect because it must be God's world. Ah, yes, but I'm being faced now with a dying person, or a poor person, a sinful person, an imprisoned person. Surely, surely that's the world-hypnotism; that's the mesmeric activity of this carnal mind presenting these pictures to me. And how grateful I am to have learned there is no law in this picture to sustain it, so it must dissolve. There's no substance, no form, no activity—it must dissolve.

Then I rest. That's contemplative meditation.

So it is, if I'm faced with a storm I realize:

God made all that was made. God is the activity of the sun, the moon, the stars, the planets. God is the activity of this earth. If it weren't for the activity of God, there wouldn't be cattle on a thousand hills; there wouldn't be crops in the ground, or oil, or iron, or steel. There wouldn't be fish in the sea and birds in the air. All of these things testify to the fact that the activity of God is infinite and omnipresent, always going on. Ah, but I've just been told about this storm. Yes, indeed, I don't doubt it either. I don't doubt it. Another form of mesmeric suggestion, another activity of the carnal mind that would claim to operate as a condition when it is only a mental image in thought, without life, without law, without being.

And that's contemplative meditation. But you can also call it treatment; you can also call it prayer; you can also call it inner communion. We use all of those terms interchangeably. Contemplative meditation means we are contemplating truth, we are contemplating God, or we are contemplating the nature of God, or we are contemplating the nature of error. We are contemplating it inwardly, silently, peacefully, understandingly. Contemplative meditation is our prayer, our treatment.

There is another form of meditation, which is beyond contemplative meditation. Usually after you have spent some time in contemplative meditation, as I have just done, you come to a place where thought stops and you just sit there at peace. There are no words and no thoughts. I'm sure you've all had the experience sometime of sitting this way with your mother, neither of you talking, neither of you thinking anything, just at peace. I know that husbands and wives often have the experience.

They don't have to talk, they don't have to think, they just sit together in a peaceful communion. So it is, after the contemplative meditation or the treatment, there usually follows a few moments of this silence, this peace. No words, no thoughts, just complete stillness. Usually it will last for a few minutes and then end with a deep breath, or a feeling, sometimes a message. Oh, it has an infinite variety of ways of ending. But the whole idea is that this latter meditation is your actual communion with God. The contemplative meditation is really your conscious knowing of the truth, or treatment. But when you've gone beyond words and thoughts, then you are in the stage of complete meditation, silence and stillness.

There is another stage beyond that. Often, after you come to the place where you can meditate almost at will, and remain for quite a while in meditation, you pass automatically from meditation to communion—and that is when the Spirit, the Presence itself, comes alive in you. There is a presence, called God or the Christ, and there is you. And it is as if there were something going back and forth between you and that presence—not necessarily words, although sometimes there are words; not necessarily thoughts, although sometimes there are thoughts—but something, a feeling as if there were a motion going back and forth between you and this presence. That's communion. There is a me and there is this presence of God.

And then there is the final stage. After communion has become a part of your everyday living, it gradually deepens into the experience where there's no longer a communion because there's no longer two. I somehow disappear, you disappear, and there's nothing left but God. And for as long as you are in that conscious union

there is no you, there is only God. When you come back
to yourself, you realize that you've been away somewhere and that this other being is the only being that
exists. That is the mystical experience. That is the
complete marriage. That is what is described in the *Song
of Solomon.* It is the complete mystical marriage where
God the Father and God the Son become one, and there
is no more Son, there is only God the Father. These are
the experiences you read about, where mystics have
transcended the human sense of life and are living in the
complete awareness of spiritual reality.

You never know where you're going, do you? Never.
And you never will while you're on the spiritual path. If
you have these major principles constantly in your mind,
you must come to a complete conviction that God is. This
means that harmony is, that the entire kingdom of God is
at peace and is at one with God. Then realize that our
only disturbance is caused by whatever it is that has
convinced us there are two powers. And when we begin
to understand the fleshly mind, or the arm of flesh, as
nothingness, that's when we dissolve the pictures of sense.

That is why the practitioner, when he's called upon,
doesn't rush like a fireman to grab his hat and coat and
run out to see the patient. If he does, he is probably
going to lose his case quickly. The one who can realize
in silent contemplation that nothing disturbing is going
on in the kingdom of God, and that which is going on to
sense isn't real and has no law to support it, no power of
continuity, breaks the mesmerism, and the picture
disappears with it. That's how healing work is accomplished.

Be sure in your own being you have given up all
thought or belief that you are going to get something

from God that God isn't already giving you. Be sure you are not looking to God for something, but you are understanding that all that God is, is flowing now. All that God has is pouring forth now. God is. God is closer than breathing, nearer than hands and feet. God is the same yesterday, today, and forevermore. So don't annoy God. God is. I don't have to go to God for supply: "The Lord is my shepherd, I shall not want." It is that contemplative meditation on this that makes it real to me. Sitting with the Twenty-third Psalm, reading it, contemplating it: "The Lord is my shepherd, I shall not want; he maketh me to lie down in green pastures. He leadeth me beside the still waters." I don't have to annoy God with my wants or needs. And there's no use anyhow.

You might as well get used to the idea: All the evils of this world are nothing but pictures in the mind. When you know this, they begin to dissolve. They begin to dissolve the very minute you know the nature of error. All evil functions in this universal mesmeric mind are not law and have no law to sustain them. They are not a presence. Since God didn't ordain evil and since God doesn't maintain or sustain evil, don't fear it, don't fight it. "Resist not evil. . . Put up thy sword." Be at peace. God is. And then you'll find how this spiritual healing work is really accomplished.

Thank you. I'm glad I told it to you!

~ 15 ~

MENTAL POWER

Good evening.

I'm sure most of you know that any teaching has to be conducted in steps because we represent states and stages of consciousness: We are prepared at one time for a teaching and at another time for something higher. Still farther along in our experience, we are ready for some of the mysteries of life. Ordinarily speaking, metaphysical teachings consist only of the veneer of the subject, the outside layer. There is very little metaphysical teaching that goes any higher than what I would call primary grades. Most of it is in the realm of kindergarten and a little of it is on the level of primary grades. I don't know of any teaching available to the public that goes any higher than what might comparatively be called fourth or fifth grade schooling. The reason is that spiritual truth is shocking. Spiritual truth can hardly be accepted at all by human beings until they have had sufficient light to lift them above that primary grade of receptivity.

This is also true of mental teachings. I don't know of any mental teachings that go any further than what would be primary grade teaching. For the same reason, if the truth were known about the mind—no, I won't say that if the truth were known, but if the truth were taught openly about the mind—there would be far too many people hurting themselves by experiments for which they were not prepared. Then there would also be the use of mind-power in wrong directions. It is probably for this reason that the truth about mind doesn't reach the public at all, whereas the truth about the Spirit doesn't reach it because it wouldn't be comprehended. It is available, but it has to be discovered, and then it isn't understood until one is prepared for it.

I can illustrate that by answering this question first—and incidentally I might tell you this: that before coming into this room I was upstairs meditating, and in my meditation the subject of this class tonight unfolded in its completeness. Then, when I read these questions, I knew right well that I was in tune with this group of students, and it was natural that these questions should be asked. But, I'm not quite so certain yet that you will accept the answers. That will depend on your own inner unfoldment and how far you've come.

Question: *How can spiritual harmony be established in the functioning of mechanical or electrical equipment? Is it possible to prevent mechanical or electronic parts from wearing out or becoming defective?*

Answer: Just think how far your understanding will have to go for you to accept the fact that to a certain degree the answer is, "Yes, it can be so." You see how at first it seems absolutely improbable and impossible that controlling the function of mechanical or electrical equipment is possible through these studies. Actually, it can't be done spiritually, but it can be done mentally.

I cannot tell you how many times I have had students tell me or write me of their automobiles malfunctioning in some serious way, and yet of their being able to go as far as a garage or the next stop–then to be told by a mechanic it was absolutely impossible for them to reach there, that the breakdown was of such a nature that the car absolutely could not have reached there–or, how many times I have been told of running out of gas and the car kept going until it reached the next station.

Of course, I know that to the human mind this is impossible, and it is for this reason these things cannot be taught more openly than they are. I'm gong to go another step and tell you that this question came up in our Seattle class, not about mechanical things, but about living things. I set out to show the students what could be done. On Sunday, the entire center was decorated with beautiful cut roses. They were on the platform, along the sides of the church, at the back of the church, and more roses were in my study. I said I could prove that the roses in the study would be just as fresh when we finished the class the next Saturday night as they were today, Sunday. And the roses remained just as they were: they hadn't opened, they were still buds, and they were still fresh. Those outside the study weren't. This is not a spiritual demonstration. This is proof that what we call matter isn't matter at all, it is mind. It is mind formation; it is mind expressed. The reason I know this is that I know what mind is, and I have seen how mind functions in the body.

Always remember, there are three states of consciousness: the material, the mental, and the spiritual. In the days before the middle of the last century, this was considered a material universe to such an extent that even the *materia medica* practice was almost entirely material. It was the application of remedies, whether pills, powders, liquids, herbs, plasters, heat and cold. But practically all of the medical practice was material, as if your body was a piece of matter and something had gotten out of order, so the doctors were going to take that material body and in some material way, get it functioning. That was the major practice of the healing arts.

But a century earlier, Anton Mesmer discovered the relationship between mind and body. He performed experiments and did healing work by the essence of mind, which in some way governed the action of the body. Evidently he was successful enough with it in Germany that he was invited to England and then to France. He must have had quite some success there because he was driven out of business by those who felt it was too competitive.

However, there was a grain of truth in his teaching, and it couldn't die. Between that and the last century a greater unfoldment took place as to the relationship between mind and body, or mind and matter. And so, there were introduced into the world teachings like the original Christian Science, which was mind over matter; New Thought, which was mind over matter, mind controlling matter; psychology, psychiatry, and psychosomatic medicine. In all of these, the power of the mind is recognized as having something to do with the harmony of the body. Now, it isn't necessary at this point to say that there are some erroneous concepts in all of those teachings. There are, and that part of those teachings which are incorrect will ultimately be corrected. But it is now recognized universally that there is a relationship between mind and body.

As the Christian Science teaching through Mrs. Eddy evolved, another step was taken, and it became known that there is a relationship between God, Spirit, and the health of body and mind. Here is a newspaper article quoting Dr. Carl Jung: "Among all my patients in the second half of life, every one of them fell ill because he had lost what the living religions of every age have given their followers, and none of them has really been healed who did not regain his religious outlook." So you see, with a recognition of that nature and a recognition of the nature of spiritual healing itself, we do know that Spirit, or God, functions in physical and mental life.

In the days when body was thought of only as matter, and remedies as matter, the world was living in that particular dimension, a material dimension, totally unaware of the fact that it was surrounded by a mental universe, a mental dimension. Oh, that was ignored. Everything was matter and materiality, material force, material power, and here we were surrounded all of this time by a tremendous mental force. Then, from the 1800's up to the present time we find more and more becoming known about the mental universe and its activities. Unfortunately for this particular era, there is a mistaken idea loose in the world that the mental realm and spiritual realm are one and the same, that the realm of God and the realm of mind are the same. This is leading to disastrous results because as long as this belief persists, there will be teachings combining the spiritual and the mental, and going nowhere—and actually preventing progress because of the failure of their teaching. One of these that I can point to is the New Thought movement, which in the last thirty years has dropped ninety percent. The main reason is this very mistake of continuously using God and mind as if they were synonymous. They are using God-power and mental power as if they were the same thing, and they're getting nowhere with it.

This same mistake was brought into the religious world during the last ten or fifteen years, and believe it or not, circulating in the churches now is the teaching that mind power is God-power. One of the tragedies that results from this is that years are lost before those mistakes are corrected. I had occasion a short time ago to mention that a minister had written about the power of prayer in plant life. A minister of the church! And in this book he reveals experiments in which he instructed a group of people how to pray for the plants to make them grow and flourish beyond their natural growth, and taught another group how to pray so as to wither and destroy them. And this led him to the conclusion that prayer can be destructive as well as constructive.

Now, when I tell you that this is tragic, you must understand why: The power of God is all good and no one can ever use the power of God for a selfish purpose, for a personal purpose, or for a destructive purpose. It cannot be done. The nature of God is good, the nature of God is love, the nature of God is life eternal, and no one on the face of the globe will ever be able to pray, or to make use of spiritual power for a selfish or destructive purpose. That is why so many of the so-called prayers of the world are powerless: prayers to do this for me, or for my child, or for my nation, or for my soldiers. There cannot be answers to such prayers because God cannot be used in that way.

God is universal good, the same today, tomorrow, and forever. And in the sight of God there is "neither Greek nor Jew, bond nor free"; and anyone who attempts by any manner or means to utilize the power of

God for a personal, selfish, or destructive purpose might just as well be touching a hot wire—they are on their way to self-destruction. God is no respecter of persons. God's rain falls on the just and the unjust. God's presence is the power of forgiveness to every phase of discord, whatever its name or nature. Now, this minister was not mistaken that plants did grow and were destroyed. His mistake was believing that it was spiritual power, or prayer, or contact with God that was responsible for the result. But God wasn't. Anyone could duplicate that experiment. It is entirely mental.

No one really knows the extent of the power of the mind. No one has ever experimented enough to learn what the actual power of the mind is. I had the pleasure and privilege of being with a teacher who taught me how to leave this body and how to travel to any part of the globe I wanted to see. And for many years I enjoyed that experience, wandering out into this world practically every night—not that it proved anything from a spiritual standpoint. It merely proved that the mind is not encased in the body. To me, that was only a step leading to the realization that I am not in this body, I am not in this room, I do not occupy space, I cannot be confined to either time or space. I can transcend either at any time, spiritually, but only because I learned first that the mind is not confined to this shell.

The mind can read other minds. The mind can read minds close at hand and far away. The mind can transcend itself, as often happens in wartime when mothers are almost living with their sons at the front, thousands of miles away. Mothers know more about their sons than the army board does because living in such identification with them, they transcend their own limitations of body and find themselves in far places. The mind is not something separate and apart from the body. The mind is not something separate and apart from that plant. Actually, mind is the very substance of body. Mind is the essence and activity of body, and it is for this reason that you can leave God entirely out of the picture and work purely on the mental level to produce healing and harmony.

Anyone who will stay away from trying to mix Spirit and mind and remain purely on the mental level can produce harmony in their bodies, in their business, in all the affairs of their life as long—and this of course is the major requisite—as they maintain their integrity. In other words, as long as they never try to use their mind-power selfishly, injuriously, or to anyone's discomfort. As long as they remain pure of mind, using this power only for the purpose of producing harmony, whether in themselves or others, there is nothing selfish about producing harmony in one's circumstances. Harmony is the normal, natural state of being. But to produce harmony at someone else's expense or to use the mental power destructively, is a sin against the Holy Ghost. It inevitably results in harm to the one who does it. It has been done. People have used the power of mind to get other people's money, other people's property, other people's business. They have used the power of mind to benefit themselves at the expense of others. It is a destructive thing, but don't for a minute doubt that it can be done. Otherwise, you will be living with your head buried in sand.

The mind has two powers—good and evil. Do you not understand that this body in and of itself can never be good or bad? Do you not realize—you probably haven't thought of it until now—the body can't be immoral or do an immoral thing or commit an immoral act? Do you know that? Of course you do. There has to be a mind; there has to be something you call I. All the body can do is carry out the instructions of the mind. If the mind says, "Give," the hand gives. If the mind says, "Withhold," then the hand withholds. And if the mind says, "Steal," then the hand steals, or tries to. The mind is always governing the body on the human level. Only those too steeped in mental inertia let the body control the mind. Then we have kleptomaniacs. Their hand just reaches out and steals, although their mind doesn't want it to. They can't help it; their mind has no control over their body. Then there are people of sensual appetites who cannot control their appetite for drink or for drugs or food; they have no control over their body. Their body has control over them, but it is because they have surrendered the power of their own mind and let the body run away with it as you might let a garden become over-run with weeds if you are too lazy to get out there and take care of it. Normally the body can't steal, the body can't overeat or over-drink, the body can't do anything of itself if there is enough control, so you know, "I govern the action of this body, I being me, acting through the mind."

So it is with health. Health can be maintained mentally by keeping the mind imbued with truth. The mind imbued with truth will create and maintain health in the body. Mind imbued either with ignorance or error permits the body to disintegrate and to develop ill health. But remember, this is all on the mental plane. Now, because there is an interrelation between spirit, mind, and body in our stage of unfoldment, we cannot reach the spiritual level without first going through the mind. There are a few exceptions to that. There have been some people who have received divine grace and are automatically imbued with the Spirit without ever having to learn the truth of being, sometimes without ever learning it in their lifetime and yet always living spiritually. But there are not many such, and it would be foolish for us to wait around to see if that particular spiritual lightning is going to strike us. We may as well acknowledge that we will have to reach spiritual levels through the mind, but not using the mind as mind-power, as you would if you were just going to heal mentally. Use the mind as an avenue of awareness through which you learn the letter of truth, and by learning and practicing the letter of truth you develop your soul powers, or spiritual powers, and ultimately get beyond the need for even the use of the mind in that direction.

Do not ever think you want to get rid of the mind. That was one of the mistakes made by Christian Science, trying to nullify the mind and body. Let's not get rid of the mind or the body. Let's have both mind and body for their proper usage. The body is an instrument through which we are now functioning. It's a very handy instrument when you want to walk down the street or drive a car or go somewhere. It's a wonderful thing to have eyes to see with and ears to hear with and a tongue to speak with. It's all beautiful. It's a wonderful thing to have a mind that functions clearly and intelligently. Let's not try to get rid of it.

The one thing taught in the Infinite Way is that if you use the mind as power, you keep yourself on the mental-physical plane without considering the highest and the real, that which is spiritual. When you reach the spiritual plane, both mind and body are instruments for God. Then there is no limit to the understanding, the inspiration, the art, literature, music, inventions, and science that can come through a mind that has made contact with God, no limitation whatsoever. You cannot do that solely on the mental plane. You cannot. You can increase your skill and ability, but only to the extent of mind itself. Once you open yourself to higher consciousness, there is absolutely no limit to what can be revealed through your mind and then brought forth by the skill of your fingers or your body.

So in answering this question, I doubt it could actually be demonstrated that it is possible to maintain mechanical or electrical equipment very long through mental means, although I am absolutely convinced it can be done throughout any period when it is necessary to our experience. In other words, if we run out of gasoline, I am definitely convinced we can run that car until gasoline is available, although I don't believe we can stop using gasoline entirely and depend on the activity of the mind to run the car. Likewise, in the case of a break-down, I'm certain that our activity would in some way hold the car together until we arrived at a place where it could be fixed. But I doubt very much if we could continue to use it very long without disaster.

The same is true of plant life. By mental means you can increase crops and by mental means you can decrease them. But to bring forth a permanent demonstration of multiplication of the loaves and fishes, it would be necessary to go further than the operation of the mind. It would be necessary to touch or reach the realm of Spirit. Then there is no limitation. But neither would there be a violation of natural law. In other words, you might double the amount of flowers on this plant, but it would not be in violation of nature because something in nature itself that is not being used would be brought into use. The full life of this plant may not now be in action and the activity of the Spirit would see to it that every seed came alive and bore fruit.

Mrs. Eddy wrote, I believe it's in the textbook, that the day will come when a thief will not have to enter your home; you will carry your goods to the thief. I'm sure that is not often quoted, and I'm sure there are not many people who believe it. But I'm sure, in view of the success that was originally had with subliminal advertising, you must now know it is true. If the power of the mind is used in that direction, you can be made to deliver yourself and your property. You say, "This is frightening!" Of course it is. Of course it is. That's why England has absolutely refused to permit the practice of subliminal advertising. The Advertising Society of Great Britain has refused permission for it to be used, the government has refused, the radio and the television stations have refused. They have unanimously refused to permit its use because if it can be used, it can be used to make you give up your money for anything they wish to advertise, whether or not you need it or whether or not you can afford it. Last month when the California legislature tried to pass a bill to outlaw its practice, they failed. The interests behind advertising were too strong. And now, if you know how, it is legal to do all the stealing you want to in California as long as you do it mentally.

When you see an exhibition of hypnotism, it is frightening to know that one man or woman can control the minds and bodies of as many people as are available. That should be frightening to anybody, and it should be outlawed. It should be outlawed in medicine regardless of the good it could accomplish. The ill it can accomplish far outweighs any good. The practice of hypnotism should be outlawed because it is an activity of one mind controlling another. Where is the freedom? You say, "Oh, but you have a choice." You don't have any such thing. If you're ill and you want to get well, and if the price is giving up your mental freedom, you'll pay it. It is frightening, and to the world uninstructed in spiritual truth there isn't any protection unless the law provides it. Even the law can't prevent individuals from using their minds in any way they want, more especially since it is possible to organize a mental activity and call it religious, and then get a license for its practice from the government.

Actually, however, there is protection against mental power, and that is the protection which you utilize when you understand the carnal mind is not power. It cannot rise above itself to accept the First Commandment, "Thou shalt have no other gods," no other powers, but the one. And as you consciously–remember, consciously–live in the realization of God as the only power, the one power, and know that the so-called human mind, mortal mind, carnal mind, selfish mind, mesmeric mind, hypnotic mind, is not power, is not God-ordained, is not God-sustained, you are protected. You can't be hypnotized consciously or unconsciously. You would never respond to subliminal advertising and you would never respond to any individual working on you with their mind.

All mental power is not a conscious evil, but that doesn't make it less harmful. For instance, you only have to use the word, *Hollywood,* to instantly think of a den of iniquity. Why? Because of what has been taking place there for twenty-five or thirty years. If you stop to think, you will ask yourself, "Are all these people who come into the movies or into the theatrical world evil, are they all immoral, are they all bad? Does it only attract bad people?" And the answer is no. That industry doesn't attract any more bad people than our work does, or any work—a dry goods store or any other activity. No. But since it caters as it does to the flesh, and as it arouses thoughts of sensuality and lust in the minds of audiences throughout the world, all directed at those individuals portrayed on the screen, never doubt for a minute that they feel that and respond to it. Then the first thing you know, they begin to act it out, not because they're bad, but because the mental activity is arousing in them that particular response.

In the same way, great stars like Lionel Barrymore, John Barrymore, and several others whom I know, have said they give their best performances if they have an audience interested in the play and in good acting. On the other hand, they give consistently poor performances when the audience's level of appreciation for the art, or culture, is not at that level, where people are attending merely to see a star. This is no different than your walking into an office where somebody is in a bad mood or angry, coming away feeling depressed; or going into the office of a person in good spirits, full of cheer, and coming away feeling cheerful. It is a fact that on the human level of life we are subject to the mental atmosphere about us. That is why fear in a burning theater creates panic. People are subject to the mental stress and strain around them, and they respond to it.

That is why on sinking ships you are apt to find more heroism and bravery, because in times of danger there are those who seem to respond to heights beyond themselves and lift others with them.

In the human picture then, a mental atmosphere is an important thing. Maintaining yourself in a mental state of purity lets the person "out here" feel clean. Maintaining yourself in a sense of mental impurity makes the person out here feel unclean, restless, and uncomfortable. In the same way, maintaining integrity in life makes the people out here trust you. Living in an atmosphere of dishonesty and deceit, you breed distrust out here. That is all mental. That is all mental action and reaction. And, as I have said, much of it is unconscious. People do not realize the extent to which their mental state affects others.

This is all on the mental plane. One of the functions of the Infinite Way is to teach you how to live so as to be unaffected by the mental atmosphere around you, by mental pressures, by subliminal suggestions of infection, contagion, danger, war, rumors of war, fear of bombs, that are floating through the air all the time. How to live above that? This is one of our major points. It comes under the heading of, "The man of earth and the man of Christ—the man who has his being in Christ."

And we're going to continue with that right after we've had a rest.

~ 16 ~

KNOW THE TRUTH

I'm going to digress for a moment to answer a very important question that came up during our break. In my former metaphysical training, we were told not to specifically treat anyone unless he asked for it, because it hurried him along too fast spiritually, like pulling a child by the arm. There were other reasons, too. But this would be absolutely true if you were working in the mental realm. In other words, you have no more right to enter a person's mental household uninvited than you have to enter his home. Each person should be permitted the integrity of his own mind, his own body, his own home, his own supply, without anyone intruding uninvited.

If a person were ill—and for all you know he might be depending upon *materia medica*—you would have absolutely no right to try to heal him by your means, any more than if you were ill and relying on spiritual means, would you want somebody to stuff medicine into your mouth or take advantage of your being unconscious to otherwise medicate you. You wouldn't want that because you have determined your way of life, even to the extent that you would rather pass from this scene under your own principles of health rather than to remain here under medication or by surgery. I've known many cases like that.

To give a person treatment through mental practice means you are entering the household of his mind and interfering with his mental processes, probably even disturbing him. You have no right to do that. If you are working from the mental standpoint of giving treatment to people, don't do it unless you are asked to. It is not your right. And as long as you are following the teaching of the Infinite Way, you will never give anyone a treatment, not only uninvited, but not even if you are invited to, because we do not give treatment to anyone. Never, under any circumstance, do we give treatment to anyone, even if they should ask for it. Why? That is not the procedure of the Infinite Way healing principles. The message of the Infinite Way teaches this: If I am a practitioner, I must know the truth. If I do not know the truth, I have no right to be a practitioner. Now, if I know the truth, it makes no difference where I am or what the circumstances are. The moment I witness a lie, I correct it within myself. If I see a person who is ill, I don't give him a treatment, not even if he is my patient. I don't give treatments. When my attention is called to an illness, I turn within myself for realization of the truth. And what is the truth? God constitutes individual being. God is your being. Your soul, your mind, and even your body is the temple of God. I'm not saying this to you; I'm not giving you a treatment; I'm repeating this to myself. This is the truth I am knowing, but it isn't only the truth about you, it's a universal truth. The only reason I'm even reminding myself of it is that there's an appearance to the contrary, and I correct that within myself just as if I saw a big sign saying two times two are five. I would inwardly say, "No, it's four." I don't give a treatment to the five or to the sign. I correct the appearance within myself.

Whether you ask for help or don't ask for help, it makes no difference to me. If I witness the discord or inharmony, my inner reaction is that God constitutes individual being; therefore all being is perfect, spiritual, and intact. This appearance that faces me is the carnal mind, which isn't mind and has no law, no cause, no effect, no avenue of operation, no channel of expression. And then I'm through.

Actually, at this stage in my work, I don't go that far because it's no longer necessary. I have been doing this for thirty years so that now when I behold an appearance of error, to me it is just evidence of malpractice. That's all it is. It's just a mental imposition touching my thought, I don't accept it, and that's the end of it in ordinary cases. But if there is no response–and I'm speaking now of those who appeal to me for help–if that does not result in healing and they come back again for help, then I may have to sit down, remind myself of this, get quiet and wait for that "click," the inner assurance that God is on the field. I'm not suggesting this to you as a mode of treatment, because you won't succeed with it until you're at the stage when it's absolutely apparent to you that the discords that touch you aren't really conditions or people; they are just this universal malpractice. Whether or not you are called upon for help, your procedure must be to remind yourself that God constitutes individual being and that God is eternal, immortal, and perfect, even as individual being. Then remember: Any phase or facet of discord, any appearance that touches you, is nothing more or less than a picture sent out by the carnal mind. And you know what the carnal mind is. It isn't really a mind, it's a belief in two powers. There is no carnal mind operating in any individual who does not have a belief in two powers. All there is to the evils of this world is the belief in two powers. That's what sent Adam and Eve out of Eden accepting a belief in the powers of good and evil. And there aren't such powers. There's only good.

Because of this human existence, we are eternally being faced with sin, disease, death, lack, limitation, wars, and man's inhumanity to man. But actually these are not evil conditions; they have no basis in reality. These are merely mental impositions that strike your thought and if you battle them or fight them, you lose, because in resisting you establish evil in your consciousness. That is why, if you struggle to overcome evil with our treatments, you can't win your case. Our treatments are based on, "resist not evil . . . thou couldest have no power over me unless it came from the Father . . . put up thy sword." We do not fight error, nor do we use truth to overcome error, nor do we use God to heal disease. Our entire recognition is that so far as God is concerned, his universe is perfect, eternal, harmonious, and we are being confronted with seeing this perfect universe through a glass darkly, instead of face to face. We are not dealing with powers to be overcome. We are dealing only with a negative appearance that has to be recognized as such and nothingized in that way. That is why I said I can only teach this to you after you have sufficient background in the writings to realize that this is absolute nonsense to the human mind uninstructed in our message. And no one knows it better than I do.

I well remember my very first healing experience. We had just received a cable from England that my father was dying. He'd had surgery and had been in a hospital for seventy-seven days when a cable came:

"Send for the body." I immediately arranged for my mother to go over and get his body. That evening I had an appointment with a friend for dinner and called at her home. She introduced me to her father who was visiting, and while sitting there for a few moments I mentioned that I'd put my mother on the steamer to England that afternoon to bring back my father's body. This man enquired, "Is your father dead?"

I said, "No, but he must be dying, or he may be dead by now." And I told him about the cable.

"Oh, no," he said. "You're a very young man and your father must be young. He doesn't have to die."

That was strange language to me. "He doesn't have to die? That's not what the doctors say. He's been in the hospital seventy-seven days."

"Well," he asked, "have you never heard of prayer and prayer healing?"

"No," I had to answer, "the only prayer I know is 'Now I lay me down to sleep.'"

So, he looked at me, and it was a very strange thing. Then I said, "Oh, do you mean Christian Science?"

"Yes."

"Oh, mind over matter. I've read about that in the paper. You don't really think that would help anybody, do you?"

He said, "Well, I'm a Christian Science practitioner. I do believe it."

Now, you know how that must have struck me, coming right out of the blue. But I said, "Well, if you can help him, it would be marvelous if he could come home."

When my mother landed in England, my father was up and dressed and ready to come home, and for

twenty-five years my father never knew a day of illness.
Never. If he had a cold or a slight fever or nausea, he
would just pick up the book, *Science and Health*[1], and read
a few pages, and he was healed.

Of course that practitioner didn't try to explain the
principles, or probably I wouldn't have asked him to
help my father. I thought he was just going to pray to
God, and if he was holy enough maybe God would
answer him. So I know how foolish this must all sound
to a person who hasn't a background in the Infinite Way
writings. Not even those who have New Thought or
Christian Science can completely understand what I say
unless they have a background in the Infinite Way,
because this principle is neither mind over matter, nor
is it the power of God to heal disease, nor is it the power
of truth over error. It is none of those things. This is a
direct revelation that was somehow unfolded within me
that "ye need not fight." There is no power in this devil,
this impersonal source of discord. Fighting it is what
perpetuates it.

That was the revelation given me, just as the nature of
God has been revealed to me in a different way than you
would ever find in any other writings on earth: a God
that you do not have to pray to, and a God that wouldn't
answer your prayers if you did pray; a God who is
always being God and doesn't have to be reminded of it
by man; a God who is the infinite intelligence of this
universe and whom man cannot instruct or influence.
Therefore, this whole teaching is not a turning to God

---

[1] *Science and Health*, Mary Baker Eddy; first published in 1875 is the
key source for Christian Science thought and healing principles.
Reprint edition, 1994, Christian Science Publishing Society.

that God should do something. It is a turning to God to be in God-consciousness, where nothing needs to be done. That is how this message differs from any of the religious teachings on the face of the earth.

Now if you ask me, "Do we pray?" Of course we do. My books are full of it. Prayer is our major mode of life. Prayer is something I am personally doing almost all of my waking hours and many of my sleeping hours, because I know how to live inside of me and maintain a contact of prayer. But it is a mode of prayer known only to the mystics.

I will tell you my idea of prayer as expressed by Dr. Alexis Carrel in his book, *Man the Unknown*[2]: "Prayer should be understood, not as a mere mechanical recitation of formulas, but as a mystical elevation, an absorption of consciousness in the contemplation of a principle, both permeating and transcending our world. Such a psychological state is not intellectual. It is incomprehensible to philosophers and scientists, and inaccessible to them, but the simple seem to feel God as easily as the heat of the sun or the kindness of a friend. The prayer which is followed by organic effect is of a special nature. First, it is entirely disinterested."—See what I said earlier about not using prayer or God for selfish, personal, or destructive things?—"Man offers himself to God. He stands before him like the canvas before the painter or the marble before the sculptor. At the same time, he asks for his grace, exposes his needs and those of his brothers in suffering. Generally the patient who is cured is not

---

[2] *Man the Unknown*, Alexis Carrel, M.D. (first published New York, Harper & Bros, 1935. Reprint, Hamilton, 1961).

praying for himself but for another. Such a type of prayer demands complete renunciation, that is, a higher form of asceticism. The modest, the ignorant, and the poor are more capable of this self-denial than the rich and the intellectual. When it possesses such characteristics, prayer may set in motion a strange phenomenon, the miracle." That is Dr. Carrel.

Now, let me read to you from the diary of Sanford Dole, the former pineapple king of Hawaii, who, few realized, was a deeply spiritual man. He is writing on the subject of prayer: "Doubtless, a great deal of doctrinal teaching of the time is a hindrance rather than a help to the spiritual life. It does not seem to me that anyone can talk to me dogmatically about God with any benefit. It is not an intellectual acquirement to know God, but it comes to us with great and inspiring force when we are in line with the great purpose and movement of the universe, which is God's activity and which we may study, and so in some measure know God. It is perhaps not easy to believe that the events which we regard as the evils of life are in the line of universal purpose. I suppose that sin, scientifically considered, is resistance to the movement of this universal purpose or neglect to join in it. It is apropos of these thoughts to refer to a text of the Bible which shows the way of progress: 'He that doeth my will shall know the doctrine,' or words to that effect." Listen: "Prayer in its highest exercise is an opening of the gates of the soul to the divine influence. The mere asking of favors from God is tiresome and discouraging."

Prayer, as we know it in the Infinite Way, is an inner communion. It is an inner abiding in the spiritual law, or spiritual presence. It is not a seeking of something; it is not a desire for something; it is not an attempt to get something. That is not prayer. Prayer is merely that inner quietness which comes from the assurance that there is a God, and therefore as long as there is a God there can be nothing wrong in the kingdom of God. Abiding in that inner assurance, a sense of peace envelops us, and that sense of peace dispels these pictures of sense.

I said earlier, we come to that state of prayer by the right mental activity. That mental activity is consciously knowing the truth. Suppose that you know there are people using the human mind both for good and evil. You also know that even those who aren't using it consciously for evil, but merely by the nature of their sensuality, or lust, or greed, are sending out subliminal activities which are harmful. Now that you know this, it is your first responsibility in the message of the Infinite Way to protect yourself. For that reason, in the *July Letter*, I asked our students to make a careful and prolonged study of Chapter 3 of the *1955 Infinite Way Letters,*[3] which is on protective work. This kind of work is not to protect yourself from evil, for you will only get into the mess of having twice as much evil, but is to protect yourself in the realization that God-mind is the only power, and that this mind of man, this mesmeric mind, mortal mind, carnal mind, is not power.

The protective work usually done in metaphysics is often harmful and dangerous, because the moment you acknowledge an evil from which to be protected, you

---

[3] *The Infinite Way Letters, 1955 to 1959*, Combined Edition, Joel S. Goldsmith (Essex, England: Fowler & Co., 1984): 39.

have made yourself the center of that evil. You achieve your protection only to the degree that you realize the world-concept of evil—the temporal powers of this world, the fleshly mind or the arm of flesh—cannot be power if the mind of God is the only power. And not one of our students has any right to start their day without a conscious realization of the fact that the mind of God is the mind of man and is the only mind, the only power, and that which is called devil, satan, mortal mind or carnal mind, is not a power opposed to God—it is just not a power. Therefore, you need not fight it, you need not rise above it, you need not protect yourself from it. You need only consciously remember it is the arm of flesh, nothingness, and then rest in that word.

When you have done that, you are completely at ease in the realization that there are no evil powers, and such as are humanly experienced are only experienced because you have given them power. Now you understand their nothingness. Now you can relax and commune within, not for any reason—not for healing, not for protection—for no reason at all. Your only reason might be the same reason for which you are in this room. And why are you in this room now? Answer that to your own satisfaction. Why? Because in this room you know there is spiritual integrity, there is truth, there is the companionship of students who are devoting time, money, and effort to living in God, not for selfish purposes, not for self-aggrandizement, not for wealth. You know that everyone in this room is giving of time, effort, and money for only one purpose: to know more about God. In this room you are safe, you are secure, and to some extent you are in the very presence of God itself and you know it. All you want is to be in a holy atmosphere.

That is the reason to go to God: only to be in the household of God, in the consciousness of God, in the atmosphere of God. When you accomplish it, you will be able to say afterward, "In his presence is fullness of joy. In his presence is fulfillment. 'Where the spirit of the Lord is, there is liberty.'" But it won't be a quotation. It will be an experience which you have had, just as all of these students who have come from so many distant places can say to you that they have been in these classes before and have found peace and harmony and love, and to some extent, health or supply. And that is why they are back again. Only to be in this atmosphere.

You, too, will find that when you submit yourself to God for no other purpose than a few minutes of resting in God, you will find that in attaining the presence of God, you have also attained liberty, freedom, justice, health, harmony, wholeness, peace, guidance, direction—all of these things that enabled Paul to say, "I live, yet not I, Christ liveth my life." Once you have attained the presence of God, you will not have to take conscious thought for "what ye shall eat or what ye shall drink or wherewithal ye shall be clothed." You will always find that this invisible presence has gone before you and prepared a way for you. You prove, "He that is within me is greater than he that is in the world . . . He performeth that which is given me to do." But remember, these are only quotations until that He has become a real experience.

It is for this reason that our first step is consciously knowing the truth. I ask our students to go through the Infinite Way writings over and over until they know the nature of God, know it so thoroughly that they'll never again turn to God for anything, they'll never ask God for anything, they won't expect God to step out of its orbit.

Then, our second step is to know the nature of error, and to know it so thoroughly that you'll never fight it again, you'll never argue against it, you'll never war with it, and regardless of what form it assumes, you will instantly recognize it as only an activity of the carnal mind. The clearest way to understand this is to understand that the ancients ascribed all evil to the devil. The devil was the source of all evil, and the devil acted as a tempter. Try to see it in that light, that there is an impersonal source of this evil and this impersonal source is the universal belief in good and evil. It acts as an impersonal tempter, saying to you, "Believe in health and sickness, believe in accident and harmony, believe in life and death, believe in abundance and lack, believe in good and evil." Your only answer has to be, "No, no, now I know the First Commandment is truth: There is no other God but one; there is no other law but the law of God, which is the law of life eternal."

Once you understand that, you can keep away from the old Hebrew concept of a God that rewards and punishes. That is the God that calls you home to himself some day and is responsible for youngsters who pass on. Once you understand there is no such God, that God cannot act detrimentally to its own experience, that God cannot be destructive to its own creation, that God is the infinite eternal life of all being and the law unto all being, then you'll know that spiritual law governs everything there is and brings it into harmony. But this understanding comes only when you have attained obedience to the First Commandment, acknowledging no other power, no other law, no other presence, no other being, in spite of the fact that you are always going to be tempted by the devil to see sickness, sin, death, bad politics, man's inhumanity to man, and all the rest of these evils. The way you respond to these temptations tells you whether you are going to fall for the temptation or pass right by untouched.

In the message of the Infinite Way we do not fight error and we do not call upon truth or God to overcome evil. We abide as we would in the Twenty-third Psalm: "The Lord is my shepherd," and I shall not want; the Lord is my shepherd and that's all there is to it. There's no more fight, and even if I walk through the valley of the shadow of death, I will fear no evil, for I know I can't die. It is an impossibility to die. Our passing from this scene will be a progressive experience into higher states of consciousness.

Now, do you see why it isn't necessary to give a treatment to anyone? It isn't necessary to correct them or improve them? It isn't necessary to tell them to be better or more loving or more gentle or more forgiving? It isn't necessary. As you consciously know the truth, the truth that you know becomes the law unto those within range of your consciousness. That is why you will find animal life is the most responsive to this work. Dogs and cats and birds will virtually respond to this instantaneously. There is no resistance in them at all. Next, plant life responds beautifully. And then children. But adults are tough. They've already learned to fear both God and devil; they've already learned about two powers, and they have to be reborn. They really have to be reborn before they can be childlike again, until they can come into absolute realization of why Jesus Christ disposed of nine of the ten commandments, outmoded them, and said there are only two commandments—and out of the ten, he used only one: "Thou shalt love the Lord thy

God with all thy heart, with all thy soul, with all thy mind." Thou shalt love God. You can't love God without trusting God. You can't trust God without a firm realization of God as the one and only power. But when you have that, you are loving God supremely.

Then Jesus dug up an old Hebrew commandment which wasn't included in the Ten Commandments: "Love thy neighbor as thyself." Well, once you have acknowledged God as the only power, you can't give power to evil; therefore you're compelled to love your neighbor as yourself because you can't introduce any evil into your relationship with your neighbor—not after you have acknowledged God as the only power.

If you understand the nature of God you can love God supremely, and your love must be imbued with confidence, trust, assurance, understanding. Then of course it's an easy thing to love your neighbor, because all you have to do to love your neighbor is know the truth, which is the truth about yourself. This is the truth about your neighbor. This is loving your neighbor. And realize that your neighbor is the child of God, whether or not he's appearing as friend or enemy. That's the difficult part. You have to follow through with Jesus Christ when he says, "It profiteth you nothing to pray for your friends." He's giving you a terrific statement. When he says that to become the children of God you have to pray for your enemies, he means just that one thing: that your prayers, which are not of course that your enemies prosper in their wrong doing but are the realization of God as the very heart and soul and mind of the individual now appearing to you as an enemy and who later becomes your friend.

So, we will not treat anybody whether they ask for it or they don't ask for it, but we will always consciously know the truth. And eventually we will pray, as Paul said, "without ceasing." We will remain in prayer even when we are in conversation. Even when we are about the activity of business, there will be a center of consciousness within us, a little area, that is always reserved for being in prayer regardless of what the rest of us are doing. It makes no difference, we can suffer it to be so now. We can do all of the things of this world, but we can always have one area in consciousness where, regardless of appearances, we are smiling in the realization that God constitutes individual being; God is the substance of this universe; God is the only law of this universe, a spiritual law of good. And we can be doing that regardless of what activity the mind and body are going through.

Question: *You mentioned no one has ever died. Please explain.*

Answer: To die means to become extinct. And so what I have said is that nobody ever becomes extinct. We pass from experience to experience, but we are always conscious and actively doing it. In this, too, I speak to you from experience. Many times I have witnessed those who have passed from sight, and in every case an identical experience took place: the individual, for a short while, was suspended above his or her body. The body remained where it was, but they were suspended above it. This, too, I know through experience, that the individual has a choice of going on or returning. And when the occasion requires it, such as a mother with a family that she cannot feel right about leaving, she will return; and sometimes that's called a miraculous healing. She chose to return. Sometimes a father with family responsibilities cannot leave his family because he feels the horror of leaving them unprotected, unsupplied, and he returns to fulfill that function. But mostly people will not return because they do not reach that point of transition until they are ready for it and desire it. That is the reason they do not return. They do not even experience it until they, themselves, are ready for it—except in cases of violence, accidents, and injuries of that kind.

We never die. If I walk through the valley of the shadow of death *I* will be there. And if I leave this plane of consciousness, *I* will be leaving it, and *I* will be conscious of it. I will never be other than *I*, nor will I ever be unaware of my *I*-ness, of my identity as selfhood. This *I* is an indestructible oneness with God, that was co-existent with God in the beginning and will be with God until the end. Therefore, even those who leave the human plane continue an afterlife which is just as human as this one until they evolve. We have the choice, we who are here, to continue to evolve spiritually so that when we leave this plane we will not live as humans but will live as divine beings. Those who do not mature spiritually still continue to live mentally and even physically, yet they have the same opportunity as we have and have always had: Any day in the week, any month in the year, everyone on earth is given the opportunity to turn to spiritual living. They may not be aware of it, but the opportunity is there, just as it was for us when we accepted it.

Therefore, as we leave this plane, we find ourselves still living and in some measure further advanced for having left here. But never forget that you cannot get away from yourself. That is why so many people go on vacation, go away for a rest, take a trip around the world, and do not benefit from it. They had to take themselves along, and it was with themselves that they were having the trouble. Just putting ourselves in another place is no cure. We witness that here in Hawaii. I'm sure all of our visitors know what a beautiful place this is: the harmony, the joy, the beauty, the atmosphere, the love and aloha. You are all aware of the beauty around you. So it may surprise you if I tell you that there is just as much unhappiness here, just as much poverty, just as much sin, just as much disease, as anywhere else. And the reason is that people bring it with them. It is themselves. There are loads of people who find no beauty in Hawaii, who are here merely because they have to be. It isn't the place that makes any difference. It's the state of consciousness you bring to the place.

So when you leave this earth plane, you will find the next plane to be what you bring to it. Don't think for a minute that you'll ever experience extinction or unconsciousness, for there is no such thing. God, infinite life, would become death, consciousness become unconsciousness—there is no such thing. Do we ever meet our loved ones again? We do if we want to and if they want us to. It is the same life there as here. We have relatives right here whom we never meet, and sometimes don't want to. But if I have anyone in my heart and in my soul here, I can assure you they're going to be right with me on my travels whether I'm on the road or whether I pass to another existence. I will never let them get out of my heart and soul and mind. Why should I if I love them? And if they love me, then there is a mutuality which means that we can never be separated. So whether it is here or hereafter, we will be together.

Question: *Will you please say something about parenthood?*

Answer: This is a very difficult subject for me. I have been a parent only by proxy and I don't have the feelings that most parents do for children. I don't know that kind of a sensation, so I can't speak about it. I love children and they love me, but it has nothing to do with that emotion of love that is ordinarily felt by parents for their children or children for their parents. It is of a different nature.

A child, to me, is very much like a bud, a blossom. It is new and fresh and has infinite potentialities, and it can be molded. Not molded to my will. Too often it is molded to the will of its parents, and sometimes unfortunately so. But it can be spiritually molded. I don't know whether parents can do that. Some can because I've seen it done, but how many can I don't know, because much of what I see of parenthood is just animal emotion. And that doesn't permit the parent to be objective or to see their child spiritually.

To see a child spiritually means to realize your child is not your child, but the child of God, another of the infinite forms and varieties of God-being sent to earth with all the potentialities of God-being. If parents can see their child that way, it helps free the child from human limitations. And as I say, never having been a parent I don't know how difficult that might be. But I have known some parents who could. Some few. To be able to love a child that way is to understand that its nature came forth from God, that it was sent to this plane of consciousness, not to be anybody's child, but to be an instrument for good on earth, just as much an instrument as was Jesus Christ, or Moses, or Buddha. Every child is that potentiality. Now to understand that a child is not limited mentally by its parents, grandparents, or great-grandparents since it is the offspring of God and its mind is of God and its source of intelligence and wisdom is God, is to free that child from the limitations of family relationships.

In the same way, to be able to raise a child without instilling fear—fear of crossing the street, fear of talking to a stranger, fear of swimming, fear of doing this or that—but rather with spiritual understanding to release the child into God, is to raise parenthood to quite a different level than normal human parenthood. Human parenthood is almost entirely selfish, and we have to rise far above that in order to be able to see that we are the caretakers of children, we are their providers until such time as they can take over that responsibility. We are their guides, and to be able to do that spiritually means to do it through inner communion with God. It doesn't mean to be a dominating person, dictating to them what they should or should not do out of our human knowledge. It means, rather, to raise them with a minimum amount of talk and conversation and a maximum amount of holding them in that inner communion with the spirit, permitting them to be God-governed instead of man-dominated.

Now, I can't speak about human parenthood because it is presented to the world through so many different methods that I feel the same way about it as I do about world peace. I don't believe it will ever be accomplished humanly. It can't be. It will have to come through spiritual means. I don't believe we are going to find a way of raising children to bring them forth into their rightful heritage through our human nature. For us in this work, the only way we have of bringing up children, the only way we have of giving them their freedom is to give them the spirit of God, to give them prayer, to give them communion, to hold them fast in that relationship, and to continually teach them the nature of these worldly evils so that in recognizing them no temptation falls into their way.

I have known children who, at the age of sixteen, when asked to go out and get some aspirin for a visitor said, "What is aspirin? I've never heard of it." They hadn't even seen an ad for it. It hadn't come into their awareness. They had been so brought up in the spiritual life, they wouldn't even know the purpose of an aspirin or any other form of medicine. I've seen that. I've witnessed over and over again, families who have gone for fifteen, eighteen, and twenty years without knowing anything about the nature of serious illness or accident or anything of that kind, merely because the parents were holding that household in spiritual realization.

It can be done. It can be done in the same way that a practitioner can hold his or her patients, whether it's twenty patients, or fifty, or a hundred, so that they are almost immune from the world's discords. A teacher can hold an entire student body relatively free for long periods of time, more especially if those students are cooperating. Why? The higher consciousness lifts the lower consciousness to its level. "I, if I be lifted up, shall draw all men unto me." As I am lifted up in this consciousness, knowing the nature of God and the nature of error, and abiding in this God-consciousness, all, or most of those who are abiding with me, rise in some degree of demonstration to better health, to greater supply, and to better human relationships.

The only reason we are not wholly immune from the world's discords is that this universal world mesmerism is a very strong belief, and we have to live on a tremendously high level—probably higher than any of us have ever been able to live—in order to be completely immune. Our blessing is that when we do occasionally fall by the wayside, we have something with which to pick ourselves up, and others, too.

It looks like there will be more to talk about, and I thought I was all talked out! I just want a minute of summary: There wouldn't be a trace of discord in this world, of any nature, if it weren't for the impersonal mesmerism that has evolved out of the belief of good and evil. And because we are born on that level, we are receptive and responsive to that influence. Therefore, some of us become sinful, others become sick, and others become poor. There is a way of nullifying nearly all of the world's discords, most of them entirely, the rest of them in some degree, through our own conscious realization of the nature of God, the nature of the evil, and of nothingizing this whole hypnotic mind, or mortal mind, or carnal mind—and realizing that since it is not of God's creating, since it is not endowed by God, it has no law of God to maintain it or sustain it.

Living in that consciousness will not only free us, but will so completely put us at peace that we can attain inner communion with God. There is nothing separating anyone from this inner communion with God except the turmoil of the mind. The mind won't let us rest long enough to get quiet inside. It is always in a turmoil about something. But understanding, contemplating the nature of God enables us to become quiet. The ability to have that faith in God enables us to say, "The Lord is my shepherd I shall not want," and drop it there. And then the realization, "I know the world is full of appearances—a thousand are falling at my side and ten thousand at the other side—but I'm realizing that none of these evils is power, they are the emanation of the fleshly mind, the arm of flesh, nothingness," brings such peace that we can settle down inside and enjoy a communion with God.

When this takes place repeatedly, then comes this—I call it more or less permanent—state of consciousness in which you are never entirely outside the atmosphere of God. And when on some occasions you are, it is only in a slight degree. Never, never after the experience are you entirely separated from God, even for a moment. There come momentary disturbances, and it would seem in those moments that you are separated from God, but you're not very far away, not very far away.

Thank you, thank you. Until tomorrow night. . . .

~ 17 ~

SPIRITUAL SUPPLY AND HEALING: AWAKENING TO THE MYSTICAL EXPERIENCE OF ONENESS

The Infinite Way is not organized, has no corporate entity and has no memberships, therefore nobody belongs to the Infinite Way. This is the result of spiritual guidance which I follow. The object of it is to enable me to present to the world the principles which constitute the Infinite Way and to permit those who respond to accept them, follow them if they like, and those who do not, to turn from them, or else follow them in whatever measure is possible. In other words, I have no ties to our students, no strings, and they are under no obligation to me or to anybody. This has made it possible for me to be invited into Unity churches, New Thought churches, even Protestant churches, and for the writings, starting with *The Art of Meditation*[1] and *Practicing the Presence*,[2] to be accepted in Protestant churches of all denominations in the United States and Canada. This enables them to embody any of the principles, any of the teachings, in

---

[1] *The Art of Meditation*, © 1956 by Joel S. Goldsmith (New York: Harper & Row, paperback edition, 1990).

[2] *Practicing the Presence*, © 1958 by Joel S. Goldsmith (reprinted 1997 by Acropolis Books, Inc., Lakewood, CO).

their individual lives, whether they're ministers or whether they're laymen, and yet remain on the path which for the present may be their religious path.

The principles that are embodied in these writings are not mine. I did not make them up; I did not dream them up. They came to me in consciousness, and therefore they are not mine. They should be made available to anyone, anywhere, at any time, who can accept them, receive them, and respond to them. And that's the way it is. By having no organization, no memberships, no obligations, those who are led to these writings may embody them to whatever degree they wish and still maintain their freedom. In this way you will eventually find what we are already beginning to witness: that these very principles are being accepted as truth in many religious fields and ultimately will become embodied in the religions of the world. And I feel that's far better than putting a barrier around the message and saying it belongs to me, and wanting either cash or credit for it. I don't. I am happy to be an instrument through which this has happened, and it brings far more joy than any glory or money could.

Because of this situation, because there are no strings on any students, there are Infinite Way students of many, many different degrees. There are those who read the books and even ask for help, and to them it is just another form of teaching that is desirable, helpful, or pleasant. There are some who read these writings, but also read everything else available in metaphysical, spiritual, or religious literature. There are those who come to classes and yet next week will be in another class down the street, and a month from now will be in still another class in the next town. That's their right, that's their freedom, and I find no fault with this because no one should ever stop their search for truth until they have found the message which is for them. Throughout my years of study, I have accepted that freedom for myself, and I rejoice in the fact that we do live in a country where everyone may follow that and no one has the right to dictate what you shall read or what your religious convictions should be or how many times you may change them.

And so it is wonderful that students may go from teacher to teacher, or from book to book, or teaching to teaching, until they find the one that is for them, the one they have been seeking, and the one they wish to see accepted throughout the world. We do have students who realize the Infinite Way is their way of life. They have been through the mill of other teachings, they have been through the search, they have found what they are seeking, and in many different ways they become more closely identified with us in this activity. It is to these students we must look for a bond, oneness, togetherness, so that this message may go forward and fulfill its destiny in the world.

Some who are at that stage become active in healing work, with tape recording work, or support this work in other directions. Each of course must fulfill himself or herself at his or her own level. But the point I wish to make is this: Those who have come to the recognition that this is their way are the ones who form the body of the Infinite Way and are helping us in every stage of this work. Therefore, as any of you come to that place in your own realization or conviction that this is your way, don't hesitate to let us know about it. Don't hesitate to let us know what advancing steps you're prepared for because the activity that is available to us and awaiting us is infinite. And as you know, at this time we haven't nearly the workers we need.

Some years ago I was invited to be interviewed on a television program in Chicago. It was in the midst of a class and I think we all took the matter very lightly, as if this were going to be a pleasant experience. But it turned out to be something quite different. The station was owned by the Chicago Tribune, and was, I think, the largest station in Chicago. After the broadcast something happened that had never happened in the history of that television station. Every telephone line was busy with incoming calls. Not a line was left open. As fast as calls were completed, more calls came in until they had received more calls as a result of that one broadcast than they had from any program that had ever gone on the air.

One of the results was the sale of more copies of *The Infinite Way* than our publisher had printed. But the second result was a flood of letters from people wanting to be healed. That was the last Infinite Way television appearance because we didn't have enough practitioners to take responsibility for that amount of healing work. It isn't merely a matter of that experience in Chicago. When an Infinite Way activity starts, it spreads rapidly. We're in an age today when if you think something in Hawaii, an hour from now they know about it in New York. If something is in demand in New York today, you can be assured it's going to be in demand here tomorrow. That means there must be thousands of students—not tens or dozens—thousands ready to respond to these calls in many different ways. Naturally, it can only be those students who have gone far enough in the

Infinite Way to know this is the message for them and wish to dedicate themselves, their time, their efforts, or their money to this activity. Then we know where we are in this expanding activity and the degree of their interest. We know to whom we can turn and what kind of help we can receive. We have no other way of knowing because we don't ask questions. These principles are turned loose and we don't ask anyone to what degree they have accepted them or to what degree they are Infinite Way students–even though we do hear many times of how little they have actually received and responded to the message.

Wherever you are in consciousness and wherever you live in this world, please remember always that your bond to the Infinite Way is a voluntary one. It is one purely of love, cooperation, service, and at no time is anyone bound to anything of a physical or material nature because with us this bond is purely spiritual.

Question: *What should the proper attitude of the Infinite Way student be when faced with economic hardships or pressing bills?*

Answer: You understand, of course, there cannot be just one answer to that question. It depends on the state or stage of consciousness students find themselves in, how long they have been students of the Infinite Way, to what degree they understand the principles, how far along they are in absolutely depending on spiritual principles alone, and what their own attitude is by now on this subject.

Actually, those who have read enough of the Infinite Way message to grasp its principles would know that economic lack and economic abundance are merely opposite ends of the same stick, and that both of these have to be overcome. They would know that economic abundance is no more stable or guaranteed or permanent than is economic lack; and as a student of the Infinite Way, whether or not they are momentarily experiencing lack or momentarily experiencing abundance, both require the same demonstration: a transition from the material sense of supply to the spiritual sense of supply.

The Infinite Way is not a message that turns economic lack into economic abundance. Actually, its purpose isn't even to turn physical disease into physical health. The results seem to work out that way, but our work is to surrender the physical, the material sense of existence, for the realization and demonstration of the spiritual life. Therefore, any problem that comes to an Infinite Way student is not a problem to be overcome. It is an opportunity to work through that particular facet of material life, or the material sense of life, to the spiritual. I have been through the experience of being faced with lack and limitation, and my attitude was—and it's going to stay this way—that I will not attempt a material solution until I work out of it spiritually, until I attain the secret of spiritual supply.

In my very earliest days I had abundance, plenty of it. From the time I was sixteen-and-a-half, I was traveling the United States and Europe, enjoying the best. But that was no guarantee of supply. And then of course I lived to experience the very opposite of that in lack and limitation. At that time it would not have been too difficult to place myself in a business activity that would have restored at least a measure of that abundance. But

I would have been dissatisfied because at no time in my life has money, abundance, or wealth been the object of life. It's not that I don't enjoy it, but that is not the object of my life. The object of my life is to find the secret of life, the secret of the laws behind this life, the secret of what makes this world go 'round harmoniously, because there must be a law of abundance for us just as there is for trees, or grass fields, or seas full of fish, or skies full of birds. It cannot be that God made cattle on a thousand hills, and billions of stars, and billions of fruit trees with hundreds of billions of fruit, and gold in the ground, and all the gems, and yet meant for us to lack. Oh, no! Our lack comes from ignorance of the law. Our lack comes from failure to understand God's law of abundance, or how to become one with God so that we can enjoy the promise, "Son, thou art ever with me and all that I have is thine." Why would we have such a statement in scripture if it weren't true? Why would the Master have tried to teach us supply by multiplying loaves and fishes to prove abundance without limit, always with baskets full left over? Why, if it is not meant for us eventually, and if eventually, why not now come into that awareness of life which is lived by the grace of God?

Therefore, my attitude at that time was to let any problem go on as long as it wanted, until I met it through understanding the spiritual law of supply, and not only understanding the law but demonstrating it. And I did. I did. I stuck with it, even to the point of having no car fare at times and walking seven miles twice a day to get to my office. I wasn't ashamed of it and I didn't hide it, and I didn't feel it was a lack of demonstration or a disgrace. I feel, as I felt then, this couldn't happen if I knew the law of God. And if I don't know the law of God, there isn't any amount of money that's going to make me happy or satisfied, because the abundance may be just as fleeting as when I experienced it before. Actually, I received my answer on the last one of those days in which I found myself without car fare, walking those seven miles. It was on that walk that the revelation finally came.

These revelations probably come to different students in different ways. I can't limit God by saying there is only one solution to the question of abundance, or that there is only one truth that has to be known. I only know the experience that took place with me. I was pondering this very question and asking myself, "How can this be? How can this be? There is an answer. There is an answer." And something within told me that I didn't know God. Well, that was the answer! "To know him aright is life eternal. It must be eternal. It must be infinite." But I thought I knew all about God. I thought I knew that God was mind, and God was life, and God was love, and God was substance, and God was spirit, and God was principle. "God is all those wonderful things that the Bible and all the metaphysical writings say God is, so how can you say I don't know what God is?" You must remember I was talking to myself. We call that contemplative meditation. Then I thought, "Yes, yes, that's right. How do I know that God is mind? I've only read it in a book. How do I know that God is law, or life, or love? I've only read it in a book. Actually, I have no direct knowledge of that truth. None whatsoever. How, then, can I find out what God is if I am not to accept what someone says in a book?"

As with all learning in life, each one of us has to find answers for ourselves. "So I must find out, what is God?

What is God?" Again I thought, "Mind. No. Mind–that's a word up here. That can't be God. Life is another word up here. That can't be God. It's a word. Love, truth, all of these synonyms are words so they can't be God. Those are just words in my mind or words in a book. You can't find God in anyone's mind or in anyone's book. Now what is God?" And the answer didn't come. Then the thought came, "'Know thyself, O man.' Hmm–that may be the beginning of it. Know thyself." But then I thought, "What is man? What is man?" Well, there again, if you just want quotations from a book, I can give you a lot of them. But I wasn't interested then in what any book said. I wanted to know, "What is man?" That shouldn't be too difficult because I am man, so I should know what I am.

At that moment I became conscious of my feet, one foot stepping out after the other. Then I stopped, and I looked down at my feet and realized, "Well that isn't man because that's not me. Those feet are mine but they're not me. There must be a me separate and apart from those feet because those feet belong to me." Then I went up to my knees, and I went up to my waist, and I went up to my chest, and I went all the way up to my hair, and actually I couldn't find myself! I wasn't there in any part of my body. All I could find was my body. Sure, feet and knees and stomach and chest and neck and face and forehead and eyes and ears, and finally a big head of hair–I used to wear it very long in those days–but nowhere could I find myself. And I really went up and down that body, right from the top of my head to the bottom of my feet without once finding me. I could not find me anywhere in my body, and that puzzled me. I said, "Now we're up against it. I can't find myself. Where am I? What am I? Who am I?"

Then the word *I* registered. "That's the secret! I am *I;* and I am not in these feet. I am not in this body. I am *I.* I can't be encompassed by a piece of flesh. I can't be encompassed by space, because the real meaning of I is God. That's why it's spelled with a capital. *I* is the spirit of me, the truth of me, my being. And that isn't in the body. That's infinite. That's eternal. That's outside the body. That must fill all space. That *I,* which is my true identity, the Master says, is one with God. 'I and my Father are one.' Oh, then that makes a different relationship. If I am *I,* not confined to a body but actually the son of God, one with God, the manifestation of God's own being, no wonder it says, 'I will never leave you nor forsake you'; and 'All that I have is thine.' No wonder. Then this *I* that I am can never demonstrate supply, because the *I* that I am must be the very embodiment of all the qualities and quantities of God, and therefore I embody supply. I am spiritual, and so supply must be spiritual. How can you think of it in terms of money, properties, investments, when it must be spiritual? If I am spirit, supply is spiritual, and it must be where I am."

This was new light in my current situation because I had quite a few human feelings toward those who owed me money but hadn't paid it and about circumstances where income was due to me. And now, all of a sudden I realized, "I–I who am one with God am looking to somebody for money, for supply, for income, when I should be the one who is able to feed five thousand and have twelve baskets full left over. I am the one through whom this infinity should be flowing, and I am acting as if I were a beggar, waiting for someone to bring me supply. And if not someone, at least God." So the position was reversed, and I realized, "Never again can

I be interested in the subject of supply except to be sure that I'm letting it flow through me and out from me. Never again dare I permit myself to think of supply as coming to me."

Only once after that did I make the mistake. Only once that I can recall did I make the mistake of thinking in terms of getting, and that was right here in Honolulu where I was living in an inexpensive hotel, and a small group of students came to me one day and said, "You ought to have a home here. Why don't you have a nice home with some ground around it so that when students want to come and visit you, or meditate, or have classes, you'd have a place to welcome them?" That was when I made my mistake. "Oh," I said, "I'm perfectly willing, and anytime the students feel they have a need for that and want to provide it, I'll be there." That night I was awakened out of sleep, and the voice spoke to me and said, "You taught them incorrectly." I sat up, "What is it? What is it? What did I do?" Then it all came back to me, and the voice very definitely said, "If the teacher is dependent on the student, then the student should be the teacher. It is the teacher's function to show forth the nature of God, the healing grace of God, the supplying grace of God. It is not the student who should be supporting a teacher. It is the teacher who should be able to feed the multitudes, whether it is food or clothing or spiritual truth. You can't be a teacher pouring out spiritual truth, demonstrating spiritual grace, and then saying, 'I am dependent on students for my material needs.'"

You may be assured the very next day I said to those same students, "I made a mistake. When the time is right, when the occasion requires it, I will have such a home." Not very long after that we found 22 Kailua Road, which we could afford and which beautifully served the Infinite Way work. Now we have Halekou, and nobody had to take up a collection to buy it. You see, my experience was brought about by the realization of my true identity. I'm not a beggar, I am heir of God, joint-heir to all the heavenly riches. I am one with my Father, and all that the Father hath is mine; and I need not take thought for what I shall eat, or what I shall drink, or wherewithal I shall be clothed. And it flows.

From its very beginning, every need of the Infinite Way has been met. Now I wouldn't exchange that year of lack and limitation for all the money our richest families possess, because not only have I had the joy of seeing the spiritual unfoldment, but I know now that wherever I am and whatever the circumstances, I need not be surprised if ravens bring me food, I need not be surprised if manna falls from the sky, I need not be surprised at whatever form of supply comes to me, because now I know that it isn't a question of being dependent on "man whose breath is in his nostrils," not even dependent on his gratitude or on his good will. It is absolute independence. It is realization of our true identity. We know we are not man whose breath is in his nostrils, that we are not beggars waiting at the gate for someone's–anyone's–favor, in any guise. We understand that God manifests itself on earth as our individual being. If "the heavens declare the glory of God and the earth showeth forth his handiwork," what about us? Why, we must be that one, that place, where God shows forth its greatest glory unto this world. We must show forth a greater glory than the stars in the sky. They're inanimate. They are not the infinite wisdom of God itself, just an offshoot. We have that mind which was also in Christ Jesus; we have that life; we have that love; we are the son, joint-heir with Christ to all the heavenly riches.

All this week our lessons have shown that none of this is true except to the degree that we are consciously aware of it, that we consciously realize and abide in this truth. That's what brings it into our experience. "A thousand shall fall at thy left and ten thousand shall fall at thy right," because they are not "abiding in the word and letting this word abide in them." Our relationship with God is oneness, and that is the truth of everyone and everything on the face of the earth, whether it be human, animal, vegetable, or mineral. We are all one with God, and there is only one life permeating our being. But until we become consciously aware of this, until we abide in this truth and let this truth abide in us and finally rest in that word, it cannot come forth into expression.

In the thirty years I have been in this work, I have had three physical claims to meet. What do you think my attitude had to be? That I must get rid of this problem, or that this is another step forward that I have to take in understanding and demonstration? It's no sin if we fall by the wayside. It's no sin if we fall into some measure of temporary relief. The sin is to become so desperate to make the demonstration that it becomes the object of our lives. It mustn't be. In the Infinite Way, health is not the object of our lives. Realization of God is our goal, and health is the added thing. Therefore, a sickness is but an opportunity to prove it, an opportunity to receive in consciousness some vital truth that may change the entire nature of our lives.

Just think. In 1921, in one of the largest hospitals in New York City, a death sentence was passed on me. I was told that I could not live longer than three months, that it was time to wind up my business because there was no help for me. Now just suppose there had been help. Just suppose some doctor could have cured me. Where would I be today? Heaven only knows! But with that verdict I had to turn to spiritual teachings, and within three months I was completely healed. And I've remained healed ever since.

I suppose by every human standard I was a tragic case at that time. Heaven forbid that I should have missed the experience. It had to be mine for all the rest of this to follow. Certainly we do know that there are people in the world for whom good health and abundant supply represent the height of happiness and peace. Of course they must have it, and get it in whatever way they can. That represents their state of consciousness. But if we are really on the spiritual path for something other than merely getting healed, then we have to face a situation like this as if God sent it to us for a blessing, because once this problem of lack is met through spiritual understanding, we'll never have it again. It can never return. It's done with. We have passed a way station, a milestone. We'll never have to backtrack over that demonstration again.

And so it is with the major problems of health. Once we have attained health through spiritual realization, we have very few physical problems for the rest of our days, especially of any great importance, unless we forget the Master's warning, "Go and sin no more lest a worse thing come upon you." If we can be tempted back into the ways of the world, then we will out-picture the ways of the world again, because our outer life is the manifestation of our state of consciousness. To the degree that we realize these spiritual principles, our outer experience becomes spiritually harmonious even though it appears to the world as a healthy body or a filled purse. It is for this reason that in this work, even when we speak of our problems, we have no right ever to actually believe they are problems, because they're not. Those are our opportunities for spiritual growth, spiritual unfoldment, spiritual demonstration, which will lift us above this claim.

Here is a note I made many months ago, but it certainly fits in right here:

"In the Infinite Way we make the transition from the man of earth, acted upon by forces, powers, and influences beyond ourselves, to the man whose being is in Christ, where the infinite invisible within, without, and all around us is the only power, the only influence, the only force demonstrating as our experience. This transition must be consciously made by declaring, then realizing, that we are no longer under the law but live by grace; that we no longer love, hate, or fear the visible universe, but yield ourselves to the influence of the Infinite Invisible which formed us and gives us dominion through grace. As humans we are under the law: legal laws, economic laws, health laws, food laws, climate laws. Bit by bit, demonstration by demonstration, principle by principle, realization by realization, we ultimately rise to come out from under the law into living by grace, which Paul described as: 'I live, yet not I; Christ liveth my life.'"

I frequently receive letters from dissatisfied students writing of their lack of unfoldment, their lack of progress.

Today a letter came from Nigeria, from a minister with whom I've been working for over a year to bring him into spiritual light. He wrote, "I am so dissatisfied with my progress that I'm getting discouraged." And I must write back to him: "In just a year? There are another thousand million years ahead of us, and no one is ever going to accomplish the transition from 'man whose breath is in his nostrils' to 'the man who has his being in Christ' merely by studying or meditating for a year."

Try to put yourself back two thousand years. Think of yourself as one of those Hebrews living under the terror of the organization as it existed in that time—and it was bad. Then, at the same time, living under Caesar. And that was bad, too. Think of their desperation and their desire for freedom. Then just imagine Jesus Christ appearing on the street one day. Now think what would happen to you if you were one of that multitude watching him, hearing him, and feeling within yourself, "This is it. I don't know how, I don't know why, but this is it," and then hearing him say, "But you must leave mother and father, sister and brother, for my sake. Sell all that you have to buy this pearl. Leave your nets and follow me." Then you'll know how very difficult spiritual attainment is. Then you'll understand why your progress is slow, and you'll be satisfied and you won't complain. You'll realize that if they had to walk those steps, so do I. If they had to die out of their old beliefs, so do I.

I only wish you could watch how slowly Peter died out of his Judaic religion and beliefs, that even years after the crucifixion he was still such a good Jew that he believed the message couldn't be given to anyone except Hebrews, that only they were worthy of it. Think of that. Think of a man who, after three years of living and working with Jesus Christ, still had not left his old religion or been able to grasp the meaning of the new. Oh, eventually he did, but it was a struggle.

For Saul of Tarsus it was easier. Once the Christ experience came to him, in that instant he dropped every trace of his Judaism except one: he kept the devil, but he called it *carnal mind*; then he went out to battle it every day. If he could have overcome that one Judaic belief of a devil, he really would have given the world a teaching far beyond anything ever known. But he didn't. He kept the devil, only he impersonalized it as carnal mind. But it still had all the qualities of the devil.

If the kingdom of God were that easily attained, if it could be reached by meditating for a year or ten, how many people would have it! But see how few have it. "The way is straight and narrow and few there be that enter." This is the most difficult life there is. It's far easier for any person to say, "I'm going to make a million dollars" and succeed, than to say, "I'm going to attain spiritual light" and succeed. It is far easier to accomplish anything in the human world than in the spiritual, because in the spiritual life we're called upon to die before we can gain what we're seeking. Don't ever forget that: you have to die before you can gain your spiritual life. You don't gain it by giving up smoking or drinking or eating meat. You don't gain it by studying for a few years or having some classes. Whew! If only it were that easy! You give it up by dying daily. Every single day of the week some trace of humanhood leaves us and is sent about its business in the world of appearances. Every problem is an opportunity to spiritually resolve whatever the situation may be. If that sounds too difficult, it's really better that you do not start. Be satisfied just to be a metaphysician who can call a practitioner and ask for help, and get it. Or, read a few pages of something inspiring and feel that you're getting close to God. But if that doesn't satisfy you and there's a drive in you that compels you to go forward, that compels you to find God, then find the teacher or the teaching that brings out in you the response, "This is for me!" Then stick with it until you attain.

Thank you!

~ 18 ~

GRATITUDE:
A SPIRITUAL INTERPRETATION
OF HOLIDAYS

Question: *Will you speak on the subject of holidays, how they are to be interpreted and observed from a spiritual standpoint, as for instance, Thanksgiving? Of course this would include Christmas, or the Fourth of July, or the Presidents' birthdays.*

Answer: This is really a beautiful experience. The Master prayed that the disciples be left in the world, but not of it. And as you know, this has been my vision right from the beginning: the word made flesh—not to leave this world but to be right in it, not subject to its false laws, but rather to open ourselves to reality and watch that reality become evident in visible form. How we understand and observe these holidays is part of that vision.

We realize of course, that Thanksgiving originated with the Pilgrims when they came to this land. They faced seeming lack and stress, yet they met their needs in many different ways. And they offered thanks. Actually, we don't know whether that really happened in the way that has been passed on to us because the Thanksgiving holiday came into existence after even their grandchildren were gone. So, we do not know whether Thanksgiving actually was celebrated by the Pilgrims or whether it was a later invention ascribed to them. But it really makes no difference because the idea itself is good. They were in this cold, barren country surrounded by warring Indians, and yet, through all of their hardships, their daily needs were met. It is logical to believe that a time came when someone would remind them of how much they had to be thankful for, and there may have been a ceremony and then later it was incorporated as a national holiday.

You know, as far as we are concerned today, we have very little feeling about the Pilgrims and how they celebrated their Thanksgiving. Today, the holiday is an opportunity for us to remember that we, too, have much for which to be thankful. It is really an opportunity for a sabbath day, a day of quiet, a day of peace, a day of reflection and rejoicing. On the human scale, nothing can be greater than a real observance of such a holiday. It is very much like the scriptural statements, "Lean not unto thine own understanding; acknowledge him in all thy ways." And of course such an occasion acknowledges God as the source of our good. "Thou would keep him in perfect peace whose mind is stayed on thee." And here, for a whole day, we have the opportunity of pondering the infinite nature and the divine nature of that which is supplying the earth and all those that are in it.

But this type of worship is minor compared to the spiritual interpretation of Thanksgiving. Spiritually understood, Thanksgiving cannot be confined to a day, a week, or a month. Thanksgiving is a state of consciousness, and it has to become a permanent state. We, as spiritual students, must realize there cannot be a minute of the day or night when somewhere within us there isn't a giving of thanks, a recognition or acknowledgment of the spiritual source and activity of all being. I can't conceive of living long without our eyes seeing some form of beauty, some form of supply, some form of nature, some form of good, without there welling up inside a deep sense of thanks for the fullness of creation. I think of this particularly when I'm seeing the sky, the ocean, the farmlands, or these tremendous green trees and plants and the abundance of flowers. You can't escape the vision of God appearing in infinite form and variety, in infinite abundance, infinite joy and peace. How could we experience all this without bringing to light in our consciousness a sense of thanksgiving, of gratitude, of rejoicing? I don't know.

By way of contrast, a barren heart is not consciously aware of God's glory manifesting in our human experience. For the world, it is a most wonderful thing to have a day of Thanksgiving because the world is barren, almost soulless. It doesn't observe the infinite beauty, the infinite harmony, the infinite grace abounding everywhere. The world takes all of this for granted. And so Thanksgiving becomes a day, at least once a year, when something within may be stirred, and usually is, by church services and newspaper articles and other programs. So it serves this purpose.

That particular day would have no meaning whatsoever for a mystic, for the simple reason that it would be a sacrilege to name one day as a day of thanks, just as it is to have a sabbath day in the week. This, to a mystic, is a mystery. How we can have a sabbath day in the week? Every day is a sabbath. Every day has to be held holy. Every day has to be an acknowledgment of God as the force, the law, the being of all that is. Every day has to be a day of rest, because in our spiritual life we are always resting. There is nothing to worry about. We know that God is running the universe, God is leading us beside the still waters, God makes us to lie down in green pastures. God sets a table before us in the wilderness, and even in the valley of the shadow of death, God is there to watch over us so that we can go through life performing its functions and resting.

Now, resting has nothing to do with the body because the body has no right ever to rest unless it needs a few minutes or hours of sleep. Aside from that, the body should be active as the mind should be active, but it should rest in that activity. Work is the finest kind of activity there is, both for the mind and for the body, and to have no work to do is punishment. To have no work to do is the next thing to a crime.

Spiritually understood then, our lives are lives of thanksgiving because of our continuous acknowledgment of the source of that which is appearing visibly. Our lives are made up of seven sabbath days every week, seven days every week in which our conduct must be holy, in which our aims and ambitions must be holy, in which our desires must be holy. It is the holiness, the resting from fears, worries, doubts, and anxieties that makes a sabbath.

We can consider every holiday in this same way. Christmas, according to our human idea of holidays, reminds us of the birth of the Christ. Actually, aside from the uses that are made of Christmas today, I can't see how the day Jesus was born is any more important than the day your great-grandmother was born. But if it means the world will have one day in the year for thinking thoughts of piety, gratitude, remembrance, if it turns this mean world to a remembrance of religious subjects one day a year, then Christmas plays a noble part in the life of mankind.

But for the spiritual student, the twenty-fifth of December isn't any different from the second of September because of that which has placed us on the spiritual path. What keeps us on the spiritual path? What is it that is performing the miracles of living: the feelings, the supply, the human relationships, the companionship, the spiritual upliftment? What is it if it isn't the Christ? Man, of himself, can't do this. Even Jesus acknowledged, "I can of my own self do nothing." And certainly all mystics have acknowledged, but for the activity of Spirit within, they couldn't perform their works. Every healer and practitioner, regardless of the teaching they follow, must certainly acknowledge that if it weren't for something transcendental, something beyond the grasp of their mind or reason, they could not perform the healings. They couldn't. And this isn't only true in spiritual healing, this is true in medical healing. I doubt very much if there is a medicine or an operation that will ever cure anyone separate and apart from the consciousness of the individual performing the operation or administering the medicine. It isn't really as funny as it sounds when you hear someone speak of a doctor's bedside manner because what is implied is the spirit of love, the spirit of confidence, the spirit of assurance, the spirit of dedication, without which I doubt very much any medicine would be effective, because medicine in and of itself has no power. It has to be the consciousness of the individual administering the treatment.

It is the act of the Christ, whether we are healing spiritually or somebody else is healing medically. It is the Christ active in and as consciousness. Do you believe for a minute that there would be a dedicated person on earth if it were up to man whose breath is in his nostrils? No. Dedication comes from an activity of the Christ, an activity of the presence of God in the consciousness of an individual. Even if it is not recognized, that is what is behind it. Therefore, we are witnessing the birth of the Christ. Actually, there can't be a birth of the Christ, there can only be a realization of that which is made evident in our consciousness. It is for this reason then, that every day of the week is December 25th to an individual who realizes that every act of good performed anywhere on earth, every act of unselfish service, of dedication, is really not man, it is an activity of the Christ expressed in individual consciousness.

To the world, it is fitting to remember the birthdays of our presidents, more especially of those few who have been great presidents, because their lives were lives of dedication. And the few who ever attain the reputation for greatness must certainly have overcome tremendous temptations to be in political office and still perform acts of service whereby all benefit. So to remember a president's birthday, again, is to have a day of thankfulness for the dedicated lives of those men who brought this country to greatness. They have the same thing in England. They celebrate the Queen's birthday, and her birthday isn't any more important than your birthday or mine. But the Queen symbolizes the head of state, and her birthday symbolizes a life of dedication. It symbolizes what every head of state, if they aren't, should be. So, celebrating these birthdays gives the nation an opportunity to have one day at least, to say thank you for a life of dedication.

You know, in our trips to England, I read the Times every morning to see the Queen's schedule for the day. I'll tell you right now, I wouldn't trade places with her. That's hard labor without union hours or union pay. It really is. They keep her on the job from early morning until late at night. That's dedication, and people should have an opportunity during the year to remember, to respect, to honor such dedication.

For us that isn't necessary. Every day in the week we think of a president, secretary, cabinet minister, or some foreign officer of government, realizing they are instruments through which freedom, liberty, and justice are being maintained on earth. Man left to himself wouldn't ever maintain it. It would slip away from him in twenty-four hours were it not for those dedicated to preserving freedom, justice, equity, especially in free countries. And in countries that are not free there are also people, not only living but dying, to bring back the freedom people have lost. How can we have a day, with the newspapers the way they are, without being conscious of that fact and setting aside at least one minute of respect and thought for those who are dedicating themselves to public service?

The Fourth of July is a day in which freedom is proclaimed. We ought to have four "Fourth of Julys" in this country so that there would be four times the reminders that we have had people in this land to give us freedom, to fight for it and die for it. This should inspire us to keep it.

For us in this work, that isn't necessary. Every day of the week is a Fourth of July because the greatest thing we have gained from our study is freedom—spiritual freedom. We have attained freedom from fears, freedom from most diseases, freedom from fear of death. We all know we're going to leave this plane one day. We know right well if there's a God, there must be a God there as well as a God here. There can't be a dividing line for infinity. The greatest quality, the greatest activity that ever comes into the experience of a spiritual student is freedom–freedom from theological domination, freedom from the law. By obeying the law spiritually we stay completely free, and we obey it more than otherwise would have been the case. We are free from the fear and experience of lack, even if it is only in a measure. Our entire work is attaining freedom. The whole mission of the Christ is to set us free. Therefore, we need no Fourth of July. Every day has to be a Fourth of July in which we rejoice in our freedom, in which we remember how it is attained and how we can give it to those who come to us.

What is it we do as practitioners and teachers when patients or students come to us? What do we do since we don't know anatomy and physiology and biology? We are not doctors; we don't know how to practice medicine and we don't know how to perform surgery. What do we do except to set them free? We set them free from physical worries; we set them free from economic worries; we set them free from theological worries. The greatest freedom that comes to spiritual students is that they know they aren't going to go to hell, and they're the only ones who know it. The rest of the world is looking at that horrible experience with dread, but not the spiritual student. Spiritual students realize that the only hell they can ever know is the one they create, and they can just as well have it here as in the hereafter, and they can just as well get free of it here as in the hereafter. Our entire work is bringing freedom to those who come to a message like this. And how then, can we wait for the Fourth of July? Of course we don't.

One thing we all learn in this work: I don't believe there is any other walk of life where there is more gratitude, more love, more sharing, more honoring than in this work. None. I'm sure that there is no other endeavor on earth, no other phase or facet of society, where so much gratitude and so much love and so much joy is expressed as in spiritual work. And why? Because, really, the only thing anyone ever has to be thankful for is freedom. Nothing else is worthwhile without freedom. With freedom, everything else is added. Therefore, freedom is really the whole of a spiritual activity.

So while we are in this world as the disciples were, let us celebrate these holidays and let us encourage the rest of the world to do likewise. Only for us, let us not limit it to those days but remember that there are three hundred and sixty-five days in the year, and every one of them is equal to the other. Each one has to include the Fourth of July and the twenty-fifth of December and the last Thursday in November and the Presidents' birthdays—and our parents' birthdays, too. Yes, I get thrills out of these holidays. I get thrills in observing them as they are humanly observed from the standpoint of remembering that, in some degree, even those who ordinarily wouldn't be turning their thought to the higher message are celebrating this one day.

~ 19 ~

REALIZE GOD AS THE ONLY POWER

I would like now to go back to the principles, and this is what is in my mind. Don't let me do you a disservice, which I could easily do if you do not make an effort to understand me correctly or if you do not insist that I clarify the situation so that you understand it. I have said to you that the ancients were absolutely right in setting up a devil or satan. They were absolutely right in understanding that there is an impersonal source of evil which tempts us, which comes to us as temptation and which never bothers us unless we succumb to the temptation. The mistake they made was to declare the devil as an opposite of God, an opponent of God, thereby giving God an eternal warfare, an eternal attempt to get rid of the devil without ever being able to succeed. Had they understood that this devil or impersonal source of evil was not power, had no law, no life, no cause, they would have freed all of us. And then verily every day in the week would have been a day of freedom—a Fourth of July.

In the same way, the earliest of our metaphysical teachers were absolutely right when they set up mortal mind and called it the sum total, the source, of all error. But they made their mistake by setting up an opposite, a divine mind, and they made such statements as, "Mortal mind causes disease but divine mind cures it."

That's a nice battle, too, if divine mind wins. You see, anything that sets up an opposition to God cannot be truth. God is infinite, and God has nothing, nobody, to war with. God is infinite. God is all. There is no power opposing God. Treat this devil, or mortal mind, as something you do not need to have a deep understanding about to overcome, as something you don't have to go to God for God's help to overcome. Then you can follow this exactly as the Hebrews did on one occasion: "And they rested in this word." Therefore, having seen the nothingness of devil or satan, having seen the nothingness of carnal mind or mortal mind, please do not let us invent some other term and then say, "Oh, help me get rid of my illusion." Don't do that. Don't set up another power against God and then want God to do something about it, or you'll just be going back to theology or the old-fashioned metaphysics.

Rest. Relax from mental anxiety. Relax from mental labor as if you had to overcome evil or contact God to do it for you, or as if you had to bribe God with a tithe. Oh, tithing's a wonderful thing, but for heavens sakes don't do it to please God. And don't do it with the idea that God is going to reward you, because it will fool you and it won't happen. Tithing is a free gift to any impersonal or spiritual purpose. Tithing is a free gift of love with no strings on it. The very moment you think of it in connection with God, you're thinking of it as a virtue. You're thinking of it as a way to help you to overcome this evil or one of its forms.

There is only one power, and if the Infinite Way is to perform a function in your life, it can only succeed if and to the degree you understand the nature of this carnal or mortal mind as a mental nothingness and illusion, a mental projection, a temptation, a belief, a suggestion, and then drop it. Drop it. Harmony comes into your experience, inner peace comes into your experience, in the realization of God as the only power so you can look out at the sins, diseases, deaths, lacks and limitations that are frightening this world and realize the only reason they're doing this is that they're being accepted as power. The only reason they're perpetuating themselves is that they are being feared and fought. I bring you back over and over again to the Master's teaching, "Resist not evil; put up your sword." I come back to it so that you may study those passages and ask yourself, "Why did he say, 'Resist not evil'?" You must come to the conclusion that if he could heal blindness with spittle, evil isn't very much of a power. If he could make the lame walk merely by saying, "What did hinder you?" then lameness can't be a law.

In the Infinite Way you break the spell, the mesmeric sense, which causes you to war or to seek a higher power with which you destroy a lesser power. You break that sense. That is the major point of the Infinite Way, that we are not a teaching that has God doing something for us, another system of a greater power destroying a lesser power. We in this work have come to the realization of one power, and of the illusory nature of everything else presenting itself to us as power. This doesn't mean that in our whole human span we will demonstrate this to its fullest extent. Probably not. There's no history of anyone ever demonstrating it fully, not even the Master. But it is the ultimate of our spiritual existence. It is the ultimate of our existence when we have transcended the cross, the tomb, the body that bleeds because a knife has been thrust into it. When we have ascended to the realization of our spiritual identity and our spiritual body, then we will have the opportunity of witnessing its fullness.

Paul reminds us not to claim we have attained the realization or demonstration of this in its fullness. Let us be thankful for whatever measure we have already seen, witnessed, and benefitted by. Let us be grateful that at least we know the principles, and if our particular airplane is only flying one hundred miles an hour for only one hour, let us at least be grateful that since we know the principles we can keep on working until our plane flies around the world at a thousand miles an hour. It makes no difference how small our demonstration is today. The tiniest demonstration is proof of the principle. From then on it is in the developing of our consciousness, the increasing of the depth and scope of our realization, that we perform the greater works. Then some day, at the point of ascension, the greatest works unfold.

The main thing is not the degree of our demonstration, but the degree of our awareness of what the principle is that is to be demonstrated. And the principle that is to be demonstrated is that God in the midst of us is not only mighty, but the only mightiness there is. Not that God is a great power that is going to do tremendous things for us, but that God is the only power and nothing need be done for us. The realization of the greatest truth ever revealed is: "Thou couldest have no power over me unless it came from God. What did hinder you? Pick up your bed and walk." As we abide in that principle, as we apply it to every facet and every phase of our human existence, we develop a greater consciousness of it and thereby a greater demonstration of it.

Above all things, as you read these writings over and over again and come to such statements as the nature of error, carnal mind, and mortal mind, please don't be frightened by them as if they were something you have to overcome. Remember they are terms for something you don't need to overcome. They are terms for that which is nothingness. And when you read them, have the same feeling about them that you have about a soap bubble: a nothingness. Maybe it would be a good idea to change those terms, carnal mind and mortal mind, into soap bubbles. Anything that will make us lose our fear of the source of error will accomplish the purpose of developing our spiritual consciousness and nothing else will. There is no way to attain spiritual consciousness while having two powers, for spiritual consciousness is the consciousness of one power. That power is of a spiritual nature—not material, not mental—whatever it is that trains us into an entirely new thought, a new state of consciousness, a new state of being. So we can look upon all of the forms of evil, whether they're thrown at us under the guise of drug addiction, alcoholism, incurable diseases, and we can throw them back into the one word or one term: carnal mind, mortal mind, arm of flesh, fleshly mind and thereby lose all fear of them. Then we find we have attained a greater awareness of spiritual consciousness, a greater attainment of the consciousness itself.

Most of you have been confronted at some time or another with a friend who said, "I have a headache." You have done a little work about it and the headache disappeared. If you have ever asked yourself how it came about, the answer is you were not very much afraid of headaches and therefore it didn't concern you too much. You weren't afraid your friend was going to die. You weren't afraid he was going to go insane. You weren't afraid he would go unconscious. It was just a headache. Therefore, with no fear of it, you turned within, you realized a few truths, and that was the end of it–and probably the end of the headache.

Ah, yes. That must be our attitude in the final analysis when we are confronted with any and every phase of discord, including the last enemy, death. We must be able to say as Jesus did: "He's not dead, he's just asleep; let's wake him up." Oh, I realize I'm talking very absolutely, and I'm not asking to be pushed into that position too quickly. But nevertheless, as we grow, we are asked for help on this, that, or the other thing, and we gradually approach each and every problem without fear, in the same way we approach the simple headache: "Oh, it's just a headache. Let's do something." Then we'll have our little realization, and it's done. Once we realize that the name or nature of the discord–physical, mental, moral, financial–is of the same nature as a simple headache, we do not fear it. Then we do the same thing: We go within, have our brief meditation, receive our click, and we drop it.

But remember: To do that, and then sit by waiting for the telephone to ring every minute to tell us how the patient is getting along, proves that you have not attained the principle. To fear to give a treatment to your child because it's your child means you haven't attained realization of the principle. Once you understand this principle, it makes no difference whether it's your child or somebody else's, or your parent or somebody else's, because you are not dealing with persons. You are dealing with a state of nothingness which you have realized to be a state of nothingness. That's what you're dealing with, not the person, not the patient. They don't enter it. They're merely the beneficiary of your understanding, if you have understanding. They're going to be the victim of your lack of understanding if you don't have the understanding. But it isn't the patient you think about, or the disease or the unemployment or the poverty, or any other phase of the error in his life. What you are thinking of is the principle of your work. The principle is God, an infinite God. The principle is that we are being tempted by a million different pictures, all of which emanate from the same old devil, or mortal mind, all of which represent the arm of flesh, or nothingness.

To the degree you can face claims that way, you can meet them. To the degree you can understand this principle for yourself, even if you can't do your own work—and that probably is the most difficult of all—at least you make it easy for the practitioner to help you, as long as you aren't sitting around fearing what you've already understood to be neither more nor less than a mental imposition.

Now, all of these mental impositions come through the human mind. Therefore, it is necessary to understand that the so-called mind of man, this mind that knows good and evil, is not a power in the sense of creating evil or being evil. Try to understand the true nature of your mind and you'll be at peace forever. God gave us our mind as an instrument of awareness. With our mind we become aware of that which is. We go to school and learn that two times two is four. We don't make it so with our mind. We merely learn through the mind that it is so. The mind is an instrument, just as the body is. In our present state of existence I walk to the door and therefore I use my body, especially my feet and limbs. If I give or receive, I use my hands. These are my instruments. But if I want to learn something, I use my mind. But I don't use my mind to create anything. Do you understand that? I don't make my mind a creative power. I make it a state of awareness. With my mind I'm aware of your presence, but I can't make you present with my mind. That is one of the errors of metaphysics; people believe that by mentalizing they can create patients and students and followers. That's a lot of nonsense. If you do it, you'll lose them because somebody else will probably do it with deeper concentration and take them away from you.

You do not mentalize to get supply, transportation, or health. Your mind wasn't given to you for that purpose. It was given to you as an instrument of awareness through which you learn. You become aware of all that is, whether it is art, literature, music, your business, or your profession. Whatever it is, your mind is the instrument through which you learn it. You don't create those things. You learn them. You don't create with the mind. But too many have been taught that thoughts are things, and therefore all you have to do is think a thought to get a thing. Don't do it. It's a dangerous practice. It can be done on some small scale, but it's dangerous. I have known people who have used their minds to work themselves into certain positions, certain places in life, and I've also seen the sorrow that comes to them because some day or other they lose. Some day or other a change comes. Some day or other somebody smarter or stronger comes into the picture, and then they find that the house they've built crumbles.

We don't create anyone's health with our mind, but we can sit down in a listening attitude and become aware of the health that is omnipresent. If we sit down in a listening attitude, peacefully quiet and receptive in the realization of God as the only power, we'll only be still a very short while until we receive an assurance through the mind that all is well—"This is my beloved child in whom I am well pleased."

~20~

PURIFYING THE MIND

Good evening.

As far as I can remember, this is the first class I have ever conducted about which I can truthfully say I'm sorry to see come to a close tonight. Saturday night has usually been the most glorious night in the world for me, and after Saturday night I could dance in the streets. There is a very definite reason for feeling this way tonight. I believe that for the first time in all the classwork that's been going on since 1947, the principles of the Infinite Way have been understood. I have never felt that way before.

You see, truth is universal. In mystical truth there is no such thing as an original idea. But the major principles of the Infinite Way, the healing principles, are an unfoldment that have never before appeared in religious literature of any nature, whether mystical, orthodox, or metaphysical. I have never been able to convey that before because students were either listening to me through their Christian Science background, their Unity background, or their mental science background, and so they were not able to clearly understand and grasp these specific principles. I know that if these principles had been practiced and demonstrated by our students, we would have practitioners in every city in the world. The only reason we haven't is because these specific principles have not been grasped, have not been understood and practiced, and therefore could not be demonstrated.

Now I don't say this in a complaining sense because it is perfectly natural. Every one of us have received teachings which we more or less accepted as divine authority. It makes no difference how mistaken those teachings may be, we find it impossible to dislodge them from our thought, our conditioned mind. In every message that embraces either mental or spiritual healing, we address the individual, and in doing this we personalize error. You either call the patients by their name, or you address them as "you," and you seek to uncover the error in their thought, or you point out to them what they lack in spiritual qualities: "You should be more loving or more grateful or more forgiving." Always, "You." Even in silent and absent treatments, the patients are the ones who are being treated. This is practiced in every teaching except the Infinite Way.

The only reason there is an Infinite Way, the only reason there is an Infinite Way book, the only reason there is an Infinite Way activity is that when these principles revealed themselves to me, I was able to uncover and demonstrate the truth of spiritual healing. But I wasn't able to convey these principles to those who were reading other literature because they missed the point. Then, after we started lectures and classes, the students attending still read other literature: literature by one person one day, somebody else the next day, and next week somebody else, and probably three or four different teachings on the same day. So it never became apparent to them that the specific principles of the Infinite Way message had to be embodied or embraced in their consciousness, and then practiced.

Now it appears, after these many years, more students are concentrating specifically on the Infinite Way writings and beginning to grasp these specific principles. There are more students actually practicing these principles in contemplative meditation and applying them in treatment, thereby opening out a way for the healing Christ presence to unfold in human consciousness.

When I first started classwork, our classes lasted two weeks, and the reason was that for the first four nights I made no progress. In front of me were Christian Scientists, Unity students, New Thought students, all conditioned by their years of study, and I would sit up here and just feel a mental wall out there. I knew I wasn't getting through. The second night was slightly easier, and by the third night there was a let-down and peace began. By the fourth night we got started with the classwork.

But here all week, the atmosphere has been completely clear, as if you received these principles and were responding to them, accepting them. And that's why I feel I could go on and on, and within another week or two we'd have this whole thing so clear we'd probably have to publish a list of practitioners too. You see, in the history of the world there have been some few hundred people who by the grace of God received spiritual illumination to a sufficient degree to make it possible for us to consider them mystics. There have been a few thousand people, or maybe tens of thousands of people, who by the grace of God received a touch of the spirit. These, of course, represent the saddest element of society. You read about these people in Dr.

Bucke's *Cosmic Consciousness*[1]: people who had one touch of the spirit and could never regain it again, who didn't understand it when it came, didn't grasp the meaning or the significance of the experience, and could never again repeat the experience. All the rest of the world has had to go through life without illumination. This isn't necessary, because with an understanding of the truth of being and a consistent living in that principle, spiritual consciousness unfolds and it is possible for everyone who earnestly turns to a spiritual teaching to receive a tremendous measure of light. The degree to which the spiritual light is received varies of course with the individual and with the use made of that wisdom after receiving it.

It is virtually impossible to receive spiritual light or illumination as long as your mind is divided against itself. "A house divided against itself cannot stand." That means as long as you are entertaining the belief that God can do something to something or somebody, or that God can do something for somebody, as long as you entertain the belief in two powers, illumination is impossible. That is the barrier that separates you from being that man who has his being in Christ. In other words, it is only to the degree you come to the realization of the nature of God as omnipresence and infinity and are enabled to think of any and every form of discord as being not a condition and not a person but a mental imposition, a malpractice, a temptation, a state of hypnotism, a nothingness, that you rise in consciousness.

---

[1] *Cosmic Consciousness: A Study in the Evolution of the Human Mind*, Richard Maurice Bucke, M.D. (first pub. Philadelphia, Innes & Sons, 1901, reprinted 1993, Citadel Press).

A barrier to this is that we think of each other as having certain qualities. Some are good and some are bad, some are spiritual and some are material. It is true that some of us are more materially minded than others, some are more morally minded than others, some are more sensually minded than others, some are more money-minded than others. But that is not true of us. That is only true of what they are manifesting under the impersonal influence of the carnal mind.

If you saw a man actually stealing a wallet, you would have to be foolish not to know that wrong is being done, that you are witnessing a form of error. But as long as you call that man a thief, you cannot open your consciousness to spiritual illumination because you cannot entertain truth while your mind is filled with error. A truth and a lie cannot fill the same space at the same time. Therefore, if you see a man stealing a wallet, be sure you have no thought about him whatsoever, but remember quickly: "Oh, yes, this is it. The carnal mind in action." And you thereby impersonalize it. You have taken error away from the person and placed it out here in space, and the moment you do that, it dissolves. It has no avenue of expression; it has no person through whom to operate.

After impersonalization, the next step is nothingizing: realizing that the carnal mind could not be constituted of God-qualities, otherwise it would be eternal and immortal and as good as God. If God did not create it, it wasn't created, therefore it can only exist as an illusion, a belief, or a state of hypnotism. With that, you have completed your treatment. You may or you may not have healed that individual. His own receptivity may have something to do with whether or not that realization heals him, but you would have kept your own mind pure, full of truth, and open to spiritual illumination, which could not have happened while you were holding a person in condemnation.

The entire basis of our healing work—and please remember that disease of every name and nature is handled in this way, and so is every form of sin or false appetite, unemployment, marital relations, employer and employee relations, capital and labor relations—is to hold no one in judgement. If you cannot do that, you cannot bring about spiritual peace. You might sit at a table and humanly negotiate in one way or another to bring peace between capital and labor, between employer and employee, but you could not bring spiritual harmony into that scene if in your mind you accept one side as right and the other side as wrong. In the entire spiritual kingdom, there is not a right side or a wrong side, there is only a spiritual side which is eternal harmony.

Consider our prison work. When we go into prison to do work of any nature—and we have no right to do prison work as Infinite Way students unless we have reached this understanding—we do not go into a prison to reform anybody, and we do not go in to regenerate anybody or to teach anybody. It is the carnal mind, the world, that believes there is good and evil, that believes there is a man or a woman who has sinned or is sinning or will sin. It is this world that sits in judgement and says good or bad, not the Christ. The Christ says, "Judge not after appearances. Judge righteous judgement." It also says, "Why callest thou me good? There is but one good, the Father in heaven." It also says, "Neither do I condemn thee." You are not the Christ-mind while you have right and wrong, good and bad, sick and well. The only way you can come to that state of consciousness is by first understanding that God constitutes individual being, God has manifested itself as individual being. Every individual in the world is God in expression, the one mind, the one life, the one soul, the one spirit individually manifesting: God appearing as individual being. It has nothing to do with appearances. This is a universal, spiritual truth. Then, if this is the truth about you, and since God is no respecter of persons, this is the truth about everyone in jail and everyone in a hospital.

The healing Christ is a state of consciousness that realizes this truth and knows that no man is evil, no man is good. Every bit of good manifested by man is God expressing itself. And every bit of evil is the acceptance of two powers, the acceptance of good and evil, the eating of that fruit from the tree of good and evil, sick and well, sinful and pure—judging by appearances. The Christ-mind, then, separates evil from the individual and places it where it belongs, in the devil that is tempting us to accept these two powers, the devil which we will now call carnal mind or mortal mind.

Having placed it there, we have taken the burden from your shoulders. You no longer have a guilt complex, no longer are sitting with a burden. If there is one individual anywhere who can look at you and look through the appearance to understand that anything you have done or are doing of an erroneous nature isn't you—it is merely the ignorance of being tempted by an impersonal source and acting upon it—you will be healed. You can't ever condemn a person for making a mistake. You can't ever condemn a person for doing something in ignorance. Every sin and every disease is ignorance of the truth that God constitutes individual being and that any and every phase of discord is the carnal mind, the mortal mind.

And so we have lifted the burden from you, from the man in prison, from the man in the hospital, from the man in the saloon, from the man in the gambling house. We've lifted it from him and we've placed it out here where it has no law, no activity, no cause, no person, and now it's dead. Now you can rest in that word. If you were sitting in an office or at home and your telephone rang every minute-and-a-half with another person calling for help, your entire treatment would take place between one call and the next. You could keep that up all day and all night because no matter what was said to you from out there, you would not connect it with a person but with this impersonal carnal mind and nothingize it even while they're talking to you. Then you would hang up the phone and rest in that word—rest until the phone rings about thirty seconds later!

Be assured of this: As you become clear on these points, that will happen to you. That is what happens to every individual who comes to the Christ state of consciousness. They draw unto themselves all those who want to be released. From what? Condemnation. Ignorance. Sin. Fear. Darkness. They are drawn to the light. You don't have to advertise. You don't have to let it be known what you know or what you are teaching. You don't have to wear a robe. Be as you are now and never speak about your religious convictions and you will still be hunted down. You will still be chased up every alley until you shed the light and share it.

All there is to the Christ-mind is the mind of an individual who does not have two powers, who does not sit in judgement or condemnation of any person or thing. It makes no difference what phase of life or facet of life it is—political, commercial, top capitalist, labor union leaders—it makes no difference. They all exist as far as the human scene is concerned. The sad part is, they always will until we learn to see that man couldn't be evil, man couldn't be selfish, man couldn't be unjust. It's an impossibility, for all there is to man is God made manifest. You are the temple of God. Your body is the temple of God, your mind is the temple of God, your being is the temple of God because God constitutes your being. We are talking of every individual on the face of the globe, every form of life: human, animal, vegetable, mineral. All is God expressing itself as individual consciousness and form.

This is the truth. Impersonalize every appearance. Don't ever tell people they can be helped if they read ten pages of a book, or go to church, or tithe, or are grateful or loving. This may work beautifully on the psychological level if human beings could change their nature. Any psychologist or psychiatrist can tell us what we ought to be and how we will be if we change our behavior, just as one of our comedians, years ago, used to tell us that he knew how to cure alcoholism. He had the sure cure that couldn't fail: whenever you lift a glass of liquor just open your hand. Well, certainly you know that would cure alcoholism. But can an alcoholic open that hand?

I've heard this for so many years: "Oh, if you could just be more loving. If you could just be more forgiving. Oh, if you didn't hate your mother-in-law so much. Oh, if you were more generous, more grateful. Ah, you've missed three Sundays in church. If you will just read so many pages in scripture." It's all nonsense, because psychologically it won't work. Individuals cannot change their nature. Only the activity of the Christ in their consciousness can change their nature. If they try to change humanly, they will repress their human nature without dissolving it, until one day it explodes. It can't be repressed; it's bound to break out.

Therefore, to be different from who we are, it becomes necessary that the Christ be introduced into our consciousness. One way of doing that is to find the individual who is not only willing but able to guide us through whatever experience it is—sin, disease, lack, or death—without criticism, judgement or condemnation, without trying to improve us, without moralizing or preaching, but is able to hold steadfast to the realization that this has nothing to do with us. This is an activity of that belief in good and evil. It is hypnotic suggestion, a mental imposition having nothing to do with a person. In the final analysis it is the fleshly mind or the arm of flesh, nothingness, that does not have to be fought or overcome, just recognized for its nothingness. Then we rest in that word.

This is actually the secret of the Infinite Way healing work. This is how it is accomplished. It has nothing to do with prayer that tries to influence God. It has nothing to do with finding somebody that is so holy that God is going to do something through them that God won't do through someone else. It has to do with specific principles. Now I can tell you that the very moment you fully grasp the idea that all evil is impersonal, in that very moment your consciousness becomes a transparency through which God appears, through which the Christ is made manifest. Your consciousness cannot be a transparency while it is doubled-minded, while it has good and evil in it. We become wholly pure, a transparency for the Christ, to the degree that we are able to impersonalize all evil.

Even though this truth was a part of my consciousness and I was doing healing work with it, I didn't consciously know it as a principle until I had been appointed first reader of Christian Science services in a prison. My first Sunday at the desk was the most miserable experience I had ever had. Every time I tried to read from *Science and Health* it wanted to jump up and hit me in the face. Finally I had to hold it down. I'm sorry, but I did. I had to hold it firmly shut on the table I was so convinced that it was jumping up at me, or trying to.

The second Sunday was just as bad, and so was the third. I tried to figure out what was wrong and couldn't. The committee in charge of that activity had told me that all practitioners in prison work must protect themselves thoroughly from sin-filled thought. And so every Friday night I'd begin to protect myself from sin-filled thought, and I kept at it steadily until Sunday morning. By that time it was ready to eat me up! It was my own evil mind coming back at me judging appearances. But on Friday night following that third Sunday, I sat down to do my protective work when it dawned on me: "Protect yourself from sin-filled thought? And man has no mind but God? Then where would the sin-filled thought be? Man is pure. Man is spiritual." Then the truth flooded me: I was the fellow who was putting evil out there! You can imagine what happened later when I learned that one of the men out there was completely innocent of any crime at all. He had been railroaded by an attorney and a judge, and here I was protecting myself from his sin-filled thought.

When I became a reader there, the average attendance at Christian Science services was eight to eleven men every Sunday. Three months later we had seventy-seven, and at the end of eighteen months we had two hundred men attending services. There was only one reason: I talked this over with our second reader, with our soloist, our pianist and our usher. We went there every Sunday, our minds purified of condemnation, purified of judgement. We went there complete in the realization that the only men we were meeting were God in expression, the sons of God, the temples of God, and that any appearance of evil was just hypnotic suggestion, just a belief of good and evil.

That's how I learned this principle consciously, through that experience. It stood me in good stead when I began some prison work here on the Island and also saw miracles take place among those men. So much so that the assistant warden here has written me a letter stating that if only a few men in Honolulu would do for the men what I have done, there would be no need for prisons. I did nothing for them. They never received money from me, or food, or anything of a physical nature. All they had was this: the understanding, the ability, to realize that regardless of the nature of their crime, it wasn't their fault and it wasn't the truth about who they really were after all. In their ignorance they accepted the temptation, the mental imposition, of all the evil floating around in the air.

But you see, we do the same thing with disease. We accept the temptation that is in the air. Somebody says there's an epidemic and we have to get sick. We accept the temptation, we accept the mental imposition which we have the power to reject. The world doesn't because it doesn't know the truth of impersonalizing. That is why it has no defense against sin or disease, lack or limitation. It has no defense. It is still being taught that you just go to church regularly, tithe, or pray upstairs. But you see, it doesn't work at all. They do not have this principle.

This is the principle by which we function. It is the reason why our meditations can be successful. It is also the reason why, when we're not successful, we can know we're double-minded and we're sitting here in judgement, criticism, and condemnation. In other words, we have not fulfilled the teaching of Jesus Christ which says, "When you go to the altar to pray, and there remember that any man has ought against thee, get up, first make thy peace with thy brother, and then return to the alter and offer thy gift." You can't go into meditation because you can't be at peace as long as you have not purified yourself. Don't forget that you can't purify yourself once and stay that way, any more than you can take a bath once and stay clean. Purification is a continuous process, and I don't mean for a year or two; I mean forever. It is a praying without ceasing because the world mesmerism is irresistible and it will reach into your consciousness unless you are alert and able to quickly and constantly impersonalize. Once you can do that, you can meditate because your mind is not warring with anybody or anything.

The mind will be still if there's no warfare, but there's always warfare if you have two powers, if you have good and evil, if you have desires, if you struggle to attain or achieve something. The mind can't be at rest. Now there isn't any reason, really, to struggle for anything, especially anything of a spiritual nature, because the struggle will prevent your attaining it. The struggle is mental. As long as there's a mental activity, you won't have the spirit. It is only when you realize what I already am that the struggle is over. The struggle is all gone if I already am. There, you see, we come back to a mystical truth which is universal. It does not appear only in the Infinite Way. Actually, it appears in every mystical teaching that has ever been evolved. Every mystic has revealed that *I Am*.

I think one of the stories that has always been very close to me is that of a woman mystic, a Muslim—and here again you see how strong the world's hypnotism is. The Muslims are taught that if only once in their lifetime they make the pilgrimage to Mecca, they will be saved forever. All sins are wiped out. Their whole life will be lived with God if only just once they can get to Mecca. And so every year, from every part of the Islamic world, there are pilgrimages to Mecca. This girl joined such a pilgrimage and had a difficult time of it because of the mountains and valleys and streams on the journey. They went through hot weather and stormy weather and cold weather. They experienced all of the inconveniences of travel that existed two hundred years ago. Eventually they all reached the outskirts of Mecca, and of course everyone broke into a run to get to that hallowed ground. But something halted this girl. She stopped and began to think, and finally she dropped to her knees: "God, forgive me for coming all this way to find you in Mecca. You who had found me where I was!" There was no need to travel. The Master said that centuries ago: "No longer shall you worship in holy mountains nor yet in Jerusalem in that holy temple. The kingdom of God is neither lo here nor lo there." It isn't any place. It's within you.

That realization brings you to the mystical truth, *I Am*. Moses gave to the world: "I am that *I Am*." After that he was no longer a shepherd. After that he was a spiritual leader of men, only because of his realization, *I Am*. I am that *I Am,* and I am it now.

Jesus repeated that: "*I Am*. I am that *I Am*. I am the bread, and I am the wine, and I am the water. I am life, and I am the resurrection." Not, I'm searching, I'm seeking, I'm hoping, I'm praying. Now I've come to the realization, *I Am*. That realization, *I Am,* makes a shepherd a great leader. That recognition, *I Am,* makes a Hebrew rabbi the light of the Christian world. It makes no difference what you are or where you are when the realization of *I Am* comes to you. From that moment you aren't that person at all. You are the light of your particular world. It really makes no difference where you turn in the mystical writings: Persian mystics, Muslim mystics, Hindu mystics, Chinese mystics, Japanese mystics, Christian mystics of the twelfth to the seventeenth century. They will all give you the same message. *I Am*.

Now in different degrees, that is the entire secret of mysticism, and when that realization is attained, it gives you freedom. That's the only thing that does give you freedom, because in that *I Am*-ness there is no longer a desire for anything or anybody. There is no longer an ambition. There is no longer strife or struggle. There is a resting in that realization. Then through that realization everything necessary for our fulfillment, whether it's person, place, thing, circumstance, or condition, automatically flows into existence. I know you will more easily rise to the mystical experience after you have made a specific practice of impersonalizing and nothingizing.

The very moment that you are not fighting powers apart from God, you are resting in *I Am*-ness. In the Twenty-third Psalm, David had nothing left to fight for because the Lord was his shepherd and he needed nothing else. But you see, as long as there is opposition or judgement in your mind, as long as there is duality, two powers, there is no way to realize *I Am*. It is only when you have learned to impersonalize and nothingize that your consciousness is so clear, so pure, so transparent, that the Christ shines through. That spiritual light shines through. It is a presence that goes before you to make the crooked places straight.

One of the reasons we can't heal everyone, and we can't heal everyone instantly, is that regardless of how true and pure our vision is, we can't remove the effect of something without removing its cause. If individuals are rigidly maintaining within themselves erroneous traits, the condition of health or supply won't change until their state of consciousness has changed. Then when the state of consciousness changes, its externalization has to change because the cause isn't there. And what is the cause? Our ignorance which makes us accept these two powers, which makes us personalize.

Most of us can be healed because we are not tenacious in our hates, envies, jealousies, or mad ambitions. Regardless of the fact that humanly we all have traits and always have had, they are not violent, they are not tenacious, and they are not what you might call deep or strong. Therefore, when you come into contact with a consciousness that is not holding us in condemnation, your consciousness is changed very easily. When, however, you hit up against those who are adamant in their evils, want to cling to them, and have no desire to be free of them, you have a more difficult time bringing the light to that consciousness. For that reason, you will notice many times that you will have to stand very fast with a patient, sometimes for a long time, until there's a yielding within them. Spiritual healing isn't merely adding health to the erroneous state of consciousness that we already are, spiritual healing is bringing us to the position of yielding our material sense, our mortal sense, our two-ness, our duality. Therefore, some of the things in us are not readily healed.

Very often as students take up a study like this, they find conditions in their bodies changing and improving, and they wonder why one thing or another persists while all these other claims have cleared up. There's only one answer. They have not yet come to the complete surrender where they are willing to grant that God constitutes our being and we are wholly pure. And that means you, and you, and you, and you, because when you come to that point you find that discords rarely abide in you except such as we bring upon ourselves by continuous violations of natural law.

Well there you are, and it's time to rest again!

~ 21 ~

LIVING IN THE LIGHT

I feel sure our visitors from across the seas have felt the aloha spirit of Hawaii and return home with joy. I am grateful for the work our students have done here throughout all of this time. I'm very grateful, too, for those of our students from overseas who are active in their own communities and have become centers of light, sometimes to their community, sometimes to their state, sometimes to their entire nation.

No spiritual light is ever given to us for our own benefit. That would be an impossibility. Spiritual light touches us that it may radiate, and each one of us, as we receive some measure of light, even a tiny measure, become active in a spiritual capacity. That is why some of our students conduct tape work, others are engaged in library activities, and some in healing work, so that whatever light is revealed in us is radiated in one way or another. We have nothing to do with that. It compels it.

There are people who are busy at work in other metaphysical activities to satisfy some sense of ego or ambition who have not been called, who have not received the light. They are not the ones of whom I am speaking. I'm speaking of those who do receive a measure of light. When they receive it, they are immediately put to work, and not by man or woman. It is by the Spirit itself that enters them. Even as Paul had to risk his life over and over again after he changed from Saul to Paul, even as the disciples risked and endured prison and persecution, so you will find in the religious literature of the world that all who received the light went out to serve mankind, even if it meant the loss of their own human life, persecution, or starvation. It is impossible for a person to receive the light and hide with it in a cave somewhere. It isn't done; it can't be done. The light itself propels one to be of service, to be active. So it is that all of us who are engaged in this work, in any way or to any degree, do not want credit or praise for it, because we are doing what we are compelled to do and would have to do even if it involved persecution, imprisonment, or death.

Remember this: As you study the teachings of the Infinite Way, the very moment you feel yourself touched with this light, it won't be very long until you find yourself engaging in some form of its activity. And this, ultimately, will be the means of perpetuating the Infinite Way message. No message will ever be perpetuated by sending out missionaries, lecturers, teachers, or practitioners who have not been touched by the light. It never will. The only way a message can be perpetuated is if the principles of that message become active in the consciousness of the student and become demonstrable. Then the Spirit itself draws to individuals their activity, and that perpetuates it. That's the way it must be in this work. So I am grateful to everyone who, in any way at all, is active in this message.

Now I believe I've answered this question about purification of our desires, purification of our selfhood. It doesn't in the beginning, have anything to do with trying to become better human beings. That is only the effect of the purification. Purification itself means the ability to have that mind which was in Christ Jesus, meaning a mind that does not judge, criticize, condemn, that does not have two powers and that can impersonalize and nothingize. That is all there is to self-purification. By this means, the act of self-purification results outwardly in a changed state of what appears as human consciousness. Therefore erroneous human traits begin to dissolve and ultimately to disappear, not leaving us perfect in this world, but probably working in that direction.

Now for the first time, I feel it is going to be easier for every serious student of the Infinite Way to attain this purification, this spiritual state of consciousness that realizes God is individual being (and therefore can impersonalize every appearance of evil) because this message is now condensed into ten tapes: the Maui Advanced Work, tapes 5 & 6; the Hawaiian Village Open Classes, tapes 3 & 4, and the six tapes of this class.[1] These three points have been presented so persistently, in so many different ways and in such concentrated form, that I am sure students with a background in the writings can complete the development of their own spiritual consciousness through practice of the class work on these tapes.

The tapes are available almost everywhere. Naturally, those who want them in their own home may purchase them. But it isn't a matter of purchasing the tapes. In every community in which there is Infinite Way activity, students will surely have one or more sets of the tapes so that those who do not have the facilities in their own home

---

[1]See Introduction, p. xv.

can certainly make arrangements to listen to them and study them with other students. I know right well what this activity does because I know the nature of this work.

Last year when Emma and I were in Holland, we were meditating together the night before the opening of an international conference seeking world peace through spiritual means. Evidently a message came to her which she did not tell me. But the next day a woman, a most beautiful and wonderful mystic who lives with the Queen of Holland and who has been her practitioner and teacher, joined us for meditation and we had a very deep meditation together. While we were meditating she said, "I have a message for you, Joel. It is, 'Joel, go home immediately. Be quiet and do not see anyone. Wait for the next message that is to be given you before you continue your work.'" As she was talking, tears came to Emma's eyes, and this woman turned around and said, "Oh yes, I know. You received the message before this." And she had. It had come the night before in those very words. And as you know, while we still had two months of lectures and class work, we immediately canceled all our work.

We returned home and I had a full month of retreat here, seeing no one. Then, on April eighth, the message was given to me, and with that this present class work began to unfold. It started with a tape, the Halekou Special Class, tape #3,[2] on one side of which was given the *June Letter*[3] on specific treatment. Right after that the work on Maui began, and then it was continued up here in this room—all of which has led to this class.

---

[2] Ed. Note: 1959 Halekou Special Class, Tape, 3, side 2, "Specific Truth for Treatments." Infinite Way Recordings, Peoria, AZ.

[3] Op. Cit., p. 104.

Oh yes, I then received a letter from this same practitioner saying, "Now leave for a trip to all of the countries in which the Infinite Way activity has been established." That letter came just about a week after I had made arrangements for our air tickets.

So you see, it all works together and convinces me that this message has been given to us in this form for the specific reason of fulfilling a need. Heretofore, even though the letter of truth as given in these classes appears in all of the writings, it has not been understood by our students, and hasn't been practiced even if it was understood. Probably it is natural to give more attention to the mystical side, to the inspirational side, rather than to first learn these specific principles and then practice them until our spiritual consciousness develops. So it follows that if our students are to attain the mystical consciousness, it will have to come through the study and practice of the principles, through purifying the human sense of selfhood, because—and this I know from within—we cannot have any degree of mystical or spiritual consciousness as long as we have two powers, as long as we personalize the appearances of good or evil, or consciously or unconsciously battle evil, or try to overcome it to heal the appearance of disease, sin, fear, or lack. I know that only to the degree that our consciousness accepts the truth that ye need not fight, the battle is not yours, does spiritual consciousness unfold.

Now, just because I've used that quotation, "Do not take up the sword," please do not interpret that to mean I believe in conscientious objection. I don't. We are all citizens of our community, of our nation, and as such we do not live unto ourselves entirely. Just as we benefit by the laws of our community, just as we benefit by our citizenship, so when we are called upon to serve it is our duty to serve. Even though we know that wars can never be right, that they are fought only because of stupidity, greed, and lust no matter who fights, and that fighting wars will not bring peace or prosperity, and never have–they have just brought intervals between wars–nevertheless, if our nation goes to war, just remember this: that for every man who objects or refuses to be a citizen and fulfill his duty, he is really saying, "You go out and get killed for me." When the government decides to draft a million men, it's going to draft a million men, and if you aren't one of them, somebody else is. Therefore, we really have no moral right to say, "Let the other fellow get killed, and not me."

On the other hand, as spiritual students we know that life is eternal. We know that the grave is not the end of our life. Therefore we are in a much better position to lose our human life than those who grieve about it, fear the experience, and think it is the end of all things. We make much less of a sacrifice than they do, for surely we cannot fear losing this human sense of existence to the same extent as those who have no spiritual vision. So it is better that we place ourselves in danger than those who fear the experience.

Beyond that, there is still another reason. With our understanding of spiritual law, it does not necessarily follow that we will be killed or wounded even if we do go to war. That has been demonstrated in World War I and World War II. For those who had been metaphysically and spiritually trained, the results of going to war were far different than the statistics. Very often the going is an act of service and of good. I'm thinking right now of a man who was a Christian Science chaplain who was on the front line during World War II. There was a machine gun nest that couldn't be located and destroyed, and it was preventing the battalion from advancing. Volunteers were called to go out and draw fire from the gun emplacement so that it could be located and wiped out. The volunteer group quickly assembled, but of course there was no possibility of their coming back. Their mission was to go out and get shot so that the emplacement could be located. This chaplain showed up just in time to go with them, but was told by the captain he couldn't go. His answer was, "I'm going to disobey your order. You can shoot me now or when I come back." And he went with those volunteers. And you know, not a single man was lost, not a single man was injured, and the purpose was accomplished. This chaplain was later decorated by our government for bravery beyond the call of his service.

I'm also reminded of another Christian Science chaplain in the First World War who sailed on mine-laying ships during the flu epidemic which took such a great toll of life. He brought thirteen ships back without a single man getting the flu. Therefore we above all others, not only have less to lose, or probably nothing, but we have tremendous opportunities for bringing this consciousness into active expression.

So I wasn't referring to being a conscientious objector when I said not to take up the sword. But I do mean that we are not to struggle physically or mentally, but rather to develop this Christ-consciousness that does not have to take up the sword or resist evil, but that can abide in the word that "thou, Pilate, have no power over me" for there is only one power and that is God.

With this understanding, our progress should be rapid, with more students doing more healing work, and those students already doing healing work should be able to accomplish it more effectively and more quickly. We should attain a greater degree of Christ-consciousness because the more these particular principles are practiced, the more Christ-consciousness is developed in us. We become a better transparency for the activity of the Christ. This, then, is the mystical consciousness.

Remember that spiritual consciousness is your consciousness when you have no evil to battle, when you are able to impersonalize and nothingize the appearance of evil. That is Christ-consciousness. It isn't some other consciousness that's going to come to you. It is your present consciousness when it is divested of personalizing good and evil, or empowering evil. Your consciousness is Christ-consciousness to the degree that you are impersonalizing and nothingizing. Therefore, there is no new consciousness to gain. There is no other consciousness to seek. It is a purification of the consciousness we now have and which, in its purified state, is Christ-consciousness. In other words, Moses, after his illumination, was still Moses, but with a purified consciousness. Jesus was still Jesus, but with the purified Christ-consciousness. That is why he is called Jesus the Christ, Jesus the enlightened. He was still Jesus, the same Jesus, but now the enlightened. And enlightenment means only one thing: the recognition of these principles. That is what constitutes enlightenment and opens the way for illumination.

The inner experiences that we have and the inner experiences that come to us, the instruction that comes, and the wisdom, the guidance, the direction that come, do so only at those times when we are living in the consciousness of no condemnation, of impersonalization.

They can't come to us at any other time. That is the full meaning of the statement: "When you bring your gift to the altar, and there remember that your brother has ought against you . . . first be reconciled to your brother."

So it is, if you hope to pray someone into health, don't try it if you believe they are diseased. Until you have come to the realization that God constitutes their being, that this condition is the impersonal carnal mind, you have no ability to heal and your prayers won't reach any further than your own mind.

That brings us to the subject of prayer. Watch yourself when you believe that you're praying. Watch yourself as if you were standing in back of yourself, and note whether you're expecting something from God, whether you're attempting to influence God, whether you're hoping for some setting aside of law. Note whether or not, in your praying, you actually believe that God is withholding something that after this prayer is to be granted. Watch yourself at prayer so that you're not reaching up to God at all, you're merely resting in the realization of this inner communion. Watch that your prayer is a realization of God's presence, and if it is necessary, utter the statement, the affirmation, the declaration of God's presence.

In one way or another, let your prayer be the realization that "I and the Father are one," that "the Lord is my shepherd." Let your prayer always remain on that level where it is not reaching out or up or within for something. Then you will find that prayer in its highest sense has no words and no thoughts. No words are used in prayer; no thoughts are used in prayer. It is an inner communion that becomes a union with God, a resting in God.

Then, you are a clear transparency through which God's grace touches the consciousness of all of those who are reaching out to you. It is exactly as if this room were filled with God but no one was aware of it, they were in darkness or sin or disease or lack—as if there were no God in this room. Then one individual realizes, "God is. I Am. God is closer to me than breathing, nearer than hands and feet. I and the Father are one. . . and all that the Father hath is mine. The Lord is my shepherd here and now." And one can rest, can be still, and be a transparency—then the presence and power of God can penetrate the consciousness of those who are in darkness. At the beginning of our prayer we do use words and thoughts leading up to that final stage of realization.

As we do world work, thinking of those in this world who are influenced by evil, those who are outlets for evil, we realize, "Father, forgive them. They know not what they do." Let us not hold them in condemnation either, but open their consciousness to this light that they may be freed of whatever it is that binds them to personal sense. With that, there is the removal of condemnation because we have declared that it is not sin, it is merely ignorance. It is not darkness, but an absence of light. So in our forgiveness, in our understanding of the impersonal nature of all evil, we are a transparency through which this transcendental presence can function in the consciousness of the world. You never know where it touches or whom it touches. You have no way of knowing how the light, which reaches earth through the transparency of those in prayer, influences legislation, how it changes decisions. You have no idea how far-reaching it is. That is why some who have attained the light do retire from this world in order, as they would phrase it, to live the life of prayer for the world—not for individuals, but for breaking down the duality in human consciousness. By remaining in their caves or remaining in their little homes somewhere alone, they permit themselves, by praying without ceasing, to be a transparency through which the light comes. And they, of course, rarely have any way of knowing who is touched by it or how, but it is evident that things do happen on earth that cannot be accounted for. There are people in hospitals about to die who suddenly get well, and no one has the slightest idea of how it happens. There are times when countries are at the brink of war and a last-minute decision changes it. It isn't always human activity that brings this about.

That leads to this: We are helped by those who have passed from our sight. You must never believe that there is a retrograde step from developed spiritual consciousness. As individuals attain spiritual consciousness on earth, they are a blessing to everyone who bring themselves within range of their consciousness, and even to some who are not aware of what is going on. But when those individuals leave this human plane of consciousness, nothing happens to their spiritually developed consciousness. Death does not touch it. You can't put it in a grave. As a matter of fact, you've already learned, those of you who have practiced meditation, that *I* can't ever be placed in a grave. If you have ever meditated with the *I,* you know that I was never born and I will never die. You know that I was never confined in a physical body, much less would it ever be confined in a tomb. "I and the Father are one," therefore, we are never limited to time or space or place. "I and my Father are one" and that oneness is immortality. Therefore, I go on forever and forever and forever. And that *I* is the state of consciousness which I am. Therefore, if anyone is benefitting by it here and now on earth, you can be assured that those same benefits will go on throughout eternity. .

If you could be made to believe that Jesus Christ was the great light that he was, that his three years in the ministry could produce an effect on the world for twenty centuries, and believe that it came to an end on that cross or in that tomb, you haven't thought deeply enough. The degree of consciousness which we know as Christ Jesus could never come to an end. There would be something wrong with God if such a light could pass from existence, if such a light could be withdrawn from the world. And I say this about Gautama the Buddha, that if at his state of elevation he could be killed or his consciousness nullified, there is no justice in the divine kingdom. Oh no! That state of development, or any state leading up to it, is perpetual, is eternal, and is forever a transparency through which God reaches this earth. That is what makes it possible for individuals on earth to attain spiritual light.

Just think of a man, a cobbler with no greater religious teaching than a very darkened theological religion who was born at a time of tremendous darkness— spiritual ignorance personified. Think of that man receiving such a light in one second that within a couple of years he was known from Switzerland to England as the greatest spiritual teacher on earth, and he became the teacher of several generations of mystics. To this very day, the writings he left behind are read by many hundreds of thousands of people in the world, and editions are continually published in England and the

United States. That man you recognize as Jakob Böhme of Germany.[4] Today there isn't a religious teaching in the world that doesn't recognize and honor him. You know that couldn't be an accident. You know it couldn't be anything other than that the illumined consciousness of someone which touched him. It may not have been one of those who have passed on; it may have been one on earth. But it need not have been one on earth for John tells us in 98 A.D. that the *Gospel of John* was given to him by Jesus Christ. Jesus Christ had ascended from the earth sixty-seventy years earlier, but John states he received it personally from Jesus Christ.

Understand that when you pray, when you commune with God, you are at one with all men and all women who are praying. You are at one with spiritual consciousness throughout the world, the worlds that have been and the worlds that will be. You are never alone because there is no such thing as your consciousness being locked up in your head, or in your chest, or in your solar plexus. Your consciousness fills all space. That is the nature of *I*. "I and my Father are one," and where I am, God is, and where God is, I am. You can't localize that or finitize that for it is an infinite relationship of infinite being. The moment you no longer localize, the moment you no longer finitize, the moment you begin to understand that your consciousness is not locked up inside of you but that it is one with everyone of us in this room, eventually you will go further and you will realize that when you are in prayer, you are in attunement with everyone in prayer, for you unite in one consciousness. The Christ-consciousness is one consciousness, and when

---

[4] Jakob Bohme, 1575–1624. German mystic and theosophist.

you are abiding in that, you are abiding in Christ, whether Christ is in a foreign land or right where you are.

You see, the error has been that we believe we are finite beings, sitting here in a body. It isn't true. We are infinite being, we are divine consciousness, we are God-consciousness, individualized but never finitized and never localized. Therefore, you are never in a place nor are you limited by a place. Never. You can be where you want to be in the realization that "I and my Father are one," and I am where God is, and God is where I am. Then you find yourself where harmony is for you at any given moment.

Prayer is a deep subject. Prayer must never be thought of as prayer is taught in churches and unless you have a complete unabridged dictionary, don't accept what most dictionaries say about prayer. All the un-abridged dictionaries do give a mystical definition of prayer,[5] which is communion. When you're communing with God, you're not limited, you're not finite, you're not in any place. You are in God. You are living and moving and having your being in God. You are dwelling in the secret place of the most High. Nothing limited about that! Nothing finite about that! We must live and move and have our being in God. We must dwell in the

---

[5] From the Oxford English Dictionary, Second Edition (Oxford: Oxford University Press, 1992):

Passive prayer, in the language of mystick divines, is a total suspension, or ligature of the intellectual faculties, in virtue whereof the soul remains, of itself and as to its own power, impotent with regard to the producing of any effects.

Prayer is the soul's sincere desire, unuttered or unexprest. Montgomery Hymn, 1819.

secret place of the most High, and the only way to accomplish that is the prayer of communion, the prayer of realization of our relationship to God, the prayer of realization of our true identity of the infinite nature of our own being, because God constitutes our being.

If you want to know more about prayer, take it into your meditation and ask for light on prayer. Ask for guidance and direction on prayer, ask for instruction on prayer, and the Holy Ghost will impart it. The spirit of God in you will come alive to be your teacher, for in the last analysis God must be your teacher. The function of a spiritual teacher on this plane is to lift the consciousness of individuals to that place where they can make contact with the Father within themselves. Part of the function of a spiritual teacher is to instruct in the correct letter of truth, but that is the least of the teacher's obligations. The major function of teachers is to live so high in consciousness that they lift those who come to them, and lift them high enough so that they may have access to the kingdom of God within their own being.

We only have access to the kingdom of God as we are lifted into the domain which is above mind, above thought, above the intellect. Only those who have gone a step beyond us can lift us to that place. Here again, all healing work is based on this. Every time you undertake healing for someone, what you really undertake is to lift them above the physical plane of consciousness to where the laws of physicality do not operate. Then spiritual harmony unfolds in them. As a spiritual healer you are not healing their bodies. You are not doing anything to the organs or functions of their bodies. All you are doing is lifting them in consciousness above the physical and mental planes to where they are in the grace of God. And the grace of God wipes out the physical and mental laws that have been binding them. That is how spiritual healing is accomplished.

Spiritual consciousness nullifies both mental and physical laws. The mental laws are those of malpractice, the laws of belief, the laws of these mesmeric suggestions. In lifting the patient above the mind, the mental laws are nullified. In the same way, there are physical laws: germs, infection, contagion, climate. But when you are lifted into a higher dimension of consciousness, those laws do not operate. Then you'll find that even though the infections and contagions may rage around you, they do not come nigh your dwelling place. You find that though there may be panics and depressions and unemployment, they do not come nigh your dwelling place. Though there may be limitations of every physical form, they do not come nigh your dwelling place. Why? Because you're not dwelling there. You're dwelling in the secret place of the most High. You're dwelling in mystical consciousness where I and the Father are one and life is lived by grace, not by physical laws, not by mental laws.

Every spiritual demonstration nullifies a physical or mental law. That's what spiritual demonstration is. It is nullification: wiping out the operation of physical or mental law. It is lifting you into a realm of consciousness where the particular physical or mental law from which you are suffering no longer operates. Therefore, to be a healer it is necessary to dwell in the secret place of the most High, to dwell in that consciousness where the physical and mental laws are not operating. This is prayer.

Living mentally means determining what you want and how you're going to get it. Spiritual living is yielding to the reign of God, the kingdom of God. It is a yielding of desires; it is a yielding of the self to a receptivity of spiritual guidance. It is not outlining and determining what we want or how we are going to get it. It is a complete yielding of ourselves so that we may be the instrument through which divine intelligence can operate.

And so we come to the end of this experience, but not quite the end because this class work started here is going to continue in San Diego, in Canada, in London and Manchester, The Hague, in Switzerland, and finally back in New York in November. And I have an inner conviction that this is a cycle of work, not just an isolated work, but a cycle of work that will lead to whatever the next step may be. It is for that reason that when this class began, I was surely more curious than you as to what was going to unfold and how, because I knew that whatever its nature, it would give us an indication of what direction we're traveling. Now that I have seen this, I'm sure that there's going to be a continuity of this activity on a progressive scale, a deepening scale, a broadening scale. In other words, we are here and we've got to keep going this way so that we finally come to that state of consciousness which is our goal.

Well, I started off by telling you this is a joy to me, and it is. Thank you.

TAPE RECORDING REFERENCES

Ed. Note: Numbers reflect IW Recording catalog numbering.

CHAPTER 1
LAYING THE FOUNDATION: THE HEALING CONSCIOUSNESS

1959 Maui Advanced Work - Tape 5, side 1, Treatment and Specific Truth
IWR/ 247 #5 side 1

CHAPTER 2
A SPIRITUAL WAY OF LIVING

1959 Maui Advanced Work - Tape 5, side 2, The Spiritual or Mystical Life
IWR/ 247 #5 side 2

CHAPTER 3
TREATMENT: KNOWING THE TRUTH

1959 Maui Advanced Work - Tape 6, side 2, Bread for the Body; Hyacinths for the Soul
IWR/ 248 #6 side 2

CHAPTER 4
TREATMENT: ITS MEANING AND PURPOSE

1959 Maui Advanced Work - Tape 6, side 1, The Reason for Treatment and Its Use
IWR/ 248 #6 side 1

CHAPTER 5
A TRANSITION IN CONSCIOUSNESS

**1959 Hawaiian Village Open Class - Tape 3, side 1,
Treatment and Meditation**
IWR/ 260 #3 side 1

CHAPTER 6
ONE POWER

**1959 Hawaiian Village Open Class - Tape 3, side 2,
The Practice of Truth in Treatment and Prayer**
IWR/ 260 #3 side 2

CHAPTER 7
THE NATURE OF GOD

**1959 Hawaiian Village Open Class - Tape 4, side 1,
The Nature of God**
IWR/ 261 #4 side 1

CHAPTER 8
THE NATURE OF ERROR

**1959 Hawaiian Village Open Class - Tape 4, side 2,
The Nature of Error**
IWR/ 261 #4 side 2

CHAPTER 9
METAPHYSICS AND MYSTICISM:
THE INFINITE WAY PATH

**1959 Hawaiian Village Closed Class - Tape 1, side 1,
The Mysticism and Metaphysics of the Infinite Way**
IWR/ 262 #1 side 1

CHAPTER 15
MENTAL POWER

1959 Hawaiian Village Closed Class - Tape 4, side 1, Spiritual Power - Mental Power
ILR/ 5923, side one

CHAPTER 16
KNOW THE TRUTH

1959 Hawaiian Village Closed Class - Tape 4, side 2, Side one continued
ILR/ 5923, side two

CHAPTER 17
SPIRITUAL SUPPLY AND HEALING:
AWAKENING TO THE MYSTICAL EXPERIENCE OF ONENESS

1959 Hawaiian Village Closed Class - Tape 5, side 1, Spiritual Supply
ILR/ 5924, side one

CHAPTER 18
GRATITUDE:
A SPIRITUAL INTERPRETATION OF HOLIDAYS

1959 Hawaiian Village Closed Class - Tape 5, side 2, Spiritual Interpretation of Holidays (part one)
ILR/ 5924, side two

CHAPTER 19
REALIZE GOD AS THE ONLY POWER

1959 Hawaiian Village Closed Class - Tape 5, side 2, Spiritual Interpretation of Holidays (part two)
ILR/ 5924, side two

CHAPTER 20
PURIFYING THE MIND

1959 Hawaiian Village Closed Class - Tape 6, side 1, Self Purification
ILR/ 5925, side one

CHAPTER 21
LIVING IN THE LIGHT

1959 Hawaiian Village Closed Class - Tape 6, side 2, Side one continued
ILR/ 5925, side two

BIBLE REFERENCES
(by first line)

~381~

G

Go and do likewise .... Luke 10:37
Go and tell no man what
      things ye have seen .... Matt. 8:4; 16:20; Mark 9:9
Go and show it to the priests .... Matt. 8:4; Luke 5:14
God has no pleasure in your dying .... Ezek. 18:32
God is the same yesterday, today, and forever .... Heb. 13:8
God is too pure to behold iniquity .... Hab. 1:13
God made all that was made and
      all that God made was good .... Gen. 1:31
God utters his voice, the earth melteth .... Ps. 46:6
God's hand is not shortened [that it has lost its power] ... Isa. 59:1
God's rain falls on the just and the unjust .... Matt. 5:45
Go into your sanctuary and pray secretly .... Matt. 6:6

H

Heavens declare the glory of God
      and the earth shows forth his handiwork, the ...... Ps. 19:1
He doeth the works .... John 14:10
He knoweth your need before you do .... Matt. 6:8
He maketh me to lie down in green pastures .... Ps. 23:2
He performeth that which is given me to do .... Ps. 138.8
He that is within me is greater
      than he that is in the world .... 1 John 4:4
He who dwells in the secret place of the most high .... Ps. 91:1
He's just asleep .... John 11:11
House divided against itself
      cannot stand .... Matt.12:25; Luke 11:17

I

I...

I am ordained to heal the sick ..... 1 Tim. 2:7; Luke 9:1,2; 10:9
I am that I am .... Exod. 3:14
I and my Father are one .... John 10:30
I can of my own self do nothing .... John 5:30

I . . . (Continued)

I go to prepare a place for you . . . . John 14:2

I go before you to make the crooked places straight . . . . . . Isa. 45:2

I have never seen the righteous begging bread . . . . Ps. 37:25

I have overcome the world . . . . John 16:33

I, if I be lifted up, shall draw all men unto me . . . . John 12:32

I live, yet not I, Christ liveth my life . . . . Gal. 2:20

I say unto you, forgive seventy times seven . . . . Matt. 18:22

I will fear no evil: for thou art with me . . . . Ps. 23:4

I will keep him in perfect peace whose
mind is stayed on me . . . . Isa. 26:3

I will never leave thee nor forsake thee . . . . Heb. 13:5

If . . .

If any man has ought against thee . . . . Matt. 5:23

If I speak of myself, I bear witness to a lie . . . . John 5:31

If I walk through the valley of the shadow of death . . . . . . Ps. 23:4

If so be the spirit of God dwells in you . . . . Rom. 8:9

If you abide in the word and let the
word abide in you . . . . John 15:4; 7

If you do not abide in my word and
do not let my word abide in you . . . . John 15:6

If you go through the waters, you will not drown . . . . Isa. 43:2

If you go through fire, the flames will not kindle upon you . Isa. 43:2

If you make your bed in hell, God is there . . . . Ps. 139:8

In . . .

In as much as ye have done it unto
the least of these brethren . . . . Matt. 25:40

In three days I will raise it up again . . . . Mark 14:58; John 2:19

In thy presence is fullness of joy . . . . Ps. 16:11

Indeed cannot please God . . . . Rom. 8:8

It is God's good pleasure to give us the kingdom . . . . . Luke 12:32

J – K – L

Judge not after appearances; judge righteous judgement . . John 7:24

Kingdom of God is within you, the . . . . Luke 17:21

J – K – L (Continued)

Know ye not that ye are the temple of God? .... 1 Cor. 3:16

Lazarus is not dead, he sleepeth .... John 11:11

Lean not unto thine own understanding .... Prov. 3:5

Least of these my brethren Matt.25:40,45

Leave them in the world but not of it .... John 17: 15,16

Leave your mother, father, sister and
    brother for my sake .... Mark 10:29

Leave your nets and follow me ..... Matt. 4:19,20; Mark 1:17,18

Love the Lord thy God .... Matt. 22:37

Love thy neighbor as thyself .... Lev. 19:18; Matt. 19:19, 22:39;
    Mark 12:31; Luke 10:27; Rom. 13:9; Gal 5:14; Jas 2:8

M

Man shall not live by bread alone .... Deut. 8:3;
    Matt. 4:4; Luke 4:4

Man who has his being in Christ, the .... Phil. 2:5

Man whose breath is in his nostrils .... Isa. 2:22

My kingdom is not of this world .... John 18:36

My peace give I unto you .... John 14:27

My words shall not
    pass away .... Matt. 24:35; Mark 13:31; Luke 21:33

N

Neither do I condemn thee, go and sin no more .... John 8:11

Neither Greek nor Jew, bond nor free .... Gal. 3:28

Neither lo here nor lo there .... Luke 17:21

No longer shall you worship in
    holy mountains nor yet in Jerusalem .... John 4:21

Not by might nor by power but by my
    spirit sayeth the Lord .... Zech. 4:6

Not in holy mountains nor in holy temples .... John 4:21

Not my will be done but thine .... Luke 22:42

Not under the law of God, neither indeed can be ...... Rom. 8:7

Nothing can enter that defileth or maketh a lie .... Rev. 21:27

Now are we the sons of God .... 1 John 3:2

O – P – Q

O Jerusalem, O Jerusalem, I would
but ye would not . . . . Matt. 23:37; Luke 13:34
Peter, put up thy sword . . . . Matt. 26:52
Pilate, thou couldest have no power
over me lest it were given thee from above . . . . John 19:11
Place whereon thou standest is holy ground, the . . . . Acts 7:33
Pray for your enemies . . . . Matt. 5:44
Pray in secret . . . . Matt. 6:6
Presence goes before me to make
the crooked places straight, the . . . . Isa. 45:2
Put it at the entrance of your homes . . . . Deut. 11:20
Put it on your forehead . . . . Exod. 28:36-38; Deut. 11:18
Put up thy sword . . . . Matt. 26:52
Quick and sharp and powerful . . . . Heb. 4:12

R – S

Resist not evil . . . . Matt. 5:39
Reward thee openly . . . . Matt. 6:4, 6, 18
Rise, pick up your bed,
and walk . . . . Matt. 9:5,6; Mark 2:11; John 5:8
Sabbath was made for man
and not man for the sabbath, the . . . . Mark 2:27
Seeth in secret . . . . Matt. 6:4, 6, 18
Silver and gold have I none,
but such as I have, give I unto thee . . . . Acts 3:6
Son, thou art ever with me,
and all that I have is thine . . . . Luke 15:31
Speak, Lord, thy servant heareth . . . . 1 Sam. 3:9
Spirit of the Lord God is upon me, the . . . . Luke 4:18
Spirit of God must dwell in you, the . . . . . Rom. 8:11; Col. 3:16
Stand ye still; ye need not fight . . . . II Chr. 20:17
Still small voice, the . . . . 1 Kings 19:12
Suffer it to be so for now . . . . Matt. 3:15

T

Take no thought for your life . . . . Matt. 6:25

T (Continued)

Take no thought for what ye
shall eat or what ye shall drink .... Matt. 6:25; Luke 12:22

Tell no man what things ye have seen . Matt. 8:4; Mark 7:36; 8:30

Therefore, I say unto you what
things soever you desire when you pray .... Matt. 21:22

There is but one good, the Father
in heaven .... Mark 10:18; Luke 18:19

They rested in his word .... 2 Chron. 32:8

They have only the arm of flesh .... 2 Chron. 32:8

This is my beloved child in whom
I am well pleased ..... Matt. 3:17; Mark 1:11; 2 Pet. 1:17

Those who live by the sword will die by the sword .... Matt. 26:52

Thou couldest have no power over
me unless it were given thee of God ....John 19:11

Thou shalt have no other gods before me .... Exod. 20:3

Thou would keep him in perfect peace,
whose mind is stayed on thee Isa.26:3

Thousand shall fall at thy right side
and ten thousand at thy left, a .... Ps. 91.7

Thy grace is my sufficiency 2 Cor.12:9

To know thee aright is life eternal ....John 17:3

Turn the other cheek .... Matt. 5:39

Turn ye and live .... Ezek. 18:32

W

Way is straight and narrow and
few thre be that enter, the .... Matt. 7:14

We have the Lord God almighty 2 Chron.32:8

What did hinder you? .... Matt. 9:6; John 5:8

What God did not make was not made ....John 1:3

What mortal man can do to you Heb.13:6

When you bring your gift to the altar Matt.5:23

When you pray, do not pray where
you can be seen of men .... Matt. 6:5

Where the spirit of the Lord is, there is liberty 2 Cor.3:17

W (Continued)

Where two or three are gathered together in my name . . Matt.18:20

Whereas before I was blind, now I see . . . . John 9:25

Why callest thou me

good? . . . . Matt. 19:17; Mark 10:18; Luke 18:19

Word of God is quick and sharp and powerful, the . . . . Heb. 4:12

Y

Ye have heard it said of old,

an eye for an eye and a tooth for a tooth . . . . Matt. 5:38

Ye shall know the truth, and

the truth shall make you free . . . . John 8:32

You are as a branch that is cut off and withereth . . . . . . John 15:6

You will bear fruit richly . . . . John 15:5,8

Your heavenly Father knoweth

you have need of these things . . . . Matt. 6:32